CHANGING CHILDHOOD PREJUDICE

CHANGING CHILDHOOD PREJUDICE

The Caring Work of the Schools

Florence H. Davidson
AND
Miriam M. Davidson

BERGIN & GARVEY
Westport, Connecticut • London

Library of Congress Cataloging-in-Publication Data

Davidson, Florence H.
  Changing childhood prejudice : the caring work of
the schools / Florence H. Davidson and Miriam M. Davidson.
    p.   cm.
  Includes bibliographical references and index.
  ISBN 0–89789–395–6 (alk. paper)
    1. Discrimination in education—United States—Prevention.
  2. Prejudices—Study and teaching (Elementary)—United States.
  3. Multicultural education—United States. I. Davidson, Miriam.
  II. Title.
  LC212.62.D38   1994
  370.19'342—dc20   94–18559

British Library Cataloguing in Publication Data is available.

Library of Congress Catalog Card Number: 94–18559
ISBN: 0–89789–395–6

First published in 1994

Bergin & Garvey, 88 Post Road West, Westport, CT 06881
An imprint of Greenwood Publishing Group, Inc.

Printed in the United States of America

The paper used in this book complies with the
Permanent Paper Standard issued by the National
Information Standards Organization (Z39.48–1984).

10 9 8 7 6 5 4 3 2 1

Copyright Acknowledgment

The tables that appear in chapter 5 are reprinted by permission of
Greenwood Publishing Group, Inc., Westport, CT, from F. H. Davidson, "Respect for Persons and Ethnic Prejudice in Childhood: A Cognitive-Developmental Approach," in Melvin M. Tumin and Walter
Plotch, eds., *Pluralism in a Democratic Society*, Praeger Publishers,
1977.

To the caring communities of the
Westtown School
and other Friends' schools,
teaching respect through
a profound commitment to love.

Contents

Illustrations

Preface

Prejudice is universal, and yet universally despised, especially where it touches children. Because nearly 40 percent of the nation's school children will be members of minority groups within a few years, school communities need to seek solutions. An atmosphere of indifference to insult interferes profoundly with everyone's learning. Minority children's consciousness of prejudice is a major reason for academic failure and subsequent disinclination to work. Strangely, those involved in the vast movement for school reform do not bring up prejudice. Perhaps some fear the power of politicians involved in social engineering, saying that crusaders for integration caused harm. Some see a need to hold a hard line against minorities' anger. Others believe that virtue cannot be taught. But for teachers struggling with plug-in anti-prejudice, anti-violence, or character development programs, a need for whole school change becomes clear.

The first step toward a sense of community might be to develop a carefully crafted charter or mission statement, focusing on mutual support, warm-hearted cooperative learning, and enjoyment of one another during many extracurriculars, as opposed to the cool sound of legally prescribed programs for those labeled handicapped or victims of prejudice. Without this increase of community attention to school atmosphere as not just the context but also the generator of feelings, more motivation to learn and more choices not to be prejudiced against those who are unpopular or different are unlikely.

Statements that draw people together are already initiating academic reforms. Parents, teachers, and administrators coming together over a period of time to create a mission statement for a school has proven power. The spirit engendered in the collaboration is more important than the page or two of resulting text. The development of caring, responsible, and committed children is generally endorsed. Parents have been far more willing to help in the school after signing such a document.

Forty years after the Supreme Court declared segregated schools "inherently unequal," remarkably little has happened to change prejudice during childhood. Segregated schools still house most minority children. Schools fortunate enough to have white, black, and Hispanic children are dismayed at the extent and the implications of the resegregation going on within their walls. To minority families, both the resegregation and the lack of attention to children's attitudes toward each other spell prejudice.

Ability groupings, special education with mainly black and Latino children, unintentionally segregated ethnic and black studies, bilingual programs, and some elite magnet programs and clubs are started with the best of intentions. Authorities may remain convinced that such programs aim at societal problems. However, these authorities are exposing "virtually every midsize school system in the country" to the legal implications of "educational victimization," according to the successful attorney following a 1993 ruling penalizing the Rockford, Illinois, public schools for resegregating poor minority children.[1] The assumption — certainly the plaintiffs' assumption — is that ethnic prejudice has caused some children to be separated for assignment to a lower status too early in life.

In segregated situations, minority students have lower test scores, lower graduation and college attendance rates, and less chance of gaining either job skills or the jobs that depend on having had association with more privileged peers. These problems are most severe for the one-third of black and Hispanic children in schools where they represent 90 percent of the enrollment. Children in the ever blacker, browner, poorer, more multilingual, and more gun-ridden neighborhoods of large cities are born into a desperate situation — one crying out for schools to become smaller, more care-oriented institutions.

Recent statements from a few black leaders that children might be better off in schools that are not integrated show these leaders' anger and deep frustration with both the low quality of urban education and attitudes of prejudice. However, researchers who have reviewed all the relevant studies think we can build better situations on the base that exists in current law. They write: "Without exception, the studies . . . show that desegregation in schools leads to desegregation in later life — in college, in social situations, and on the job."[2]

While the country's wrenching attempt at urban desegregation has proven this point and raised the national consciousness regarding minority children's right to the resources and channels of social mobility, it was poorly planned. We charged ahead, spent millions busing children from one poor city neighborhood to another, and hoped that their natural friendliness would succeed in reducing prejudice where adults had failed. Busing for racial balance was a crude and partial response to a number of complex and intimately-related social and personal problems, all of which still exist. Because of neglect that was far from benign, social problems have worsened: Urban schools are resegregated, violence is entrenched, and interracial understanding is even more lacking. When schools fail, the phrase "equal opportunity" is hollowed.

Still, the national debate over how schools can be made more effective and more fair to minorities has come a long way since the 1960s. We simply did not see the enormity of prejudice and the insight and effort required to change it in children. There is much to learn from both educators' experience and the psychological research carried out since that time. It has become clearer that the Civil Rights reforms most notably neglected curriculum, school atmosphere, moral education, and smaller school size as four means of creating a caring and welcoming atmosphere for minority children. These children sense that dominance allows distribution of resources; they naturally push, shove, and argue to get some feeling of power. They need to learn that self-dominance gains real resources later.

Childhood prejudice is linked to immature moral judgment focusing on power. Moral judgment can be educated, even as moral behavior is encouraged by an atmosphere of support. As adults join to create the statement of the school's mission, they gain strength from each other to tackle the misunderstandings that will arise when they later begin thinking about an anti-prejudice curriculum. They must agree on its outlines, as well as the necessity of delaying its use until a moral, caring atmosphere can be established.

Reform comes in patient steps. Agreement on outlines delays discussion of particulars while understandings are built. Social scientific debates about "whose morality?" may be set aside when there is agreement on confronting prejudice with love, not with an intellectualized approach to every moral issue. Teachers have traditionally known better than social scientists that simply described virtues and rule-oriented behaviors are appropriate in the early grades.

The anti-prejudice curriculum should be developed locally. It must go beyond a bland "let's appreciate diversity" to dealing with prejudice itself. This essentially negative subject matter risks evoking powerful emotions not only in meetings of adults but also in unprepared classrooms; teachers know they could easily have a bad time. Only embedding such a curriculum in the prior positive accomplishment of bringing out caring in every student, teacher, volunteer, parent, janitor, cafeteria worker, principal, and superintendent who has anything to do with the school creates support for the goal of serious moral education. It is a goal enhanced by a school's diversity.

The well-taught child's ability to analyze controversies in fables and stories and a high growth potential arising from childhood's obsession with "fair" and "no fair" are seldom brought together. To know what to do about the discomforts and evil potential of prejudice and lack of ethnic mixing in a school, we will contend that it is necessary to look at children's capacity to morally analyze actual social situations.

In the early questionnaires that psychologists used to study prejudice, the focus on unstable and overly negative attitudes reinforced some simple and polarized conclusions about human nature. Children were either prejudiced or tolerant, but seldom in the process of perhaps transcending a narrow outlook or identity. Prejudice was thought to be a fixed trait, directly related to parents' attitudes. In 1974, a large federal study to determine how much prejudice existed among children was withdrawn midway in its course because of the belief that prejudices belong to families, and because of the fear of parents' potential reactions. The trait view of prejudice, transmitted like germs mechanically through a family, solidified a sad underestimation of human nature and of children as unadaptable when defensive.

It is true that identity, including ethnic identity, is a basic human attribute defined by a somewhat negative exclusivity: If I am this, then I am not that, and I think and hope that is not as good as what I am. But the need to empathize with other people and to indicate interest in friendliness is as much a part of human nature as the need to define one's reference group or call oneself independent. Questing for meanings, including moral meanings, is a universal and precious part of human development. Young humans not only want to experience fairness but also want to give it, according to their perhaps dim but brightening intelligence. Most want to grow toward some ideal that they consider good.

That much is easily demonstrated, but consensus in the research community about how childhood prejudice differs from adult prejudice is still lacking. Traditionally, reseachers have been split into communities of clinicians, developmentalists, educationalists, and sociologists or social psychologists all of whom, then as now, must narrow problems into manageable bits in order to arrive at describable degrees of certainty about the outcomes of tests of hypotheses. Important variables are often omitted from what is tested, and so will appear in neither the results nor the discussions of their implications. A partial solution lies in the value now accorded wide-ranging anthropological field studies and psychological case studies. Cognitive psychologists are also more aware of the importance of interaction between attitudes and carefully arranged contexts for raising the upper limits of what a child can understand.

Social psychologists summarize the causes of prejudice under such broad categories as economic competition, sexual apprehensions, cultural styles, broken homes, and the sociohistorical background of racism. Unfortunately, each of these causes is one level removed from the responsibility of educators paying attention to individual children and particular incidents. Unsophisticated media commentators still connect these intractable causes to school children by way of the influence of their parents. We now know that parents have less influence in this area than was thought. But the popular false assumption of parents' power has allowed educators to believe that there is not much they can accomplish. They may teach group characteristics under a solution called multicultural studies, but when individual students' prejudices remain unknown and untouched, parents should not be blamed.

Studies of how school desegregation might more effectively reduce prejudice recommend strong leadership, affirmative action hiring, continuous programs to increase contact between groups, programs integrated with the rest of the curriculum, more focus on getting to know individuals and attending to individuating characteristics rather than group ones, reinforcements for choosing to work with a member of another group in class and in extracurriculars, setting up intergroup cooperative education, developing materials for classrooms and for parents of young children, and teaching minority children skills to cope with prejudice. Translating these ideas into comprehensive programs and studying the characteristics of partial programs that seem to help is just beginning.

Still, what is missing are the important effects of an atmosphere of supportiveness and care not focused on deficiencies. Teachers show prejudice when they believe that certain children cannot learn. Administrative help for proving the opposite should encompass teacher empowerment, parental presence, smaller group and school size, listening and negotiating skills, and knowledge of how children think morally. Respect cannot be engendered where disrespect exists.

Yet, the difficulty of a paradigm change in a naturally conservative institution such as a school cannot be underestimated. Some are so large that older children are treated as enemies in a war zone or as an army only slightly friendly. We see innocuous and "politically correct" ethnic studies become a lightning rod among people who urge that children develop character, work harder, and know western history. Minority parents express rage concerning the neglect of their cultural accomplishments, their points of view, even their physical existence. Politicians and radio talk-show hosts expand the tensions between races and the political left and right. The hope for this book is that it will carry the multicultural torch into conservative territory, use psychological tests to expose the harm that overly legalistic and moralistic politics inflict on children, and emphasize both the caring, empathic atmosphere the left desires and the moral and character development wanted by the right. A school with heart, high moral purpose, and a sense of direction is also much more likely to attain the academic success desired by all sides.

In a few reformed schools described here, warmth, fairness, and respect facilitate academic learning and self-esteem as much as moral learning. Those serving the poorest minority children defy the implications of the trash, glass, and discarded needles in the streets around them. The atmosphere created by hard-working teachers and parents drawing energy from students' successes is nothing less than charismatic. Parent volunteers and mentor-tutors who connect the school with the larger community are as vital to these schools as their dedicated faculties.

Evidence is also accumulating that giving young people a chance to help resolve problems in their communities helps change both the atmosphere of schooling and the child's ability to morally analyze what needs to be done. A child's surprised awareness of unexpectedly generous feelings and concerns undoubtedly raises moral level better than a lecture or sermon might. Behavior-based discussion helps children and young people effect the difficult leaps from unconscious prejudice to insight to the kind of resolute behavior that can become commitment in adulthood.

This book begins with a survey of what is known about moral development and prejudice in childhood, then describes research that ties them together. This is done in two ways — by showing how childhood prejudice is often radically different from the adult kind and by elaborating carefully researched stages of respect. We urge that different approaches to moral and anti-prejudice education are appropriate at different ages. An atmosphere of caring can draw in families and meet their need to learn more about child development, which could still further influence and extend education's influence on values.

Teachers as well as other adult mentors must be given some of the training for mutual support that counselors, school psychologists, special education teachers, and social workers could pass on to them. Close listening is a rewarding skill because it brings on mutual recognition. Another powerful means of change in the clinician's repertoire is a skit used to open a discussion, a technique with which this book's authors — mother and daughter — have some experience, and so begin their book.

Introduction

A scene from 20 years ago brings back the smell of chalk dust in a fifth-grade classroom on a hot afternoon in early June. The children, shifting restlessly in their seats, glanced at the playground and green fields beckoning from the window. Summer vacation was close, and the students could think of nothing else. The teacher looked at the clock and sighed, closing her book. It was useless to think of the class doing any more work that day.

The teacher decided it would be a good day to let Florence Davidson lead the children in a role-playing experiment she had been wanting to try. The students were well acquainted with Davidson. As a child development researcher at nearby Harvard University, she had been playing games, asking questions, testing, and interviewing the children and their families all year. They rather enjoyed being called out of class to meet with her — it was more fun than studying. This time, the whole class would join in a game designed to provoke thought.

"Let's pretend," the psychologist began, "that this whole classroom is a swimming pool at a fancy country club."

"Yea!" The children liked that idea. They described the possibilities of such a place ("Ice cream in a glass dish afterward, with chocolate sauce!"), then began moving slowly around the room, making swimming motions with their arms.

"Then let's say that this country club is very snobby, private, and exclusive. The rules of the club are that no outsiders, including Turks, Asians, and people with dark skin, are allowed."

This late in the year, the children knew Mrs. Davidson well enough to know that she was interested in finding out what they thought about different kinds of people. They were not surprised to learn that this game had a deeper purpose. But there was a reason they did not know for adding then unknown Turks and Asians to people with dark skin. Ethnicity, not just racism, had to be emphasized because parental permission for research had been given without a meeting to discuss its pros and cons. The prevailing ethic of the public schools, which prevails still, is that all people are created equal, and, therefore, it is better not to call attention to group differences, especially black-white differences. Troubling minority children with painful issues is problematic, depending on the age of the children, but when their individual and cultural differences are ignored they feel diminished or invisible. Davidson had to be careful, but she knew from experience that most children of this age hunger to investigate the truth.

"One of you will be the swimmers' black friend who is outside the fence. And I want the rest of you, all his friends, to give your reasons for why he should be let in. We'll have a couple of pool guards, too, to give reasons why your friend should not be allowed in. They do not have to say what they really believe, because they are paid to be guards."

The children immediately picked Roy to be outside the fence. Roy was one of three black children in this class of 22 students. All three were bused as part of Metco, a state-funded program designed to give inner city children the chance to attend a volunteering suburban school. Roy was a handsome boy with a quick smile that just as quickly turned to anger. He had a reputation as a fighter, but his playfulness and happy-go-lucky style made him one of the most popular boys in the class. As Roy's best friend, an older white boy, explained, "I don't know, he's just so *alive*, right? He's always running. He's something."

Roy took to the role of the excluded swimmer immediately, moving back and forth around the edges of the room and keeping up a lively patter about how hot and ready he was, and how he knew his friends needed him. He seemed to be saying that his ability to transcend the obvious insult should be enough to get him into the pool. The other children continued their swimming motions and began calling out less subtle reasons for why Roy should be admitted.

"He's our friend, and we belong to the club, and we want him to belong, too," said Jo, a bright, voluble girl who had overcome earlier shyness to become one of the most outspoken fifth graders.

"No one deserves to be excluded. It's not right," offered Tom, an athletic, popular boy. Tom was remarkably thoughtful and low-key for his age. He dropped his gravelly voice: "You gotta be fair, and do what's important."

Another child, Beth, came up with the rationale that a tanned white boy's skin was almost as dark as Roy's, so why not let him in? "Look at Sal!" she said, referring to an olive-skinned boy from an Italian background. Classmates joined in general approval but added nasty comments about the stupidity of prejudiced people who judge only by color.

Ella, one of the other two black children in the class, saw the game as a chance to be serious. "All people are the same," said the quiet girl earnestly. "Why hurt people? Everyone should be let in."

The designated pool guards, meanwhile, were coming up with reasons to keep Roy out. "The club is private. The people who own it say they get to decide who belongs. They spent the money. They built it," said Sal.

"Rules are rules. You can't change it. They have to be obeyed," yelled Meg, another pool guard. Meg had blond, chopped-off hair and a saucy air. Her teacher described her as tough, precocious, and a good choice for guard.

After the arguments had gone back and forth for awhile, Mrs. Davidson asked the children to sit down and tell what they felt like as they played their roles. At this point, the third black child in the class, Leah, who had been quiet during the exercise, suddenly revealed her pain and anger at "the way black people are always treated. There's hatred and hate and more hurt." She refused to listen and interrupted each subsequent speaker, who also interrupted her. "The people who built the pool have the right to say who uses it," insisted a boy named Pat, an aggressive cherub who often took on Leah.

Although in the end everyone agreed with Jo's summary, "I'm not prejudiced and the people at the country club shouldn't be, either," the intimate knowledge of prejudice's effects held by Leah, Roy, and Ella went unexplored. Still, two years later, when Mrs. Davidson asked the children to comment on what they had learned from this exercise, Leah's sincere emotion was what most of them remembered. The white children denied that the game had lessened their prejudices because, they said, they had none in the first place, but they thought Leah had said some important things that they could not quite recall.

Leah's mood swings confused the other children. She was outgoing, smiling, and very entertaining with her pranks behind the teacher's back, but she could suddenly withdraw into herself, become manipulative, or cry. In fifth grade, several of the white girls, including an especially extroverted girl named Jan, had been attracted to Leah. But by seventh grade, the black and white children had separated. Jan said, "I used to invite her home to sleep over. To be nice, you know. But I don't know if she appreciated it."

The implication of superiority in this remark is clear, and it shows how pervasive the effects of prejudice are, even among these privileged suburban children who insisted that they were free of prejudice. Although school desegregation had brought them in contact with black peers, they still lacked awareness of their own prejudices and of the experiences of blacks in society. Indeed, many people are observing that, despite the gains achieved since *Brown* vs. *Board of Education*, prejudice among American children is as rampant as ever and may even be growing. We seem entirely unprepared for the certainty that more than one-third of our school children will be non-white by the turn of the century. While multicultural curricula are debated as divisive and taking time away from other studies, it becomes increasingly difficult to ignore differences, to devalue them, and to place minority children in separate programs, whether these be special education, persistent language groupings, ethnic studies, or our enormously stunting lower tracks.

PREJUDICE AND MORAL JUDGMENT

What causes prejudice in children? Most people assume it is the simple result of family molding and the influence of a prejudiced society. In the words of a New York subway billboard depicting black and white children hugging each other, "Nobody's born a bigot." This billboard seems to be saying that children are born innocent, and they only become prejudiced because parents and society make them that way. To many people, the implication of this view is that prejudice is an intractable problem about which little can be done because of the privacy and power of parental influence as well as the endemic nature of racism in society.

Parental modeling and societal influences do have a strong effect. However, recent research has taught psychologists that there is a third cause of prejudice that underlies the other two. The studies in this book demonstrate that childhood prejudice stems in the first place from cognitive immaturity — that is, from children's inability to reason about and value the idea of respect for other people. This finding has important implications for educators, because it means that through understanding how children see themselves, how they think, and how to stimulate their moral judgment, they can gradually be taught to recognize the fallacies in their thinking and their prejudiced assumptions.

Just as many diseases could not be cured prior to medical understanding of whole-body health, childhood prejudice also needs to be put into the larger context of children's morally-related thinking. Prejudice is an aspect of moral values and beliefs, in that it can be defined as how much (or how little) respect we have for people of other races, religions, and cultures. Thus, the three leading theories of how people develop morally can also be applied to the question of how prejudice is caused.

The first and most widespread theory is that morality and its seeming opposite, prejudice, are socially learned. This theory maintains that children learn their values by imitating others — their parents, siblings, friends, and such important influences as television. The second theory grew out of the psychoanalytic model, which argues that subconscious factors like anger and fear prevent children from developing morally and frequently cause them to become prejudiced. The third theory is that it is chiefly cognitive factors that underlie both childhood morality and prejudice. We will argue that, although all three theories have merit, failure to address cognitive and related behavioral aspects of moral growth is a chief source of persistent childhood prejudice.

In the 1920s, the father of the modern study of childhood cognitive development, Jean Piaget, began to demonstrate how young children are unable to reason about moral concepts. For example, he found that younger children tended to judge naughtiness or blameworthiness in terms of the amount of objective damage done, and to leave out entirely the intention of the deed. Thus, they found a child who unintentionally broke 15 cups more guilty than a child who broke only one while committing an implicitly naughty act. Older children, however, are able to consider motives and intentions. Piaget described two stages of moral judgment, the second taking into account how others think.[1]

In the 1960s and 1970s, psychologist Lawrence Kohlberg used his own made-up stories to discover and describe additional stages, each evolved from its predecessor but comprising a whole new set of interlocking structures of reasoning.[2] His tests uncovered three levels of morality: self-centered, then conformist or conventional, and, only much later if at all, principled. Each level has a less advanced and a more advanced set of structures totaling six stages.

Kohlberg's theory began as a common-sense building on the model of Piaget. Piaget separated the underlying structure of assumptions at each stage from the more superficial and perhaps forgettable contents of thought. Structures are defined as the instruments and organizers of content, transforming between stages according to their own laws. Very young children have fewer structures and more limited points of view. As they develop, they are able to coordinate more viewpoints (a structural operation) and, thus, enter into the conventional level of morality. The stages and the differences between the structure and the content of ideas are described at length in later chapters. Briefly, at stage one the fearsome power of authorities implies that harshness of judgment is right. At stage two, this "might equals right" point of view is mitigated by awareness that standards for behavior are not set in concrete but are being influenced by other people. At stage three, it is known that each person influences the other in a mutual way; and at stage four, a neutral outsider might judge human transactions differently. At stages five and six, which are beyond the understanding of school children, morality is determined not by rules of conduct but by abstract principles of fairness to all.

The levels and stages that Kohlberg discovered empirically are uniquely penetrating and careful, although criteria for the principled level are still hotly debated. The tests and scoring systems he developed with others over many years have now been used in thousands of published studies. Kohlberg demonstrated in a number of cultures that all but his principled stages constitute an invariant sequence, so that attaining a higher stage is always preceded by attaining all lower stages, step-wise and in order. The stages are only roughly linked to age; not everyone progresses on schedule. Some people never achieve the conventional level, and, even in complex societies few progress beyond it. A majority of school children operate at stage two.

Kohlberg's work is criticized by his colleague, feminist scholar Carol Gilligan, who pointed out that caring is as important to becoming moral as reasoning. Where Kohlberg would describe the highest form of morality as a personally disinterested choice (in which the decision maker in the overcrowded lifeboat does not know whether the person he indifferently chooses to throw out will turn out to have been himself), Gilligan would retain the personality and personal history of the decision maker who knows she must act but must not lose herself in her caring. She says the decision-making process of such a person is based in the "psychologic-logic of relationships," rather than "the abstract logic suitable to hypothetical dilemmas." Explanations are constructed by caring people as part of a process of interaction that probably would raise issues not only of friendship and family but also of gender, age, class, and race relations.

This is a valid point, but by itself, Gilligan's scheme probably cannot provide a fair and nonsexist means of measuring institutions or the people in them, because explanations and categories are located in the very emotion-influenced processes by which family, gender, race, and other social-political relations are created and maintained.[3] It seems preferable to conduct research using Kohlberg's stages, and then use Gilligan's theory to try to overcome the limitations of Kohlberg's abstract bias while making use of the data.

OUTLINE OF THE BOOK

Working under both Kohlberg and Gilligan, co-author Florence Davidson undertook to compare children's prejudices with their stages of moral judgment. If a relationship between low moral stage and prejudice were shown, perhaps more specific educational strategies could be devised to raise children's moral stages and strengthen their moral development and consciences in order to lessen their prejudices.

Davidson designed her study in two parts — a broad, cross-sectional study of 154 students in several city and suburban schools around Boston to test for an inverse correlation between moral stage and prejudice; and a long-term study of the 22 students in the previously described fifth-grade class during the rest of their public school years. Both studies relied on her invention of a Parchesi-like board game called Comments, which was designed to elicit remarks about various ethnic groups. The game is described more fully in Chapter 3. The Comments game was followed by private interviews using unfinished sentence stubs derived from comments by local children of similar age, some standardized questions to reveal prejudice (E Scale), and three of Kohlberg's moral dilemmas (concerning the value of property, human life and slavery). The long-term study also included the children's I.Q. and achievement test scores, the Tasks of Emotional Development (a stories-told-to-pictures test), and the results of child, mother, and teacher interviews about each child's feelings, behavior, and life history. The results of this study are covered in Chapter 3.

Throughout this book, case studies describe the ten children already introduced. The stories of Roy, Jo, Tom, Beth, Ella, Meg, Sal, Leah, Pat, and Jan (changed only in names and details to protect their privacy) provide an intuitive understanding of how children think that cannot be gained from a purely statistical study. They demonstrate just how complex the causes of prejudice and arrested moral growth are. Although the research was conducted in the 1970s, it is still relevant because of both the persistence of prejudice and the universality of findings having to do with structures of thought. Furthermore, no other long-term study of ethnic attitudes among school-aged children has been published, and it would probably be impossible to replicate this study in today's more apprehensive environment.

The book proceeds as follows: Chapter 1 looks at the cognitive roots of prejudice and some of the structural problems that prevent young children from reasoning about prejudice; Chapter 2 addresses the emotional and social learning aspects of prejudice; Chapter 3, as mentioned earlier, gives the results of the study connecting prejudice and moral stage; chapters 4 and 5 connect moral stage to prejudice in more detail in order to emphasize how children think; and chapters 6, 7, and 8 offer educational strategies for reducing prejudice based on the findings presented earlier in the book. These chapters also examine what some schools are already doing to create a caring atmosphere.

Research into subjects as complex as these must not be taken as definitive, but rather as pointing in new directions. It may be especially risky to combine scientific reports with prescriptions about prejudice and morality, lest the persuasiveness of the former be undermined by doubts about the latter. Yet, there is a need for simultaneous examination of researchers' and educators' experience. The urgency of the need to address racism in our society and to challenge the morally borderless wandering of our youth seems to justify the risk of prescribing.

While the educational strategies presented in this book can overcome neither society's failure to concentrate on children nor the economic factors that influence the most devastating expressions of racism and prejudice, with sufficient care, they should raise students' moral development. The value of life must be reasserted and tolerance of violence abandoned. Over time, a morally educated populace could determine more consciously the social factors that dictate when and how our society becomes more just.

CHANGING CHILDHOOD PREJUDICE

1

The Cognitive Roots of Prejudice

In Boston, an eight-year-old white boy called out, "You little African boogers!" to a group of black girls on the playground. "Whitey brat, I hate you!" "You're a fat pig!" "Pink pig!" the girls yelled back. The one who started the teasing said later, "We were only playing; it doesn't mean much." A few months later, in the same city, a group of white teenagers on trial for shooting and paralyzing a black football player offered the same excuse. "We were playing, shooting at pigeons," one said. In that case it seems certain that more than play was involved.

When people speak of prejudice in children, they ought not to mean the same as when they say of a teenager or of an adult, "He is a real racist." Teenagers and adults, in order to be prejudiced, must deny their understanding of the rights and respect all people are due. Little children have no such problem. Although children are thinking and reasoning, their predispositions are less organized and less stable than those of older adolescents or adults.

An unfortunate view of prejudice is that it is a personality characteristic that becomes crystallized at an early age. Prior to the 1970s, researchers too often assumed this was true. Overly-narrow hypotheses were generated by theories of learning socially from others or being affected by unconscious personality dynamics. Since then, as cognitive-developmentalism revolutionized psychological research, it began to seem more likely that children are different from adults in their kinds of prejudices even when surface manifestations are similar.

RESEARCH ON PREJUDICE

The early research of the 1920s tended to conclude what was assumed — that if children's negative ethnic attitudes are not the result of adopting the parents' attitudes, they must be just the slow copying of observed sociological patterns.[1] In the 1940s, clinicians tended to focus on how these attitudes become malignant. *The*

Authoritarian Personality, published in 1950 in reaction to the ethnocentrism of Nazi Germany, held that homes that are oppressive, rigid, harsh, and critical tend to produce prejudiced children.[2] Authoritarianism was defined as an early-appearing central structure with a determining role in personality. Its counterpart — prejudice — was described as a semipermanent trait that organizes thinking. Because of the appeal of a simplified explanation, the trait idea survived a torrent of criticism of the research in the book. It has persisted even in the face of consistently low correlations (accounting for less than 15 percent of variation) found between early and late childhood for personality, attitude, and other noncognitive traits studied by Kagan and Moss and later by other investigators. Traits found early are seldom found later in childhood, except for aggressiveness in boys, which is culturally rewarded.[3]

In 1952, Bernard Kutner, the first psychologist to research cognitive problems in prejudiced children, held to a trait theory in that he assumed some seven-year-olds already had "true prejudice." This emphasis led to item choices for questionnaires that produced results based on the original assumptions. Ethnic stereotypes were dictated to the children by a teacher to see whether the children agreed with the stereotypes. Children who simply acquiesced to prejudiced items while not revealing any doubts or countervailing views (12 percent of the sample) were called "clearly prejudiced." Kutner, in further testing, found these children less able to form concepts, more ready to jump to conclusions, poor at dealing with ambiguity, less task oriented, and more rigid in their approach to problems.[4] The reasons for these attributes were not investigated, and some children may have been merely avoidant, shy, or overly compliant.

Mary Ellen Goodman, who investigated childhood prejudice in the 1950s, referred to the Kutner study as her basis for assuming that "true prejudice begins as early as seven years of age."[5] Independently, Helen Trager and Marian Radke introduced the term "crystallized" to describe the prejudices of seven-year-olds, mostly because children, by this age, are able to offer rationalizations and a philosophy behind their attitudes.[6] No later study showed whether these children's philosophies or prejudices changed, which now seems likely.

In 1954, the same year as the Supreme Court's prototype desegregation decision *Brown* vs. *Topeka Board of Education*, Gordon Allport published a landmark review of research called *The Nature of Prejudice*. He defined prejudice as overly generalized and inflexible conclusions: "A negative set toward another ethnic or racial group or its member because of the fact of his membership which leads to judgments that are usually based on a number of faulty and inflexible generalizations."[7] He rejected any theory of inborn prejudice or its "instinctive roots," replacing that with a theory of learning "the home atmosphere" as the chief cause of prejudice.

Allport further speculated that childhood prejudice has three stages: an early period of faulty and inflexible judgments, a middle period of total rejection of other groups, and then a period of rationalizing prejudiced ideas.[8] But the middle period of total rejection has more recently been found to be one of some cautious acceptance. Existing surveys are mostly of children too young to report their mental processes, but their faulty judgments clearly do not remain inflexible. Children feel little obligation to behave consistently or make permanent decisions. Allport was strongly interested in the oversimplifications that characterize childhood thinking but had available only a single report on prejudice during the middle period of schooling, one from the deep South describing total rejection of the colored.

Allport noted that, when parents forbid interracial play or society separates people, young children assume there is something very wrong with people who have dark skin. He wrote about the cognitive problems that could perpetuate this view. He observed older children rationalizing their prejudices by talking democratically but not acting so. By what he called "the principle of subsidiation," many adopt attitudes that conform to an existing self-image and fulfill its needs.[9]

In the 1960s, Kenneth Clark's findings agreed with Goodman's that prejudice begins very early. Clark found black children to be conscious of color at age 3, "usually before white children begin to think about it." Very light skinned blacks sometimes showed difficulty in identifying what race they were before age 5 or age 6. Other children "know about race" at least a year earlier.[10]

Attitudes are also taken early. Goodman and Clark separately found that four-year-olds of both races preferred white dolls to colored ones, and black children were already upset by awareness-questioning that brought out the differences between which race they were and which they would prefer to be. Researchers agreed that young children already have a nebulous sense of inferiority associated with dark skin. Some children gave a clue to their feelings of rejection — childish notions of aesthetics, unfavored colors, and association of color with dirt. Others indicated that elders had conveyed a value judgment.

As cognitive psychologists revised some of the conclusions from this early research on racial awareness, they observed that while urban American children by the age of three or four can nearly always label their racial category they do not have a true racial awareness. Their categorizing really consists first of simply labeling skin color and hair differences between blacks and whites. It is now clear that, for every child, racial awareness comes step by step as elaborations of understanding are added to the original color-naming. As awareness changes so does the level of any self-esteem that has a root in race or ethnicity, and attitudes toward others from different groups may change along with it.

Race awareness parallels gender awareness in young children. Knowledge of what sex one is also comes step by step, as Kohlberg affirmed. "Forming gender identity is not a unique process . . . but part of the general process of cognitive development."[11] Even at age 6, correct self-labeling as to gender does not imply classification in terms of numerous secondary sex characteristics nor always a notion of the permanence of two-sex categories. At six, many uninstructed children still believe that a change of hair style and clothing can change a girl to a boy and vice versa. The same notion of mutability applies to race.

The child's difficulties in establishing a stable gender or racial identity are reflections of problems with constructing stable definitions of physical concepts. Piaget demonstrated with clay, sticks, and water that quality, number, and volume seem to young children to change when only their outer appearances are actually manipulated.[12] As the child's mental structures mature, new ideas of inner and outer qualities and their relationships and values develop. Only then can the child begin to understand what race and ethnicity really are and to choose to modify transient attitudes. Most prejudices expressed before this time are hardly serious from the child's point of view and, in many cases, can be labeled playful. This most common kind of childhood prejudice is produced by the characteristics of immature thought: its lability, tendency to generalize, inability to categorize by simultaneous variables or deal with contradictory information, and, very probably, its quick expression of emotions, such as anger or joy in labeling, calling names, and holding onto irrational beliefs for the pleasure of self-assertion. The following sections discuss these cognitive difficulties in more detail.

LARGE, LOOSE CATEGORIES

Allport suggested that the major problem in prejudice at all ages is "overcategorizations in which everyone placed in a class is assumed to behave similarly."[13] All through life, understanding can improve through differentiation of categories. At first, the baby has only the one category — self. Reactions are evoked only by immediately present sensory events, and whatever happens is interpreted in terms of feelings about the events. Inner reality is known first, and only later does the inner merge with the outer. As the baby learns to accommodate expressions of need to a caretaker's response, the self-centered expressions remain related to two categories — self and not-self.

This polarization of thought into two major categories sets the favored paradigm for some time to come. Categorizing by good and bad or by race and color and grouping like with like and unlike with unlike is inevitable in childhood. Observed groups may change in their membership and, yet, remain within the polarized category.

Stereotypes and prejudices are an inevitable aspect of simplistic thinking. Walter Lippman wrote of the stereotype in 1922: "It precedes the use of reason. As a form of perception, it imposes a certain character on the data of our senses before the data reach the intelligence."[14] This is most obvious where intelligence is still in its early stages and before children are able to imagine the motives or take the perspectives of others.

Differences are apparent to young children before similarities are. They create tag labels, as if for easy mental filing. "Mexicans fight bulls." "Italians eat spaghetti." "Indians wear feathers." Whole nations are thus classified by a single behavior, and the stereotypes tend to persist. More than 80 percent of the second graders in our study and many of the older children in the city and suburban groups reported the very same tag ideas. Some of the stereotypes were innocent, but others were ancient cultural canards with childish extensions because of a typical "all bad" way of categorizing: "Jews like money. They cheat. They fight, too."

A white boy, age 7, said, "I'd like all white kids because the other guys fight a lot. I seen them; they're bad." An eight-year-old black girl, echoing a friend, said, "Keep the whites out of our school? Yeah, I think so, because they might start all the trouble." This girl offered a historical context for her conclusion. She continued, "Especially they did, I hear, so far as I know, in Alabama, Selma. It was so fun when all the black people were in Africa, and I wasn't even born yet."

The child's attempt to create order out of a confusing world tends toward overuse of the categories of good and bad. Appearances and occupations by which people are classified are given value as if they implied some moral imperative. A doctor may be automatically good. A slum dweller (one whom the child does not know) is bad. An eight-year-old suburban girl surprised herself one day by realizing that people in slums are not bad, but she clung to valuing by occupation: "It's not their fault they live with rats. They can be good people. (long pause) Like they might even kill a rat; that's good. Or somebody from there could become a doctor."

Henri Tajfel found that differences between groups are often exaggerated to make them clearer, and when contrasts are enhanced so are prejudices. Tajfel described three ways to process mental data: categorization, assimilation, and search for coherence. Stereotypes are the result of the first process — categorizing — when it is based on exaggerating characteristics so as to minimize differences within a group.[15] Errors in the assimilation of ideas among both adults and children result from the need to simplify the world in the search for coherence.

ASSOCIATIONAL THINKING

Loose and free chains of ideas are often used by children in a situation that an adult might say calls for a more thoughtful resolution of an issue. Children turn up one idea or image after another, often to no evident purpose. Illustrating this is a set of judgments by a seven-year-old girl: "Blacks and Jews and Chinese are all bad. But God's nice. If you don't believe in God, you should never be a teacher. A teacher should not be a bad person."

At seven, notions abroad in the environment are often taken in by assimilation in an undigested condition. The child probably did not wonder whether God related to blacks, Jews, and Chinese or whether teachers might have belonged to those groups. In response to careful questioning, she failed to produce a reasoned chain of ideas, including any doubt about the badness of these groups or subsequent amplification of their badness because "God's nice." Rather, she described a simple word association of bad versus good. The distinction between very bad and very good was what suggested the thought of God, followed by the thought of the necessity of authorities (teachers) to uphold the goodness of God. Then came the badness of those teachers who do not.

Such talk is related to playfulness, which involves assimilation of the new idea without accommodating it to previously accepted related thoughts. A new and surprising thought not fitted to old ones sounds playful and creative. Prejudice may not have occurred to the urban 13-year-old Irish boy playing our research game who acted like a younger child in saying, "I like Italians; the kids are okay. . . . Except for their grandmas' humongous noses!"

Many studies have noted the value of play as a rehearsal of competence, a release of tension, a means of not taking self too seriously, and a creator of joy as well as an expression of it. Associational thinking has a creative potential that is obvious to teachers of art, poetry, and music. Psychologists also see benefits in playful fantasy. Along with the similar process of free association, fantasy is useful in play therapy for correcting mistaken approaches to human relations. Indeed, young boys who are overtly violent make less than average use of fantasy play.[16] They, and many other children from overburdened homes, are psychologically damaged by the partial loss of this essential outlet and means of feeling fully alive.

Groups also use playful associations of ideas and humor as a natural therapy for reconciling tensions and disagreements without having to expose them to serious analysis. Many jokes rely on putting down an out-group to increase playfully the cohesion of the in-group. These jokes are enjoyed and passed on by children. However, ethnic jokes may also foster an attitude of petty aggressiveness toward minorities, as well as stereotypical false conclusions, as in a seven-year-old's extension of "Poles, it takes three to change a light bulb. One to hold on, two to twist the guy. They ARE that stupid."

Children are likely to reason that if such a joke is abroad, there must be something to it. Unfortunately, they later become aware that even where there is no ethnic or outside threat, types and degrees of humor are integrally related to many cultures' behavioral code that implies other cultures can be devalued. As the child learns the language, stereotyped attitudes, and even the graffiti of his own subgroup, he may use them to reinforce his enjoyment and belongingness by excluding those others, the butts of the jokes.

Joking laughter in a group of older children is usually not so free as to violate each individual's sense of complicity with peers. The joke must be correct. But the desire to conform often causes the child or early adolescent not to care whom he hurts, so long as peer pressure makes the listener accept the majority's enjoyment. This kind of cruelty is widespread and easily extends into intimidation. A 13-year-old city boy confided, "Kids come into the room and yell, 'Is anyone Jewish?' So they can tell a joke. Nobody ever says 'yes.'"

Consciousness of what peers are thinking and a desire to gain their approval thus allows play to overcome fairness. It is easy to hold onto playfulness as an excuse for prejudice long after that childhood period when loose, associational thinking is natural and unavoidable. Cruelty, no longer playful, becomes an increasingly senseless habit when careful thought is not insisted upon.

City children, in particular, are more likely to choose playfulness over reasoning as a means of approaching social relations. One obvious reason for this difference from their suburban peers is that they must live in close proximity with a number of threatening attitudes from other groups. Retaliation follows when they express irritation outside of a context of play or ambiguity. They rehearse verbal aggression. The result may be avoiding consideration of moral issues regarding prejudice in the depth available to their powers of reasoning.

ACCENTUATION, INTERPRETATION, AND CENTERING

None of us notice all that goes on in our environments, and each of us must accentuate and select information according to some internal criterion. This information must then be interpreted. How the child thinks is determined by interaction among three areas: biological programming, what information the child has already absorbed and mentally structured, and what the child selects to accentuate and then assimilate in the way of new knowledge. Biological programming dictates the search for coherence. At an early age smartness becomes confounded with goodness because the two are central, and, for the same reason, being stupid is confounded with being bad.[17] Each child has much in common with others at the same age and stage in the way information is selected as well as in how it is processed.

Goodman considered a physical bias to be the major social origin of the race prejudice she observed in four-year-olds. Largely because of mental immaturity, attitudes condense around visual cues. Once having made a mental connection, often unconscious, between black-ness or brownness and undesirable or feared aspects of life, the negatively inclined white child may go about selecting from all observed behaviors of his dark-skinned playmates those that tend to confirm the bias centered upon.[18]

Many young children hit and chase each other, but the frequency of such observations as "black kids hit" is striking. A minor offense may be overlooked when it comes from one's own group, but it is likely to evoke a protest if there is already a need to categorize and to defend or assert one's rights against those of another group. In this way, evidence is selected, exaggerated, and then interpreted in a biased manner.

Even though early categories and reasoning are inevitably biased, the child-mind constantly strives to make some sense of things. Nega-tive and positive impressions contend, and the resulting tension needs to be resolved. Piaget first described accentuation as the effortful process of bringing order from a welter of associated ideas by lighting on one as most important. Then this is followed by a serial focus on single attributes of a situation.[19]

In the same way, children who select only one or two attributes of other groups to retain in memory use these tags as evocative images that become the nuclei of attitudes. Phyllis Katz and her collaborators observed white children changing previous perceptions of pictured dark or white faces after they had begun to accentuate some tags or labels they had learned from the experimenters. Black children did this less, since color cues were, for them, more salient than the labels that were provided.[20] Eventually, the idea of human nature and of group nature may take over as more inclusive. Centering, accentuating, and interpreting take their places in more rational thought processes.

RATIONALIZING AND OVERGENERALIZING

The need to create complex meanings from simple categories and ideas obviously brings initial distortions. Unknown groups may be summed up in the single word "strange" by the young child. The admo-nition, "do not speak to a stranger," is interpreted as a strong condem-nation of all who are not known, especially those least like the child's family. Later, the problem of labels intensifies. "Indians are good because they have ponytails," said a seven-year-old, who sported this hair style herself. "At least Navajos. I don't know about the other guys, they might fight." Many children's categories are built around such nonessential but appealing particulars of appearance. This changes as the child gains new information and notions of value. Overgeneralization may then at least originate with valid facts.

Emotionally powerful categories have the capacity to hold more generalizations. Categories of abstract meaning having to do with authority, personal appeal, fairness, and so forth impinge upon and may take over lesser categories based on simple facts. "Italians are okay — our teacher is Italian," said a first grader, perhaps implying that he looks up to teachers. Here the category of "teachers," or powerful authorities, seems to be drawing together other categories and dominating a supposed lesser one such as "Italians." Likewise, the categorizing power of color was found by Katz to be "blinding" in the sense that from an early age, members of minority groups are not perceived as individually as are members of one's own majority group.[21]

Once a child reaches an age when it is important to him to philosophize, sometimes as early as six or seven, larger and more meaningful categories begin to monopolize the others. Without such a process, mental organization would not progress. "Shoulds" are important in philosophizing about behavior, although somewhat undisciplined children may ignore their own conclusions when an insistent wish surfaces. Shoulds then lead to rationalizing a greedy or a hostile act, as in "They should not have started it." Shoulds are also useful for pleasing someone important to the child. "You shouldn't hate," surely an adult formula, was used by one boy as a way to bring not only others but also himself into behaving acceptably on the playground.

Children young and old overgeneralize or philosophize in seeking explanations to tie together observable phenomena, as shown in their constant "whys" and unique theories. A ten-year-old city boy said, "God is up there watching us through the roofs, like he wants us to do a good show. It is like he's watching TV, so he can pick what to watch, which family, and like all the people. That's why he made us, I think."

Explanations of what goes on in cosmology and the social world range from this highly original theory to uncritical quoting of an authority. Simple reference to authority is less frequent after midchildhood. There is still acceptance of adult domination in order to feel secure, but once a fabricated justification follows a child's unfair behavior, the parent can be sure that the child has also begun to think for himself.

Childhood is, nevertheless, a period of strictly limited thinking, lacking knowledge of facts or awareness of rules of evidence. Take, for example, the statement aimed at various groups: "Everybody hates them. There has to be a reason!" To many children, this seems to be a piece of compelling logic. Ignorant of the vast realm of history and of responsibility for hatred, they find it easy to acquiesce to what "everybody" thinks or does. Exceptions to logic are permitted if they are needed to fit a previously biased conclusion, or conclusions are extended in the face of contrary evidence. Often a whole group will agree to preserve some simple self-favoring bias without being aware of its own collusion in rationalizing.

EGOCENTRISM

Piaget also described the role of egocentrism in the child's mind. By egocentrism, he did not mean a nasty selfishness but rather a structural inability to take into account systematically the viewpoint of another person.[22] This egocentrism is never absolute. From the earliest months of life, the infant is social. The baby learns to take turns in speaking and responding, and an intuitive feeling for what the other person will do grows out of an apparently inborn empathy applied to experiences, especially good experiences.

Younger children cannot verbalize awareness of other people's feelings. Nor can they, as preschoolers, give correct answers as to what an experimental doll on the other side of a papier-mâché mountain sees. They imagine that what they see must also be what the doll sees; that is, all perspectives are the same as their own. Because each child's understanding of the world involves only what has been directly experienced, at first the child naturally assumes that others attach the same feelings to the same experiences. The case is often the same with more subtle social perspectives, but, here, children begin to vary according to what they have learned.

Imaginative children often carry egocentrism so far as to engage in lengthy monologues or interrupt with continuous questions, unaware that their perspectives are not the only ones that matter. Early egocentrism can soon be modified. Experimenters have found some preschoolers take others' viewpoints with ease and competence. Egocentrism turns into selfishness only when limits are lacking; when parents are uncertain, overly indulgent, and, perhaps, self-effacing; or when the child is not given enough sweetness, to use Winnicott's term, and must take over and manage his own gratification.[23] Whether behavior remains selfish and narcissistic, the structural egocentrism of the mind always lessens with age and experience, so any biased thinking becomes more voluntary.

The change away from egocentrism is called decentration. As egocentrism describes a subjective point of view, so decentration is the gradual loss of subjectivity through a new ability to consider multiple perspectives. A number of researchers have compared perspective-taking in the physical realm (such as recognizing differences in opposite views of a mountain) with the social viewpoint-taking of older children. John Flavell and Robert Selman described what they called stages of role-taking, the successive changes in the child's ability to take into account other peoples' thoughts, intentions, wishes, and emotions.[24] Some recent studies have linked cognitive development with a lessening of prejudice. In 1980, Semaj noted the effect of maturing thought structures on minority children's own-group attitudes.[25]

Children under the age of seven can label others' overt feelings, but they have difficulty distinguishing between their own and other people's social perspectives. Being emotionally aroused in a negative way can make such distinctions all the more difficult. From ages six to eight, children are usually aware that people have different views, but they focus on one perspective at a time. They become more reflective about their own ideas at the next stage. By eight, nine, or ten, the child is biologically ready to develop skill in mutual role-taking, if the environment is right. Mutual role-taking is defined as awareness that others can simultaneously consider one's thought while one is considering theirs.[26] With the advent of mutuality, there is a new opportunity to escape prejudice quite apart from moral considerations, because actions can be judged by purpose, intent, and taking into account the reaction of the other to one's own or others' prejudices.

VERBAL AND MORAL REALISM

Egocentrism at first leads the child to a world view that involves what cognitive psychologists call "realism," the unconscious assumption that one's perspective is the right one, objective and absolute. A simple example is the young child's typical certainty that his aunt is everyone's aunt. Such a child may also have an inability to comprehend left and right, in the sense that a person to the left of him could simultaneously be to the right of someone else. She thinks left and right, like good and bad and aunt, are immutable categories: "I would not help a slave. I'd make him my slave, instead," may not be a hostile statement, even though it came from a socially retarded, white ten-year-old. Eventually, the child understands that some properties belong to movements or relationship, not persons. When he also grasps that the properties or characteristics of persons are also changeable, and that groups of people are not inherently good or bad, he is old enough to think about prejudice.

Through the age of seven, some children carry verbal realism to the point of believing that words, once uttered, can take on a kind of magic that makes them the truth. This makes the child not a liar, no matter what others might say. A second-grade black boy in our study said he was born in Ireland. He had no intention of telling a bad lie, as his mother later called it. For an hour he seemed to believe in his fantasy, as he had believed in his pretend playmates when he was younger. Perhaps he found it pleasant to imagine himself as white. He expected others to accept his words and was upset that his teacher in an overly serious way endorsed the objections of two of his white classmates. This "black child participating in being white" phenomenon has been documented in other research on prejudice. While Goodman notes that this kind of verbal realism is the result of unfortunate societal patterns, when accepted without feelings of threat, it protects the child's imaginative playfulness.

Unfortunately, verbal realism also adds to problems that result from the labels, stereotypes, and taunts children typically toss about. Because of it, labels may seem to a child to have absolute significance, even while their meaning is unknown. A meaningless taunt on the playground, "Chew gum, Jew gum," upset an unprepared second grader. The young child's reliance on a small vocabulary may contribute to allowing verbal realism to take over. Allport called the early grade school period the stage of linguistic precedence to emphasize the importance of words at this time. Children chant, "sticks and stones may break my bones, but words will never hurt me," to shake off the magical effect of name-calling.

"Bad words" cause shudders in many small children because verbal realism produces a kind of temporary symbol phobia. Fear of words or symbols makes them more exciting. "My mama thinks I don't know 'nigger'," said a white six-year-old. "But I heard it lots of times on the bus. She [mother] whispers, but I know!" Parents and teachers may exploit a child's verbal realism, reinforcing it in order to preserve order. "If you swear, you'll be severely punished." Unfortunately, when older children continue to regard a mere word as an absolute evil, they may fix upon their symbol phobia and avoid deeper thoughts about prejudice or other moral evils. Therefore, when disciplining small children, one must take seriously the limits of their stage of thought and simplify one's response.

Moral realism is a structural problem of thinking that is parallel to the verbal realism of absolute right and left. Social dictates about such behaviors as wearing clothing are, for the young child, crystal clear and absolute: "Of course Indians should wear pants!" The reason that Indian partial nudity seems wrong is that it cannot yet be related to other people's subjectivities — the intentions and social meanings within a variety of cultures and climates.

Moral realism is a strictly literal interpretation of rules received from without or, as William Damon described it, making an abstract moral idea into something concrete.[27] "Mama, he touched two silvers," a five-year-old said loudly, pointing at a stranger across a hushed restaurant. This child had been taught that it is impolite to bother others by toying with the silverware between courses. She equated impolite with bad, making a moral issue out of a mere custom, and then assumed the rule applied to all. Egocentrism is again the cause, producing confusion between the subjective (parental rules) and the objective (order of nature). Parents mirror and reinforce this error when they become upset over minor violations of their standards, as they, too, confuse custom with morality.

During the period of moral realism, until at least the age of eight, duty does not imply responsibility to develop one's own reasoning conscience. Rules and duties are given from without and are forever. Children may be likely to label all those who do not know or conform to the rules not as just lapsing temporarily, but as bad persons. Noting that "Koreans chase you" or "blacks hit" may justify and explain the prejudices against these groups under a system of moral realism. Younger children usually intensify their negative observations. They typically advocate harsh punishments for those who break the rules, even when they are among the offenders.

Sometimes a child learns as early as three or four to try to be excused by rote repetition of "I didn't mean to do it" or "I'm sorry." He does not really understand why these empty words change parents' feelings. Only much later can he examine rules in relation to others' motivations and impute motives similar to his own to excuse them. Meanwhile, he simply compares the shape of outer events with the rules he believes to be centrally established, and apologizing fits a rule he was taught. Realism's origin in egocentrism is, again, a lack of differentiation between the self's own accepted rules and an outer reality that includes the views and feelings of different kinds of people.

SOCIOCENTRISM

Egocentrism is not a problem of early life only, for some egocentric attitudes toward family, ethnic groups, and other races and nations persist indefinitely among normal adolescents and adults. They seem to be psychologically necessary to a simplified sense of personal identity. Piaget found that in preadolescence "egocentrism re-emerges in new guises farther and farther from the child's initial center of interest."[28] This guise is no longer just that of the physical body, its beauty or ugliness, or safety from life's pushes and shoves that seem unfair. Gradually the story of self becomes one of a more imaginative identity that includes belongingness, ethnicity or nationality, ownership of goods, and even its attendant class consciousness. Social awareness vastly increases social group consciousness.

The constant slipping into sociocentrism, in which all is scaled in reference to one's own group, undoubtedly has something to do with the adolescent's growing need for an identity beyond what the family has provided, a process described at length by Erik Erikson.[29] Belonging to a group, perhaps preeminently to an ethnic group, gives context to who one is and what kind of life goals one may choose. It frequently motivates achievement. Each new positive discovery, not only about one's self but also about one's group, adds to the richness of emotional life and the meaning of individuality.[30] Adolescents who drift away from weak communities become even more desperately conscious of their friends' characteristics than is typical and make use of pressure from peers to help them abandon an identity more pleasing to their families and to adults at school than to themselves. They want to leave childhood and all its bad feelings behind.

However, if the bad feelings come from a current situation, there is a real danger to integrity when an upsurge of positive emotion about one's ethnic group is accompanied by ignorance of the real worth of the larger human group and, perhaps, some doubts about adult integrity and the worth of one's background culture. Beliefs for which there is no evidence can be defensively accepted by adolescents and adults who should know better.

Ethnic neighborhoods tend to be friendly and culture-preserving places where older and younger children mix. With the advent of drugs, they have become all the more the turf of aggressive and undereducated teenagers who go to extremes to preserve the group's ownership of the ground beneath their feet. Often, these adolescents lose their own "groundedness" in any larger truths. Turf battles resemble national wars, especially as irrational social and emotional statements are made to vaunt the worth of one gang, group, or ethnicity over another. Prejudice becomes a deliberately chosen recentration of ideas selected to counter alienated feelings. These ideas are used as a filter to exclude any contrary evidence.

"What else can I do? I'm going to go with my friends," said a white 13-year-old boy while hesitantly planning to reclaim a playground in a Boston neighborhood that was changing from white to black. He would assert himself, become somebody, even though "not an important guy." He denied any prejudice and expressed the typical dismissive and inadequate reasoning of his group when he said:

I don't care about blacks, but it don't hurt anybody if I do or don't, because I'm not an important guy, the president or somebody. It's not my business if the courts want to do all that stuff. Blacks're here. But this is our neighborhood. Irish are best. They can come here if they want, but they'll never belong.

CONCLUSIONS FOR EDUCATION

In recent years, social psychologists have accepted that prejudice is a phenomenon different in childhood, and at each stage of childhood, from later life. The cognitive roots of prejudice discussed in this chapter are normal aspects of the way all children start out. They try to fit their experiences and what they are learning into the assumptions they have, but as their ideas of human nature and their partially-reasoned world views prove inadequate, these assumptions must change and be influenced by new perceptions. Biased categories and other structures of childish thinking become rearranged in the process. The child also wants to appear more mature as changing brain physiology makes equilibrated thinking possible. Kohlberg showed that children's basic philosophies typically reorganize themselves several times. Thus, prejudiced judgments can no longer be seen as part of an early-appearing fixed trait, passively absorbed as certainly and trustingly as mother's milk and almost as early.

Children cannot gain the ability to structure complex thoughts until they have first taken in the world in an overly simple way. Stereotyping is simplifying. But stereotypes of different kinds of people and their differences (that stand out for the very young more than similarities) naturally lead to negative judgments of them. Negativities may then persist, either innocently because they are good for teasing others and for bolstering self-confidence or more malevolently because the child experiences negative emotions. Defensive emotions, left unattended, can overcome normal needs to seek social meanings and stronger coherence among moral judgments. There is, then, a second type of prejudice that is emotionally driven.

A third, socially-learned type of prejudice results from the kind of persistent desire to belong and conform that shuts out others. This may impact moral progress, as well as result from the lack of it. The stories of Ella, Jan, and Meg illustrate the role of the family as it influences the emotional and social factors that inhibit cognitive and moral development, at least for a time.

ELLA, JAN, AND MEG: EMOTIONAL AND SOCIAL BLOCKS TO MORAL GROWTH

Ella's Story

Ella was a pretty, light-skinned black girl who looked and acted older than her ten years. The teacher said that she had "a ready smile, sophisticated dress, and a good social manner. These gain her much approval from the suburban children." Ella had a tendency to prod the other girls as if she were the teacher's helper. She particularly disapproved of Metco children who did not keep in mind that they were "guests of the community."

Ella's mother was admired for her modesty and diligence as a kindergarten aide at her daughter's school. In Ella's teacher's words, Ella's mother showed "total dedication" to her daughter and to Ella's recently adopted sister, the child of her adolescent cousin. She rode the Metco bus with them each day to prevent them from being exposed to any disorder. At her job, she seemed overly quiet, no doubt carrying within her the internalized role conflicts of a black woman in a white setting.[31]

Ella's teacher thought that "her poor mother silently suffers" because her eldest daughter's school work was not quite up to the class standards. A deeper reason for her suffering was perhaps grief, because she had lost her first husband, Ella's father, in an auto accident when Ella was six. She married again, but briefly. Ella, too, seemed somehow grave or at least lacking much childish enthusiasm.

Ella's tested I.Q. score was below average (88), but this kind of poignant family history typically inhibits test-taking skills and invalidates such a score. Being black in a white school after a history of personal loss, including loss of neighborhood friends and having to seek all new friends in the suburb, made Ella inhibited, according to her mother.[32] Friends back in the city warned her that the pervasive racism in suburban America, no matter how disguised, would be destructive to a token black child. But she decided that the child's future lay with the better education of the suburb.

In grade five, evidence of fear of white racism and of loneliness in the suburb did emerge in Ella's projective testing. In two of eight Tasks of Emotional Development (T.E.D.), stories to be made up about neutral-looking pictures, the main character's feelings were, "She feels sad. She has no one to play with — probably no toys and no friends, if they're white."[33] But two teachers told the investigator that Ella was well liked "even though she does not reach out for friends."

To one card depicting only white children, Ella said at age 10:

These four girls are talking and this black girl is over here. She is wondering how come they won't let her into what they're saying, because she feels terrible about it, being all by herself. The others think it's fun to have her being left out. After that they play jump rope and leave her standing there. She goes home and finds something to do. Maybe some day they'll see they're selfish and let her in.

The story evoked by the mother-trust card, which depicts a woman offering a cookie jar to a child, was particularly positive: "Take a few cookies. Take some more."

At age 10 Ella displayed stage one ideas about the dangers of the world. She described her resentment against blacks who increase dangers in their own neighborhoods. Subservience to white authority seemed at her young age the obvious course. Lacking knowledge of history and a raised consciousness about her own group, she stated that slavery would not be bad if slaves were well treated. She also said:

Segregated schools should be left the way they are because black people might not get very nice to whites. They want their own way, and they don't like white people. But the whites want to be friends. They should like the white people. They are all nice. Like we had the militants, and so we have hardly no stores to go to. The other stores are burnt down.

At this age, children do not yet understand how societal forces constrain paths of economic advance to maintain the present and future status of those in power. Such subversion by the esteemed authorities could hardly be imagined. Children begin by accepting the injustices of the stratification system.[34] A black child in a fine school may imagine that all other families could choose to have their children there, too, and that the avenues of upward mobility are wide. The message from adults to do your work, do not bother people, and you will succeed was constant and eventually effective in Ella's case. However, the corollary seemed to be that those who do not succeed deserve to fail. Perhaps the fact that both Ella and her mother were slim, light, and pretty encouraged them all the more to cross-identify with white people.

By age 13, Ella had changed. She believed she must respond to her own home community's pressures and the opinions of the more forceful Metco children by joining them in drawing apart from whites. As she made more friends among other black girls, Ella was troubled by her own previous simplicity in accepting that Metco students should behave as grateful guests. At the same time, she moved into the self-assertiveness of stage two. She was not yet at the stage of conciliation in which she might educate her white classmates.

Testing in the fifth grade brought many instances of silence on her part when probes suggested problems that touched upon her conflicts, but during the seventh-grade testing she spoke more freely. She reduced by half her numerous fifth-grade prejudgments against blacks and the few against whites and others. Her 15 percent of tolerant statements in fifth grade increased to 45 percent in seventh. Her quiet, gentle, fearful personality had begun to change in accordance with her new value system. Growth in assertiveness, along with some continued identification with middle class values, is shown in the following examples.

Probe: Lots of black people don't go to school, even though it's against the law.

At age 10: 'Cause they don't like school. In the city the teachers holler. We can't do nothing. And the children won't obey there.

At age 13: They either get in trouble or they can stay in their house and do nothing. If they want to, they should. If they go out, they'll take drugs. Just to be around.

Probe: Many Indians have different beliefs from whites or Americans.

At age 10: Indians are a different kind of people, and sometimes they don't like the white man.

At age 13: If one got hurt, a white man could give some medicine, or we could always show them our ways to see if they believe in them. Then they might be good to us.

At age 10, Ella made more careful observations than about half the class, but upon entering adolescence her expressions became more disorganized. She was the only class member to be thus affected, dropping in percentage of thoughtful responses from 50 to 29, while the rest of the class rose in this percentage. A reason for her disorganization may appear in her typical question, "Why do the black kids have to make a fuss, when we are not poor people here?" For Ella, being middle class meant keeping a low profile; but this maintained sad feelings.

To the T.E.D. picture of the girl standing apart from a group of others, Ella said at age 13: "There's four girls and another by the house. She feels left out because they won't share secrets with her. (very long pause) Then she starts to cry. Then the girls tell her to go home, because they don't like the things she did. That is all."

Worries about prejudice and the way people see poverty (and perhaps the presence of her mother in the school) made Ella different from noisier Metco students. She seemed to want to favor gentleness and tolerance. However, in rejecting "the way black kids act," she had to deal with a growing desire to fight back, a vital part of her own identity. It has long been known that typical children in certain immigrant groups devalue their nationality, their original language, and even their "ignorant parents," so it is not surprising to find a child in a devalued racial minority seeking to avoid a derogatory identity by joining with attractive, middle class whites. Had there been black teachers in the school, she might well have felt differently.

Jan's Story

Jan was the fourth in an Irish-American family of eight children. An attractive older sister was in the same school in the class above, and two brothers were in high school. Their father, a plumber, and mother, a part-time bank teller, were devout Catholics. Jan's mother appeared warm, sincere, and idealistic, and Jan benefited from growing up in this positive atmosphere. She was called "our future stage star" by her mother.

Expressing happiness and correctness was central to this family's value system, but putting God in charge caused some strain. When faith represents the unquestioning acceptance of deliberate prejudgments, even if for a positive purpose, certain defensive superstitions, stereotypes, and prejudices may appear. Although children were taught to believe in God's love for themselves and for all races, they also believed in Satan and hell and so rooted some of their faith in fear. Some of Jan's comments about black people indicated a sense of danger unwarranted in this suburb.

Jan described her early life in a delighted way, but there were signs that not only "group thinking" but also the distractions of numerous siblings close in age may have interfered with her individualization. She quoted her mother about her future career on the stage as if it were quite settled. Jan was slow to separate her opinions from her next older sister's ("she knows everything") or to develop a conscience somewhat independent from that prescribed by family and church. She lacked an autonomous sense of responsibility to lead her to think about societal problems. Moral realism, exalting rules, was the result.[35]

Both her intelligence (I.Q. 105) and her achievement scores (average, fifty-fourth percentile) were normal. It was, therefore, notable that she seemed "at a total loss when given thought questions" (comment of the fifth-grade teacher). For example, when asked "What can be done for the poor people in the city?" Jan said: "I don't see why they can't help themselves. The ones that are strong and healthy can just start to dig, and get to work. They might be digging, and they might hit oil! And then they could help the sick ones."

With a child as extroverted as Jan, one cannot be sure that such a response was not given as a crowd pleaser, but, whatever her reason, she was unquestionably naive and underdeveloped in the range of her social considerations. Jan's sweet, naive role seemed deliberately played in contrast to both her mother's harsh certainty and her older sister's more questioning, school-oriented style. She constantly sought "should" answers, easy prescriptions for complex problems. Jan's fifth-grade teacher wrote of the "strange rut she thinks in, with only dogmatic and rigid beliefs" and that she is "unable to give reasons for them."

Her T.E.D. test and her teacher's evaluation of her ego development both rated her above average in positive outlook and general social skills with peers. Instead of stressing the loneliness of the outsider when presented with a T.E.D. card showing four girls talking apart from another child, she had the lone girl find new friends to start up a better game. The four girls then wanted to join in the new game and were immediately accepted. This answer would score high on ego strength. However, on more complicated questions requiring good judgment, she did poorly.

Jan, at age 10, really wanted to be as sympathetic and kind as her star image probably dictated. But her favor-trading stage two values appear in the following comments on slavery: "Slavery is wrong, because it caused the Civil War. People were getting treated so mean that they stole ammunition, and that's how it started. But segregation, it's okay, except when the blacks get jealous because their schools are so bad. If they don't mind, then it's okay."

Ideas that later led Jan into goodness-oriented stage three, such as an attempt to have considerate feelings for Leah and other black people and the overriding importance of kindness, are evident here. She felt a sentimental sympathy, but her underlying racial attitudes were still suspicious of those who cause trouble. They lacked all conviction as to the necessity of social reform, and attitudes toward taking action are a necessary part of morality.

Most people are fair, except to blacks. Blacks can do whatever they want, because they need to get confidence. And whites should all help. But they don't have to help clean the slums, unless they were part of the cause. If you want to make a black friend, you should make sure he isn't carrying hidden weapons. If he is, he better be shipped to some island.

This statement shows how Jan's stage two concept of fairness, in which the exchange of favors is instrumental to one's own wishes, limited her reach for idealism. By age 13, Jan had developed a stage three idea of respect and had nearly attained that stage: "Black people are just the same as white people, they want to do right, so you should give the benefit of the doubt when they start a riot."

By this time, Jan was more idealistic, but she was still more sentimental than truly conscientious. She ended her friendship with Leah with impulsive remarks painful to Leah because her own feelings had changed. "Leah is a baby," she explained. "She is just too difficult. She didn't do anything to me, but I don't know why we were ever friends." Jan vacillated in such commitments because she did not yet own her values by understanding or generating them, however strongly they were pronounced.

Jan often spoke in normative terms, with standards taken from majority views. Her moral realism embodied more sense of the value of rules than of responsiveness to others' needs. At 13, she opined,

Kids should not make fun of other colors of people. It's terrible that a rat could bite a baby. My mother made me quick go in the other room and cover my head when that came on TV, because I always have nightmares anyway. If I had to decide what to do about the slums, if I was in Congress, well, I'd go by what the majority thinks. I represent them, so I'd give them ideas, but I'd use their ideas. If there's going to be a riot, then they would think of something to prevent all that suffering.

In Jan's family, smoking and drinking were forbidden, even to the extent of having the children pledge what they would do later as adults. Where life was so prescribed, it was not surprising that Jan developed rather primitive personality defenses, including denial and some counterphobia (firm, phobic-sounding affirmations for warding off fear, the result of the "head under a pillow"). These defenses appeared in some considerations of black people, such as shipping them to an island if they carry weapons. Likewise, with use of the defense called projection, the investigator was accused of purveying prejudices. "By mentioning such words as Jews, blacks — did you say retarded? — you make me want to be prejudiced!" This is an example of a counterphobic protest of lacking prejudice herself. Because she feared prejudice, she projected it onto the interviewer (who did not say retarded).

Nevertheless, Jan was a delightful, gregarious, and well-behaved child. She valued impulsive generosity. Her prejudices were variable, not fully adopted, and apparently more the result of cognitive confusion than an aspect of her identity. She is the kind of child who would presumably benefit from an intellectually oriented, questioning form of moral education.[36] She was efficient in schoolwork, except in areas of social judgment, and she gained the approval she sought from peers. Her tolerance and openness increased from 58 percent in the fifth grade to 74 percent in the seventh, and her numbers of observations rose rapidly from a low 22 percent in fifth grade to a more typical 74 percent in the seventh. Her family's affectionate coerciveness did not prevent her from developing to stage three in high school, although it was an excessively moralistic variation of stage three that presaged neither autonomous thinking nor a total lack of prejudice in the near future.

Meg's Story

Meg, as a fifth grader, had the confident air of a girl who knew she was smart and pretty. She had full, pouting lips, blue eyes, and short blond hair. While her individually tested I.Q. was 130, she missed the top quartile of achievement in fifth grade because she valued a show of protest against restrictions more than spending time studying. Her teacher wrote that she could make a good written assignment if she tried, but she often did not try. Thinking by freely associating ideas in loose generalizations or overly large categories was not a problem for such a bright girl, but she held onto rationalizing as a means of covering feelings wounded in her parents' divorce. She also seemed to be more prejudiced than most classmates.

Meg's fifth-grade teacher called the child "sexually precocious, longing for a boyfriend." More likely, Meg wanted intimacy of the comfortable, cuddling sort because she had not had enough of this at home. Her father had remained detached from the family and far away since she was eight but continued his child support payments. Meg said she wanted to be older to be more the equal of her two popular older brothers and less like her younger sister.

Meg's parents were divorced when she was seven, and the children moved with their mother, now a secretary, to a new state, where Meg entered third grade. The teacher describes Meg's mother as "steady, tries hard, but seems bitter and not open to any discussion or helping. She may be lonely." Meg's statement was that she would like to get along with her mother, "be happy!" and do fewer chores at home. Although lonely herself, she thought the solution would lie in creating a lifestyle more exciting than that of her burdened mother.

Meg's fifth-grade teacher found her lacking in "being a child," in ingenuousness and innocence, and admitted that she felt put off by this girl's critical nature. "She acts superior to everyone, but she is unaware of this problem, and considers herself part of the group. She can be flip and sarcastic and not see it at all." Meg's show of being popular made her seem happier and less overly sensitive than she actually was. Her classmates disliked her covert taunting of less-bright students, her occasional scuffling with other girls, and her negative prejudgments about black students.

At age 10, four of Meg's comments about blacks while playing the Comments game were: "A long time ago blacks were slaves. Some people call Negroes something else! Some Negroes have fuzzy hair and big lips and some don't. Some blacks have Negroes' flat noses."

Many of Meg's fifth-grade comments were scored as prejudices because she expressed herself sourly. During the sixth-grade interview at age 11, Meg said, "When there was trouble in the high school, the stupid principal blamed whites. The blacks never get punished for anything in these schools. They brought knives into our high school, and who gets blamed? White kids."

Meg stated that her racial attitudes did not come from her parents. "They don't care. In New York we sold our house to a black family. Some people around there were mad. In New York also, people don't like Jews. Me either, probably."

In spite of her high intelligence, Meg's moral stage remained transitional between stages two and three up to graduation from high school. At the beginning of adolescence, her values became more openly egocentric as she chose less frequently to consider the viewpoints of others. She was one of only two children in the class whose percentage of tolerant remarks dropped significantly between fifth and seventh grades — from 84 percent to 65 percent. The class as a whole gained an average of 15 percentage points during this period. Only a few children revealed negative emotions that inhibited attitudinal progress.

Meg's ego strength consisted partly in being aware that she had the toughness and intelligence to prevail. She created a story about an ostracized and lonely new girl who was befriended by a pitying adult, although the test card that elicited this story had no adult pictured. Her story hinted that she received an indifferent reception in this new school two years before, after the move from New York. Some of her other stories also had themes of a child's rejection being based on poverty or regional differences, to which she opposed the benefits of new clothes and wealth. In her stories, the child was always strong and found a way of overcoming handicaps.[37]

Meg was capable of penetrating psychological observations in conversation, for example, when she spoke in sixth grade about Leah. "She wants it both ways. She expects to get what she wants because she's different and black, and she expects everything to go wrong for the same reason. And then she can have sympathy." Having made this shrewd remark, Meg lost touch with empathic feelings and proposed a manipulative solution. "If I'd come here as a black, I'd put on two personalities, so I wouldn't act like a jerk, the way those kids do. I'd mix in, pretend I was OK, act like other people, try to forget my color. But not really do it." Perhaps this represents a double story-line that Meg was inventing to compensate for her own sense of being an outsider.

Meg was determined not to be conned. At 13, she said, "I can see right through a kid who pretends to like blacks but really doesn't." As for her own feelings about blacks, she said: "Metco gives smart black kids a chance, but it can make whites temporarily more prejudiced, like me last year. It would be permanent, though, if we never knew one. Last year we hated Leah, so we hated blacks. But now it's more cool around here. I'm sort of glad we have the black kids."

Meg upset some adults, but she was also considered sophisticated. She moved toward more positive statements after age 13 because her good mind and mastery of "being cool" were more appreciated by her peers, particularly the boys, and her popularity improved. Her candor was admirable. Still, she made few tolerant remarks.

In summary, Meg's racial attitudes at age 10 were related to her irritability, induced perhaps by the fighting and divorce of her parents and a difficult and lonely move. There was also the influence of her older siblings, who seem to have triggered Meg's reaction to occasional tensions in their school. Her high intelligence fostered independent judgment, and her school achievement improved over the years. Cognitive development was somewhat slowed by her negativity and defenses, not so much in schoolwork as in social judgment.

Meg's case also illustrates how emotional issues interfere with learning, particularly social learning. Her unmet longing for intimacy was thinly covered by psychological tarps to keep out pain and vulnerability, but these defenses also caused her to form and express some very negative opinions. Although she was easily able to imagine others' motives, including Leah's, Meg's bad feelings prevented her from reasoning well about fairness.

2

The Emotional and Social
Roots of Prejudice

Ella, pretty and shy, had lost two fathers and was caught between valuing the middle class culture of the suburb where she went to school and the very different culture of her home neighborhood. The emotional and social conflicts she lived with prevented her from enjoying her own attractiveness, as Jan did. Jan lived in a family that, for religious reasons, chose to think simply. Whatever prejudices she had were, in part, socially caused, for her cognitive confusion seemed perpetuated by her family's rigid style of expressing their accepted beliefs. Meg, on the other hand, had suffered emotional damage from her parents' divorce. Her frustrated anger at them may have been displaced sometimes and expressed in the form of prejudice.

The stories of Ella, Jan, and Meg show how the three roots of childhood prejudice — cognitive, social, and emotional — overlap and influence each other. There is no separate part of personality that determines whether other ethnic groups will be favored or rejected. Just as the word "ethnic" may cover differences in race, origin, culture, language, beliefs, or religion, the word "prejudice" is a kind of shorthand for no one trait but, rather, a number of possible negative attitudes, judgments, and predispositions to behavior. This chapter will examine the emotional and social factors that either cause prejudice or keep a child from abandoning the normal, cognitively-caused prejudices of early life. We will see that, while children, especially young children, do not, as a rule, directly copy their parents' prejudices, parents have an enormous influence on the child's level of moral judgment and its implied degree of respect for people that affects prejudice.

EMOTIONAL PREJUDICE

The study of emotionally-caused prejudice has its roots in psychodynamic theory, which views prejudice as reactive, rather than directly copied from cultural and parental ethnic attitudes. Because emotion is ephemeral, these roots of attitude are far less accessible than those of conscious thought. Psychoanalysis assigns them to the unconscious mind, a place where even Freud sometimes feared to tread. In that tradition, Kovel wrote that "excrement becomes symbolically associated with the ambivalent feelings a child has about separation from his mother . . . dirt becomes, then, the recipient of his anger at separation. . . . Racism involves the separation of people, so it must become involved with anal fantasies."[1]

While theories relating to infancy wander far beyond the limits of possible verification, the insights of depth psychology have a core of important truth. The problem is that unconscious encodings may be expressed differently in each individual's thoughts or behavior. For example, the experience of extreme separation anxiety some babies have when parting from parents seems often to reappear in later attitudes and behavior. One baby remains anxious, but another overcomes it with assertiveness and anger. A third baby, for the most part, seems to forget about bad feelings as she learns some useful defenses in order to cope. Unless we know something about what an individual's thought process does with any experience or strong feeling, its future effect remains obscure. The angry child may become prejudiced. The anxious one may hold back from judgments, showing the anxiety in guilt or self-disparagement. The early-coping child may be shy in some situations, yet not be prejudiced. Habits of coping tend to persist, but not always, because they can be altered by new ideas and circumstances, including character-training appealing to the child's social interests.

In a less delving and more plausible psychodynamic approach to prejudice, ego psychologists such as Harry Stack Sullivan and Erik Erikson described the strong human motive to form social groups that exclude others in order to increase the self-esteem of their members. Nonmembers may then become targets for any frustration-induced aggression, regardless of its real source. As in Meg's case, the unconscious part of the mind may harbor repressed hostilities that can be unleashed in varying intensity to enhance the sense of self.[2]

PARENTAL AND PEER INFLUENCES

Psychodynamic theories especially emphasize the role of parents. These theories allege that early anger at parents often results in later scapegoating of others. The thesis of the classic tome on prejudice, *The Authoritarian Personality*, is that strong attitudes of prejudice represent hostile or aggressive tendencies that are inhibited or repressed in their direct expression toward the in-group of one's own family and then displaced onto an out-group of persons toward whom it seems more legitimate or permissible to display hostility. Children in punitive homes are not allowed to express their anger directly at the parents who cause it. As a defense, the child becomes intolerant of ambiguity and identifies with the frustrating authority figures, idealizing them and displacing aggression on to weak others, who then become despised.[3]

Early researchers studying child-rearing practices supported the displacement theory of prejudice. In 1950, Harris, Gough, and Martin concluded that suppressive, harsh, and critical home slants children's later behavior.[4] A psychoanalyst, Frenkel-Brunswik, added evidence that rejecting, neglectful parents produce prejudiced offspring who resolve ambivalence by not allowing themselves to think about both sides of an issue.[5] In 1967, Coopersmith found inconsistent discipline to be even more related to emotional prejudice in childhood than parental harshness is.[6] Inconsistent discipline causes children to nag — and perhaps to hinder — their own development by becoming less enjoyable to themselves and others.

Psychologists agree that self-image is at first a mirroring of caretakers' faces and behavior. Some parents dislike parenting, or perhaps disciplining, especially after a long day at work. Others are chronically depressed, uncertain, or disappointed. They may then honor their own parents by imitating how they fought, hit, or scolded. Young children who are told too urgently that their behavior is bad decide that they are bad, unable to understand a statement often made to them that there is a distinction between self and behavior. They recall anger, mainly, and exaggerate its meaning. As the self is devalued, so eventually may be other people. High intelligence, because of its consequent oversensitivity, can actually add to this problem.

Children react strongly not only to parents but also to each other. They spend, on average, twice as much time interacting with siblings as with parents. A frequent problem is that successful children and bullies may tease, intimidate, or cause jealousy in siblings and even peers with shy temperaments or lesser abilities. If the stronger child is the younger, the insults are more undermining.

Although Milner, in 1983, summarized early research (1938–60) as mostly demonstrating that children's racial attitudes and behavior show similarity to those of parents,[7] in 1991, Aboud made a claim more like our own — that divergence from parental thinking is more likely when the child is younger or more cognitively immature. She found at least a dozen confirming studies in the past quarter century.[8]

Contributions to children's developing models of self come from all aspects of experience, including their own temperament, emotions, previous behavior, comparing themselves with others, and the behavior toward them of models they value. As important as these models are, the constructions children's own moral judgments put upon parental and societal norms also influence their attitudes and behavior. Paradoxically, it may be that parents far from the norm have the most lasting effects — positive as well as negative.[9]

Although some children are temperamentally aggressive without being in the least negative, perhaps heaving at their mothers' ribs even before birth, a child of three or four who bites, grabs away toys, knocks down others' buildings, and goes into paroxysms of temper usually has an inadequate sense of his power to create enjoyment and love in the people around him. He then seeks another kind of power, developing habits that persist if the environment does not change. Grade school children who are deliberately rough, disrespectful, or rude and who start fights are in general five times more likely to be convicted of crimes by age 30, according to a large study.[10] Some learn to manipulate people to gain attention of the kind they became used to from acting in a hostile or frightening way. The feeling of power mixes confusingly with the bad feeling of self-disapproval, causing a secret diminution of self-esteem and perhaps defensive rage. Such a child needs soothing and playfulness. Neither the adults who react with anger nor those who ignore or inconsistently give in do the child a favor, because early ability to pacify and discipline oneself may be one of the best predictors of future happiness.

Rosalind Gould's study of play showed that it can be a diagnostic tool for assessing young children's comfort as well as their aggression toward family members. Those who are more proficient than others in their ability to become the other in play are also the ones most likely to fantasize happy scenes. She found this imaginative ability already somewhat lacking in those four- and five-year-olds who, playing roughly, identify with an aggressor.[11]

It now appears that playing out scenes of power and hostility (getting out anger) does not help a child to gain empathic ability and can have a negative effect if not sensitively handled and abbreviated. In particular, firing at a video screen or a plastic soldier seems more likely to increase identification with a punishing adult or perhaps a violent character on television.

Anna Freud had a provocative hypothesis regarding the way negative personalities develop. She argued that anger from too many aggressive experiences is not the whole story, because sad or angry children often simply lack enough support, fun, and positive experiences to balance out their negative feelings. This helps explain the observed ability of abused children to right themselves in a more adequate environment. Not enough happy attachment feelings in childhood can lead to not enough conscious celebration or desire for fun, followed by a delay in ego development.[12] Again, the emphasis is on the child's interpretation of the feelings. Empty and depressive thoughts lead to low productivity and then low self-esteem, which has been repeatedly correlated with prejudice (most notably by Judith Porter and Phyllis Katz).[13]

SOCIALLY LEARNED PREJUDICE

Because of the strong influence of culture, social psychologists, sociologists, and anthropologists have traditionally been social learning theorists. They stress that ethnic stereotypes and corresponding attitudes are learned from socializing agents through the same processes by which anything else is learned — direct instruction, modeling, reward, and so on. Prejudice, like morality, is said to be learned socially in a framework of imitation, passive assimilation, and conditioning. The interdependence of groups in society, with the dominant exploiting the weaker, creates unfortunate attitudes that children then pick up. Institutionalized racism, for example, is as important to address as individual variations in attitudes, according to Pettigrew and Milner.[14] Children assume the underlying attitudes of their culture by imitating behavior modeled by others and copying ideas that prove rewarding, say social psychologists.[15]

While the role of television and the youth culture in the development of children's ethnic attitudes is still largely unknown, because only the roles of parents and the desegregation process have received much attention, social learning theorists are clear that a prejudiced society will produce prejudiced children. Even the acquisition of new meanings is believed to come about through association with culturally favored ideas. For example, a child's attitude about skin color might be based on an association of two concepts: light versus dark and clean versus dirty. Light is already associated with clean and dark with both fear of the dark and dirt. Thus, light skin becomes favored, while dark skin can be invested with notions of unpleasantness and disapproval, at least until children are exposed to contrary opinions. However, black children who have learned the beauty of their own skin color illustrate how prejudices can change and how socially learned ideas are more operative in later childhood and adulthood.[16]

In the 1970s, John Williams demonstrated the negative color associations just mentioned, attaching observations of the human diurnal rhythm to the theory that various attitudes to darkness reinforce each other. He and his collaborators used their Color Meaning Test to demonstrate a childhood bias toward light colors, as well as to show that white children with stronger color preferences have a more pro-Caucasian, anti-black bias.[17] Since that time, societal reinforcements of such attitudes may have changed somewhat, because of increased interracial contact, more ethnic groups being portrayed on television, and changed attitudes in adults. However, color preferences among children remain.

Culturally reinforced ideas bring about other specific prejudices as well. In the following discussion of a game among city fifth graders, Pam and Lou both seem to be justifying some prejudices and establishing their own identities by offering opinions based on supposed facts.

Their ignorance has left them open to influence from culturally-biased views.

Pam (white): Puerto Ricans are poor people.
Lou (black):   But we're not. I like me black, and black friends! Because we tell you if we don't like something. No "nice-nice" and lies, and that.
Bob (white):   The Indians were here first. That's the truth. So I like them.
Pam: Whites belong in this city, not blacks. As far as I know, the first people were the cave men, and they were white.

In this discussion, the culturally-biased assumptions are that being Puerto Rican means being poor, that blacks among blacks are more honest, that being there first creates virtue, and that whites deserve precedence from the order of creation. These city children's comments illustrate how their attempts at reasoning reinforce ethnic loyalties that include myths of superiority. The in-group notion that a right to the local turf has something to do with its owners being better people also underlies attitudes about prior possession. Sensing conflict, white children may come up with reasons why black people wanted to move north or to their part of the city ("the Southerners want them to be slaves again" said one), but they are generally ignorant of adults' real or imagined reasons for fear and aggression.

Henri Tajfel researched the tendency to organize the world of known people into groups, which people do in a healthy way because it helps bring into focus the unique attributes of in-group membership and a comfortable feeling of social identity. The process nonetheless implies easily exaggerated standards of intergroup comparison. Tajfel and others found that children so like grouping that even when they are arbitrarily assigned to comparable groups with neutral names, such as blue or red, they assign more rewards, such as coins, to their own group members.[18] Tajfel also described how the need for an identity dictates more own-group preference as the child grows, regardless of ethnicity.[19] Ashmore and DelBoca added to this the norm of social reciprocity, namely, that one is often handsomely rewarded by members of one's own group for favoring them.[20]

Hall and Jose concluded from their research that, although the struggling or prospering of one's own socioeconomic or cultural group exerts a pull of loyalty upon the preadolescent, the child's cognitive stage of ability to think about distributive justice exerts an even stronger pull on behavior than the sociological status of the child's family. Most older children, regardless of their own family's status, take others' apparent merit and seeming good intentions into account. Cognitive stage seems to overwhelm the influence of social class, at least in middle childhood.[21]

SOCIAL INFLUENCE OF PARENTS

Children seem to accept their parents' political opinions more readily than their negative racial attitudes. Perhaps this is because the immediacy of fairness brings on more questioning of moral issues than of political alliances, and instances of the unfairness of prejudice are publicized. Preschoolers show only moderate correlations with parents' scores on measures of prejudice, and many are definitely more prejudiced than their parents, probably because of cognitive factors.[22] Negativity is shown in the following quotation from a seven-year-old city girl: "My mother thinks since years I don't know the word 'nigger.' She's no help when they bother me so terrible. She would put me to bed. But there's lots of them all over, so why not call them what they are? I hate them."

Some older children describe their parents as more prejudiced than themselves: "I'm not prejudiced, but if I was, it would be their fault," said a black boy of 13. "They're always going on about hippies." Much of the evidence on this is equivocal. Patchen found that parents' education and socioeconomic status had almost no effect on children's interracial friendships, but that parents' racial attitudes did.[23] Ashmore and DelBoca pointed out that there is no evidence of direct teaching of prejudice at home, but there may be rules about playing with certain others, or overheard remarks and embarrassed changing of the subject. If another culture is unknown to a child, negative features may be attributed to it from these behaviors of adults.[24]

One thing is sure: As children grow older, the overall influence of the home tends to lessen and that of the school, friends, and personal thinking grows. Middle grade school may be the period of highest compliance with parental ideas, but one study of prejudice found that among 145 Midwestern families with third- to fifth-grade children, father-son combinations had one out of three agreements, mother-daughter combinations had fewer, and father-daughter and mother-son combinations had no agreement above the chance level.[25]

PEER INFLUENCE

The powerful influence of peers has increased. Two studies in the 1950s revealed that between ages 12 and 18, peers already outweighed parents in influencing both values and acts. Bowerman and Kinch found fourth graders more parent-oriented, but a shift took place by seventh grade toward valuing what peers said.[26] Ten years later, Condry and Simon found the shift occurring earlier and more markedly as the culture underwent changes that increased the gap between generational values.[27] This accelerating shift has also been confirmed by more recent studies.[28]

The shift is unfortunate, but friends often present new viewpoints. Wherever prejudiced or authoritarian attitudes (especially those related to feeling either superior or unfairly treated by society) might be maintained in the privacy of a home, the peer group may provide some correction to children's preoccupation with what parents feel. It is with peers that children learn reciprocal relationships. Like Kohlberg and Harry Stack Sullivan, Piaget believed that peers' mutual influence is an indispensable socializer of children, introducing them to altruism because sharing can offer as much pleasure as selfishness. He wrote that friendship is essential to the understanding of how one's own personality is similar to others.[29] This overcomes the common misconception of believing that one is unique and, thus, either inferior or superior. The greater the maladjustment, the more likely the prejudice that supports it, which consists in bolstering poor self-esteem by falsely putting others down.

Friendship, however, does not necessarily change this tendency. Narrowly based friendships with like-minded persons may reinforce it. Condry, Simon, and Bronfenbrenner, examining 766 sixth graders, found that it was the most peer-oriented children who had negative views of themselves, of their future prospects, and also of their peer group. The researchers attributed this to parental overinvolvement in adult affairs and consequent neglect, especially through a father's absence. When parents neglect their role, susceptibility to group influence during grade school can create an antisocial child.[30]

While there is no evidence that children discuss whether to dislike or to favor certain ethnic groups, a subtle, but devastating, form of mutual consultation goes on in judgments of classmates. For example, Ralph, a sixth grader from a suburban school that had no bused blacks, described the kind of friend he would like to have:

A nice kid, somebody who cracks jokes and doesn't get mad very easily. Race, well, it would matter to a lot of people. I guess it matters to me a little, 'cause of what other kids might think, and everything like that. What his father does doesn't matter much. But once everybody hates a kid, everything matters. Kids get on the lookout and notice every little thing, once the rumors start. I think maybe rumors start with the older big kids, and what they don't like. Then in our grade, or anyone older, they follow the example of the big kids. Somebody didn't like his looks, and it grew. Those ones you have to avoid as friends. Don't talk to them, or you will be considered one of them. There's about five in our class.

Observers have found that categorization works exactly in this way to produce discrimination against a group who are "out." Labels and perceptions interact, even where there is no overt intergroup competition. This hypocritical avoidance of the not-liked children is especially noxious as an expression of the status consciousness that lies behind much socially learned and polite suburban prejudice.

Like Ralph, each child in our study was asked, "What kinds of friends do you like? And what kinds of kids do you not like?" Sixty-four percent of city second graders criticized fighting in their answers, and 72 percent of suburban second graders did likewise. "I don't like to fight, but I do when I have to," was the most frequent attitude reported, even by girls. The girls expressed the most prejudice against people who fought too much. There was a larger percentage of reported dislike of roughness in the suburb, but there were fewer actual reports of beating up as opposed to pushing and fighting. By fifth grade, 56 percent of city children spontaneously protested fighting, as did 37 percent of suburban children.

Children commonly reported that blacks fight more. It was also, but less frequently, said that Jews fight less. Some middle-class boys, a group that included most of the Jews, refused to engage in typical games of bluffing and fighting, because, as a Jewish boy noted, "these things are no fun for the one teased." Such compassion apparently won Jews no admiration among the toughest boys. Prejudgments against Jews were frequently based on the seeming aloofness of some who attended to their studies, which was interpreted as cowardliness or condescension ("they are all yellow," or "they are all smart"). Such remarks may also be interpolations of adult stereotypes.

Over the past decade, social learning theorists, observers of feelings, and cognitive psychologists have been building on each others' work. Aboud concluded that cognitive development causes a movement away from self-centeredness at age 8, which leads the child to care about groups and, thus, to minimize intragroup differences. Another major shift at age 12 results in maximizing these differences because the child becomes more interested in the attitudes and beliefs of individuals, while still wanting to belong to a group. She speculated that the younger the child, the more likely is emotion to dominate cognitive processes, then these predominantly affective processes are replaced by perceptual processes, while only later does cognition take over.[31] This is suggestive, in the sense that the better structured cognition of older children invites more belief in his or her own thought products. However, all three processes — feeling, perceiving, and thinking — occur at all ages; indeed, rapidity of cognitive development is more obvious the younger the child.

INFLUENCE OF DESEGREGATION ON PREJUDICE

Amir describes an "almost mystical faith in the 1960s" that getting to know one another would be the solvent of racial tensions.[32] Excessive optimism was in part because of short-term reductions in prejudice in small social learning experiments based on the theory that working together for a goal in a situation of equality creates friendliness. This contact theory has generated research ever since, and has been much elaborated and revised by field studies of desegregation. In some of the first desegregated high schools in Georgia, Bullock found that interracial contact and crossracial friendships created racial tolerance.[33] However, subsequent research more frequently reported no effect or negative effects from contacts that lacked "supraordinate goals of high appeal."[34]

By 1973, hopes that children would overcome prejudice with friendly play were dashed, as summed up by Billig and Tajfel's explanation that unless there is some proposed reason for behaving otherwise, people generally prefer to interact with people like themselves, whether in race, status, perception, or beliefs. Contact even intensifies initial attitudes, especially if they are strongly held.[35] A book-length study by Glock and others of 5,000 adolescents in the 1970s found that prejudice was as rampant as ever among integrated high school students.[36] This study measured the backgrounds and attitudes of eighth, tenth, and twelfth graders in three schools within 200 miles of New York City. The schools had different racial and ethnic compositions but were not undergoing major changes such as court-ordered desegregation at the time of the study.

Nevertheless, studies by Hawley, Schofield, Armor, and many others about how school desegregation has fared refute any popular impression that the moral imperative of the 1960s had, by the 1980s, given way to pessimism and pragmatism among educators. Most teachers have risen to the challenge. However, many non-educators still assume that the noble experiment of desegregation has failed. The authors of these studies say that this is because the belief that children of all backgrounds learning side-by-side would bring an end to prejudice and social inequality was disappointed. They termed that belief "the old myth." While it is sad that busing between urban schools has helped lower-class blacks so little, there is hard evidence that desegregation has not undermined the quality of education as much as have other pervasive problems: the anonymity of huge schools; the presence of gangs, weapons, and drugs causing fear and anger among students; and the lack of authority and burnout in adults. Armor wrote that it is loss of hope for educational excellence, not prejudice, that has driven approximately half of the white parents in nine large cities to remove their children from the school systems.[37] However, white flight and resegregation within schools have not destroyed interracial contact. Desegregation is proceeding better than it would have without *Brown* vs. *Board of Education*. A new myth, that voluntary desegregation would work better than the court-ordered variety, is also resoundingly refuted by Hawley and his colleagues.[38]

CULTURAL AND ENVIRONMENTAL INFLUENCES

The effect of social class on prejudice seems to be smaller among young people than among adults. Many studies of adults have shown that the deprived are the most frustrated and prejudiced. Although a poll showed that adults who occupy blue-collar and low-income strata displayed anti-Semitism at a two-to-one ratio over those more privileged, the large Glock study found economic deprivation among adolescents accounting for only a small amount of the variation in prejudice within any particular school.[39] The expectation that relatively deprived teenagers would be prejudiced as a reflection of their parents' prejudices also was not fulfilled.

Nevertheless, by adolescence, family status indirectly influenced a number of important measures, including I.Q. and academic achievement. These are related to prejudice, because, as the Glock study's authors wrote, "Youths with motivation and abilities to perform well in school are typically affected more deeply by sophisticated understandings of social life and arguments in favor of democratic values, both of which militate against prejudices they may hold." Failure to be thoughtful in bringing positive values to bear on attitudes correlated with a lack of interest in school and a lack of learning. Sophisticated understandings were less often offered to lower track students. As a result, the authors concluded that "it is academic deprivation which appears to be the major source of prejudice."[40]

Another way to approach the study of the social variables in attitudes is to ask the children about influence on their thoughts, even though answers offered with little insight can hardly be conclusive. Each child in our long-term study was offered five choices of possible influences on ethnic attitudes. In all groups at all ages, "Thinking for Self or Own Experiences" was chosen by about one-third as the reason for the ethnic attitudes they held. Averaging all scores, the groups "Parents" and "Kids" each received 17 percent, but only 6 percent of the city seventh graders and 13 percent of the suburban seventh graders credited their parents with the primary influence. Nearly a quarter of the older city children chose Kids. A subgroup from public housing, which was highest in prejudice, was also highest in choice of Kids as their main influence. Most suburban fourth and seventh graders denied that peers most influenced them. School was said to have the least influence of all, being selected by only 7 percent, which may have been because of the absence of any program to deal with prejudice or recognize differences. Twenty-seven percent of the children chose television as their major influence, demonstrating its educational power.

SUMMARY OF INFLUENCES ON PREJUDICE

While no single theory can adequately describe the complex processes by which attitudes are formed, recent studies by social psychologists see attitudes toward different groups of people developing in conjunction with the child's striving for cognitive competence and coherence. Phyllis Katz was one of the first to integrate some of the disparate early theories.[41] She proposed eight stages of childhood prejudice, four of which are relevant to school-aged children. In the earliest grades, she observed a stage of consolidation of concepts about a group. Next, children favor their own groups while relying on their perceptions in judging others. In middle childhood, cognitive elaboration is still based on experience, but comes out of previously formed opinions and the child's ability to reason.

Katz's last stage is a speculation beyond her evidence, one with which we disagree. She says that in late grade school, attitude crystallization must occur "because of the seeming intransigence of adult attitudes. Though diversity may be beautiful, the child-mind does not remain open indefinitely."[42] Still, secondary school students can be educated, and moral development takes place, often rapidly, in college and in later life.

Katz's stages recognize that children and adolescents reconstruct events and, through reasoning, build them into a complex model of the world that defies a simple learning-theoretical description. In seeking the roots of each child's model, we may trace complex events back to some of their simple beginnings, but the path in the other direction — explaining complex thought structures on the basis of conditioning or instructional principles — is more difficult. A cognitive approach is required to uncover the operations, rule systems, or thought structures available for organizing experience. A depth-psychology or clinical approach is subsequently necessary for understanding the role of personality and family-induced defenses that stand in the way of moral stage progress, defenses evident in our case studies.

Walter Stephan proposes an appealingly complex social model of attitude formation, although neither moral development nor personality defense is emphasized. It begins with beliefs derived from experience, which then lead to motives and intentions that have to be checked against one's own norms or ideals, as well as the norms and ideals of important others, before behavior can be decided upon. The imagined cost versus the reward for performing the behavior will then determine whether it occurs. The acts that are actually performed and the feedback that results continuously influence attitudes.[43]

One could say that the "factual" beliefs with which this sequence begins may originate with television; the family's involvement with another group; warnings about strangers; overheard discussions about crime, jobs, or affirmative action; and especially the child's own experiences in school and neighborhood. However, they are then influenced by the child's personality and judgments, the latter often made according to the structures of the child's moral stage. Stephan hints at this by emphasizing norms, standards, and ideals. Among personality factors, the motives and intentions that develop depend on empathic imagination, ability to pay attention, learned self-discipline, intensity of convictions and feelings, the sense of personal identity from awareness of past thoughts and habits, and desire to imitate what other children are doing.

Inclination to action is particularly important. High moral judgment is of little use without it. In active children, impulsive reactions to insults or how *they* look may short-circuit the expression of the moral stage at which a fairer judgment takes place. Such actions in opposition to the child's better judgment present opportunities for moral and anti-prejudice education.

CONCLUSIONS FOR EDUCATION

The three main branches of psychological research on childhood — the social learning, the psychodynamic, and the cognitive-developmental — have their counterparts in the three types of childhood prejudice. Although different types of childhood prejudice may respond to corresponding educational initiatives, the surrounding atmosphere probably most determines how much prejudice finds expression.

As children grow older, they learn socially to respond to other peoples' wishes and behavior, fitting into the atmosphere of the home and school. Children imitate each other's behaviors to gain acceptance, but they also learn from adult instruction the values for which their school stands. Focusing a grade school around caring can result, after enough time, in a supportive, enjoyable, carefully crafted atmosphere in which personal attention is the norm and blaming others is avoided.

When children suffer the second type of prejudice, the kind that is emotionally driven, their defensiveness holds off easy acceptance of other people. Still, in a school arranged so that every child feels successful rather than ignorant, favorable self-judgment should erode their fears and defenses. There can then be progress in learning respect for others. Children need to feel that they are enjoyed, not just graded and judged, before they can commit their affections to their own friends and their school. Committing to a wider community comes later.

The earliest type of prejudice in childhood, from cognitive under-development, is probably the most common and the most amenable to education. One way to pursue the claim as to its prevalence and relation to children's structures of thought would be to show a correlation between higher stages of moral judgment and fewer statements of prejudice in several populations. This is the path on which our research set out. Its findings, described in Chapter 3, are that significant numbers of children do abandon prejudice or decide not to give evidence of negativity toward others as they achieve moral growth. Before describing this work in detail, the stories of Sal, Beth, and Roy are introduced as examples of how cognitive prejudice dissolves when education in a favorable atmosphere produces the ability to think more clearly.

SAL, BETH, AND ROY: PREJUDICE REDUCED BY MORAL GROWTH

Sal's Story

The whites certainly did start the world! Otherwise, who started it? There must be more whites than blacks. Weren't we the ones who brought them over to the U.S.? I can't see this world being started by the blacks!

Sal was ten and in the fifth grade when he made this remark to some white classmates. They all seemed to like him, even though to adults he appeared confused, antagonistic in a silly way, and prejudiced during most of grade school. His fifth-grade teacher called him "big, messy, and warm." Perhaps it was his warmth that best predicted his progress. The most unusual thing about this otherwise average boy was his progression from cognitive confusion at age 10 to a well-structured reciprocity in social judgments and a good moral awareness only three years later. He reversed the usual pattern of difficult children becoming more so with the onset of adolescence. As an adolescent, Sal pleased his teachers with his helpfulness and cheerful attitude. He had, from an early age, garnered support with such non-verbal social skills as a direct gaze, a relaxed body, and a frequent smile.

In the fifth-grade classroom, Sal acted overly sure that some of his bizarre opinions were correct. Perhaps he sensed that he was confused or emotional and wanted to cover this up with a show of confidence. He may have thought it a handicap to have olive skin, a square build, a foreign name, and a Latin family in a suburb that was strongly Yankee, intellectual, and homogeneous. However, his family was also affectionate, worked outdoors, and stuck together. In time, the boy seemed to appreciate all this: he spoke glowingly about his family when other teenagers scorned theirs.[44]

Sal's mother emigrated from South America to marry an Italian-American who had grown up on a local farm. They met when he was in the Navy. They built a successful nursery business on what was left of the farm after selling off a number of house lots at fine prices as the suburb encroached. Sal worked, too, and the family prospered and became more like the neighbors. His mother, speaking good English, said they were against every kind of prejudice. She undoubtedly felt displaced and somewhat lonely, because she clung to her two sons and feared that an accident or ill health might take them from her. She forbade participation in all sports "until you have grown some." She described Sal as a particularly sweet, obedient child: although stubborn, he would give in with a rush of affection.

Sometimes, a single incident can affect or arrest a child's development for a time. The following statement by Sal at ten cannot be literally true, but his emotional exaggeration of whatever did happen seems reason enough for his subsequent anxieties:

In fourth grade, I was left alone for four days in a hospital. Doctors one after the other gave me shots all over me and in my spine because they were fighting and did not like each other. And I had a terrible headache, so I begged them to leave me alone, so they did. Later they told me it was all my nerves! My dad said I should forget it, but I can't.

Sal missed one-third of his fourth-grade year. His mother would say only that he had "a broken collar-bone and a headache after surgery — anesthesia." Somehow, Sal fixed his mind on the experience. In the fifth grade, Sal's social cognition was impaired by associational — rather than logical — thinking, a dominant imagination, immature accentuation of ideas, and overgeneralization leading to prejudice, as in these examples:

If you're tannish, it depends on the trees and the sunburn. A computer said so; there's a computer that does all that. Water on the black's hand looks white. One kid put his hand in the mud and he was going to touch me, but I couldn't tell if it was cleaned. If a guy who hates blacks gets to be president, he will send them back to Africa. Some of them snarl. But some help. If a slave ran away, I wouldn't help him, if I lived then. A slave is a slave, so that's just it. He'd be my slave, if he came to me.

This statement, in its essential verbal realism, is more typical of a first grader than a fifth grader. On a test for authoritarianism, Sal marked most items in the prejudiced direction. His playground pronouncements surprised some of the children in this liberal community, but he either ignored their taunts of "Boy, you're prejudiced!" or insisted he was right. Nevertheless, because of his friendliness, classmates continued to rate him well-liked.

Sal showed anxiety by tapping his foot throughout the first interview, but his inadequate judgments could not be attributed only to transient anxiety. Egocentric and rationalized assumptions caused a selection of facts and ideas about people that made up a defensive web of meanings. To use Carter's summary of the implicit notions in childhood's frequently defensive philosophizing, Sal already had "a metaphysical system, however ragged and incomplete."[45]

Sal said of Indians, "If you know the true religion, you won't worry and get heart attacks, you won't think a spirit is going to attack you. We should convince them that spirits are only the wind in the tents." Sal's immature assumptions about power relations seem tinged with self-reassurance: "Indians want to finish the trouble, if somebody starts it. But they are too weak, and the good guys win!"

Even while shutting out others' opinions, Sal did not lack curiosity. His I.Q. was average — 108 — but his percentage of analytical statements about ethnic groups during the Comments game, when added to those in the subsequent interview (75 percent versus a class average of 52 percent), predicted his emergence from confused egocentrism.

While Sal's early anxieties undoubtedly slowed down and inhibited the structural changes in his social thinking that later appeared, an incentive to take the viewpoint of others existed in the family's mutual supportiveness and shared enjoyments. Apparently, unfortunate events like the hospital stay or early parental mistakes, such as overprotection, are not so damaging to a child as a lack of emotional support.

In the happy climate of this home, Sal did not become angry at his mother for worrying about his health or side with peers against her about playing school sports.[46] He probably struggled unconsciously with these problems, using the primitive defense called denial, which made him appear overly simple. When his father brought him into the family business of selling trees, Sal came to identify more with him, which may have helped resolve whatever intellectual blocks were associated with the unconscious denial of differences between his mother's ideas and those in the local environment. At this point, Sal became able to listen to classmates and teachers. He developed new thought structures as he practiced taking the viewpoints of others. While in fifth grade he had stated that Jews swear a lot and always try to get out of work and that Mexicans should be kept out, in seventh grade, he said:

Mexicans see pictures of our suburbs. They end up in cities, but it's our prejudices and no jobs that push them there. We should allow all immigration. We use their place for vacations, and we stay there, so let them come here. Jews have more holidays and some of my friends don't like that. But I do. I think they should be allowed to, because they are created as equal as Christians, Catholics, and so on. They might keep their store open on Christmas.

Sal also made an imaginative statement about Indians. It incorporates the sentimentality often seen at the beginning of childhood conventional thinking, when pleasantness, rather than might, becomes important:

If we had left the Indians in charge of the land, we would have half as much pollution. They used one deer for 50 people, lasting a week. For us, one deer is for eight people in one day. We should never have fought them. It was their land. I would have fought back, too. I saw an Indian in a TV commercial going across a lake, and I thought how they love wildlife and they don't like to kill humans, either.

Instead of emphasizing the differences between self and other, Yankee and Italian, Mexican and American, Sal moved away from the normative judgmental viewpoint. His new relativism brought out the ideas of others, which increased their interest for him. Sal soon recognized that unusual values can be perfectly legitimate for other groups.

Beth's Story

Beth was born into a corporate manager's family that was especially pleased to have a girl. She had brown hair and gray eyes, and she developed all the social graces that ensure popularity. Her mother, a former teacher, believed in showing care and altruism toward others but was apparently not free of a suburban type of prejudice called "symbolic" that tends to think of people as symbols of their group and situation, rather than as individual humans who feel their problems.[47] The effect is to maintain the value of social harmony over consideration of the need for change. Beth recognized the contradictions in her mother's ideas, and, yet, in the end, she accepted the same assumptions. She provides insight into how symbolic prejudice begins with a certain pride.

Beth, at age 10, reported that two foreign students had been invited to live in her basement, "because Mom wants me more aware of other kinds of people." Mixed feelings about this caused confusion: pride that her mother cared so much about her attitudes but annoyance at the inconvenience. "I don't like them being there," she concluded. The foreign students were disturbing, real people, not just "kinds of people" whose lives could be used to teach an abstract lesson.

The feelings that emerged illumine the mutual vague suspicions that this devoted mother-daughter pair each had of the other. Beth's mother thought of her child (and perhaps of herself) as selfish. She made a strong effort to counter this defect at the price of her privacy. Apparently, that caused some resentment in Beth, who said she was bringing the problems of the outside world into the house. Outsiders can all too easily be kept as such, not just by keeping them in the basement but by relating to them as people in need. That increases the importance of the giver and, by extension, the in-group. Beth sensed this problem. She further explored her reactions: "My mother is a mother and a teacher, and she can do it. She can do about anything. She talks me into feeling sorry for people. She always brings this up, when we're just sitting around. It gets boring."

Beth's mother proposed that her child might be "too spoiled, because she has no understanding of less privileged people." For her part, Beth attempted to be pleasing by at first agreeing with her insistent mother on "feeling sorry for people" and afterward rebelling to a degree that seemed calculated to maintain harmony by showing just a little assertiveness while not appearing too spoiled. She remained more reactive to adults than willing to compose her own ideas.[48] The abrupt shift of attitudes toward blacks from positive to negative in the following statement seems to be an example of her uncertainty:

People don't start riots on purpose, as prejudiced people would think. Like, you know, the blacks who are left out might get someone to be our president who orders, "Let the whites be our servants, let all the blacks out of jail." If we give them what they want, they'll parade all over the street. Martin Luther King didn't go too far, so all were sad at his death.

It can be questioned whether Beth felt some insincerity in her family that she wanted to avoid by rebelling, or whether she simply expressed her own version of her mother's ambivalence. Beth's mother put limits on her own "do-gooding" by, for example, opposing low-cost housing in her suburb. "It would ruin our schools," she said. "I'm for everything that can be done short of bringing down what has been painfully built up. When it is a matter of your own children, you dare not go too far."

Beth said on this subject: "Mama thinks it's awful that the churches should talk about bringing poor people here, because that is not a church subject, and it is not their business. And religion is very important; they should preach about that."

Beth's grades and test scores predicted her high marks (standardized achievement seventy-second percentile; I.Q. 122). She was considered mature by her teacher and "particularly secure." The teacher rated her highest in the class in ego strength. Over the 32 months of the main study, her moral maturity moved from stage two to a high stage three, and her percentage of tolerance from 45 to 85. Beth assumed a leadership role in the class during this period. She adopted and enjoyed conventional attitudes that made her feel mature, and she shared them by moralizing.

It may have been ambivalence that kept Beth from extending much friendship toward the bused black children, although she felt somewhat drawn to Leah. She embarrassedly and quickly confided that she was glad her mother was not chosen as a Metco host parent. "I asked my mother what to do when kids say, 'You're standing up for that creep Leah!'" Then Beth added that she does not dislike anyone, "not really." Keeping up appearances and having a well-rationalized conscience were as important to Beth as to her mother.

Identification with a parent or other idealized person represents a strong motive to become still more like that person, especially if she is predictable, rather than too complex. Kindness, competence, and power are desirable characteristics to copy, because the feeling "I am good" calms anxiety and gives pleasure. Beth's mother was not predictable. The fact that Beth's impulses confused her and were not particularly generous might have represented the partiality of her acceptance of her mother's self-justifications.

Later, some judgments of Beth's character by her mother may have allowed Beth to think with more independence. Conflicts between them continued to develop in adolescence as a result of Beth's strength and her mother's controlling nature. Beth began to think more freely, with less patronizing prejudice, as the progress shown between the following quotations reveals.

Fifth grade: You shouldn't break the law if you could ever get it changed. So I don't know if I would help a slave. You should go give some talks in the slave markets, to try to end slavery. But there's always troubles, you can't stop them, like hunger and slaving. So do your little bit. Slaves aren't really doing any good. They aren't saving lives, or really helping people. One or another might become somebody, if he could choose to. Like a surgeon. So they should be free, in case they might choose to.

Seventh grade: Of course you should help a slave get away. Slavery is wrong. Forcing someone to work or be whipped is wrong; it doesn't matter who it is, black or white or purple. It's a person, not an animal, and working should be by choice, or because you need something.

Beth's progress by grade seven was encouraging in regard to her future attitudes. However, even at age 13 she said, "*It's* a person," as if black people might still be as strange and remote from her privileged self as purple people.[49] While her mother may not have created all the generosity she might have liked, her direct teachings succeeded in stimulating Beth to be aware of the importance of life's moral dimension, as Beth shows here: "When I was eight, two black girls, bad, knocked me and my friend off our bikes and took the groceries we were taking home to my friend's. She nearly got hit by a car. My mother said, 'Just because those two are bad doesn't mean all black people are bad.'"

Roy's Story

Roy was a lively, good-looking boy with a small, neat build. His father, although unemployed for medical reasons, took care of his six children with evident affection and generosity. Their attractive mother scrubbed floors at a hospital at night. Roy said his parents were "real religious. But my father doesn't feel real good." His father was born poor in the rural South; his mother was hardly better off in a northern city.

Roy's normal style was to seek enjoyment throughout the school day. His ready smile, aggressiveness, and "cool" image brought out playfulness in other children. A lightning temper, with the flash soon over, built his reputation during his first two years on the Metco bus as one who would fight (and win) for his friends. Both black and white children admired him. As with Black English, which has no passive voice and keeps its action in the clear present indicative, Roy's whole demeanor said, "Here I am! This is my truth, and you will never paint me white."[50]

In the fifth grade, Roy's projective testing showed him to be unsettled and angry underneath. With joking, verbal dancing, and charming avoidance of probes, he produced vignettes, rather than stories, about the Tasks of Emotional Development pictures. To the self image card, depicting a boy with a mirror, Roy said, "Here is a boy who sees in the mirror he has a black eye, so he barricades himself in a room and throws himself on the bed." No further details were forthcoming. Roy's prejudices were likewise somewhat fragmentary and incomprehensible to himself. On the E Scale, Roy at first checked most stereotypes as true.

A lively preschooler whose experiences seem fleeting, disorganized, and overchallenging may become restless and impulsive in school. Roy's sensitivity may have been overcharged by the many stimuli of urban life, but also enhanced by a large and economically insecure family crowded into a few rooms. Roy's tests showed considerable vagueness and lack of integration of forms, which indicates defenses less stable than his school successes and popularity would predict. However, beneath the hyperactive defense, one could sense in Roy a persistent struggle for fair values and a more organized mind. No half-hearted evasions of problems would do for him.

Regarding school work, Roy's teacher complained that he tended to "act, rather than evaluate," but he managed to stay in the top group in math, where he had been placed to increase his confidence. His observations and directed thinking increased sharply from 11 percent to 91 percent over the months from age 10 to age 13. His tolerance in the same period rose from 32 percent to 85 percent, and his moral stage from one to two. His I.Q. tested at a probably inaccurately low score of 91, and his achievement scores were at the thirty-ninth percentile on local, suburban norms. He had attended an inner city school through the third grade and was one of the better students there. In the suburban fourth, fifth, and sixth grades he held his own without special help.

In the suburban junior high school Roy adapted less successfully. His father died of tuberculosis during the first term of seventh grade, and Roy's grief was sharp. He cried during an interview. He seemed to cope by increasing his habit of laughingly pushing and assaulting other boys in the halls and playgrounds. Soon, anyone who afforded him the slightest excuse (such as remaining angry after the last fight) was in danger. "I'm sorry, I just love to fight," said Roy, smiling shyly to the principal. "It's a good sport." Between flares of temper, Roy was so good-natured that the school staff and some white boys remained sympathetic. People seemed to sense his holding back, perhaps rehearsing being tough while not becoming overly antagonized, as city boys do with their rituals of insults. The majority of his fights were with black boys, anyway. "Blacks mess around too much," he said in a despairing tone.

Despite the increased fighting, Roy's prejudices lessened from fifth to seventh grade. In seventh, he checked only half the stereotypes on the E Scale as true, distributed equally between anti-Semitic and anti-black remarks. About Jews, Roy said, "Jews. . . . My brother got gypped so he called it by a Jew, but I don't know. I hear lots of people teasing Jews. In Boston they say Jews gyp people, but I don't know, 'cause I don't hear that here."

About blacks, Roy was more confused. The seventh-grade interview took place soon after a disturbance had occurred in his neighborhood. Roy was attracted to the "bad black" image of power, even as he found power in his own fists. Consciously, he denied the attraction.

The Black Panther Party I hate. My uncle got crushed in an elevator because of them. They got investigated. They held up stores, that's how they got their store on Blue Hill Ave. They start their meetings by a yell, "Black Power." If anybody belongs to it and tries to get out, they better not, 'cause a car could go over the curb. Most blacks — well, most that are bad — they start riots and grab a lot of stuff. I seen it. (to himself) We're going to have a riot, soon.

In seventh grade, Roy was more able to tell stories than before. To the Tasks of Emotional Development aggression card, which depicts boys confronting each other, he said:

It could be more fair. The one that's going to get hit by the bully, he didn't want to swap something. I guess they're going to get into a fight. If he doesn't, they won't call him bully no more. The boy, he might have called him that. Then he might beat the bully; you can't always win all your fights. Me, I never saw any bully. He picks on people, and scares people, and fights. (big smile)

This story showed Roy's increasingly false style of dealing with the white world. From his point of view, he was still real, using performance criteria (not acting white) to judge his involvement with his black identity. However, from the school's viewpoint, he played at a charming, teasing innocence while he was becoming anything but innocent. Fighting — being a bully — was one delight in Roy's life because it was a way to live openly and intensely. A second was the paralyzed dismay of the middle-class school authorities. In the early years of so-called integration, they were prevented from dealing as harshly with him as with some of his white classmates because of their liberal sympathy toward his usually well-veiled hostility. Roy's ego had been formed and supported by the pleasure others took in his forceful activism, his charm, and his brand of success. He enjoyed tuning in to other people and being well liked.

However, Roy was unhappy with the contrasts between his home environment and the suburban school. He made this clear in conversations around the time of his father's death. Roy confided that he fought so much because:

From the place I live; that's the real reason. It's so different from here, and I'm not from here.

Segregation wouldn't be good, because if we were separated for a long time, we might get to only like our own. Especially if we studied black history, we would start to hate people. It happens around my way, and the school I was in. Whites get beat up a lot. My sister goes to high school; what a mess. All "protection" in the school, kids carrying things. Last week two white boys chased her swinging a TV antenna, all the way to where the police are. Her friend brings a big butcher knife in her purse for protection. She got it out after she bet two dollars she could split a cookie, and the whole table laughed. That's how it is, all the time.

Later in the year he said:

I'd never steal nothing, 'cause I'll get caught. I know our history. Huey Newton, he killed a policeman, October 28, 1967. Cleaver, he took off his clothes to show he had no weapons, and got arrested for that. Willie Stone in New York, he did a lot of shooting for nothing. It would be a better nation if everybody was allowed to have their own customs. But around where I live, they have whiskey parties on the fire escape, and the police, they're always surrounding them, or they're chasing kids that hook school, or steal purses. The last one I knew, my friend, she got off.

Perhaps the intensity of Roy's desire to fight back against someone, whether it be the less-successful black boys at school or powerful whites, frightened him. He used maxims, such as "once you steal, you always will," to keep himself in line, but their continued effectiveness depended on stage one structures that he was now too advanced to maintain. He knew and disliked the danger in ghetto streets long before the prevalence of crack cocaine, yet persistent idealism attracted him to becoming more ideologically militant. The idea that fighting the law is reasonable because law is part of the system (of oppression) led Roy to study the black militants of the 1960s. He had yet to decide whether to suppress his sensitivity, his own dangerousness, neither, or both. Beneath self-aggrandizement was the need to keep feelings of hopelessness and the collective lack of power of his people out of mind, and Roy felt successful in this self-defense.

Roy probably felt tension between his background, which included al his mother's loyalty and love, and coming to somehow prefer the experiences in the white school to those in his neighborhood. While Roy was too morally aware for simple anti-white prejudice, choosing to fight any and all boys demonstrated a compromise adherence to his accepted values of "being a brother," flirting with danger, and seeking popularity. Roy needed someone to recognize his strong leadership potential and devise a way for him to shine before the school, in speeches, in debates, in sports, in performing arts, in teaching black studies, in almost anything he could have done with charm and individuality.

Sarah Lawrence Lightfoot describes the distressing difference for most lower class black children between the profound and deeply etched learning from their families and the style and attitudes of schools. Lightfoot writes that the asymmetric power relations between schools and ghetto parents need to be harmonized around the truth that the child's self-image is crucial to educational progress. The parents need to be in the schools, both advising and learning from the counselors and teachers, so that "as the first and primary educators of the child, their effects will not be undone, but elaborated on, enriched and expanded."[51]

Alienation from good, but struggling and preoccupied, parents and alienation from conceptualizing and confronting social evils currently troubling the child are the effects of schools that unknowingly attempt to counter, etherize, or distort the ethical perceptions that mean so much to a confused adolescent identity.[52] In Roy's case, no one was available at school to acknowledge and admire his attempts to learn black history and to establish and ground his own positive strivings. He needed to sort out these issues and he needed support to deal with his father's death. In ninth grade, Roy was suspended from the suburban high school for stealing another boy's shop project. His former teachers were shocked to hear that he stole it to give to his mother as a work of his own.

3

Prejudice Tied to Moral Judgment: A Study

The stories of Sal, Beth, Roy, and the other children illustrate the ways in which unique events and family constellations sometimes foster and sometimes inhibit personality and moral development. Personality emerges in the narrative each child inwardly recounts about ongoing experiences and adventures that star the self. The child's limited interpretive ability colors the story but expands with the support of others as the narrative continues.

Sal's history shows that cognitive problems, even when severe, can be overcome with the help of a warm and supportive family. He moved past the confusion of his hospital stay, and structural changes in his moral reasoning took place. Beth was critical of her mother, yet internalized many of her suburban attitudes of superiority. Paradoxically, she began to overcome these copied attitudes because of the stimulus to think morally that she received at home. Roy, so alive and struggling to find his place in the world, showed promise despite his father's death and the hardships of his background. His moral growth seemed to derive from his alertness and will to constantly test and think about his environment.

Like Roy, each of the case-study children was part of a long-term study of 22 fifth-grade classmates tested repeatedly through junior high school and high school. This study sought to correlate the children's prejudices and moral development with I.Q., achievement, and Tasks of Emotional Development (T.E.D.) test scores, as well as the protocols of child, mother, and teacher interviews. Although small, the long-term study helps us to better understand how a child's family, culture, experiences, and emotions influence moral stage progress.

A second study of 154 children in second, fifth, and seventh grades in several city and suburban schools also hypothesized that there would be an inverse correlation between moral stage and prejudice. It was not possible to meet these children's mothers or teachers or to obtain I.Q. and achievement scores. They were tested over two weeks only. Both the short, broad study and the long-term study involved playing a game called Comments, responding to some one-sentence probes about prejudice during a private interview, answering standardized questions, and then responding to three of Kohlberg's moral dilemmas — those concerning stealing to save a life, euthanasia, and slavery. To avoid as much as possible promulgating prejudices, the probes came from remarks by a set of younger and a set of older grade school children in the suburb during pretesting with the Comments game. Most children found them rather foolish, but not "horrifying," as one child described the classic E Scale probes used in a pretest.

THE COMMENTS GAME

The major difficulty in prejudice research is finding an indirect technique to evoke attitudes that there is much social pressure to conceal. All the traditional ethnic attitude measures for children older than seven are either too direct or too circumscribed: Bright children can easily discern the aim of questionnaires or doll-choice games, and the compliant, or less-bright, may too easily assent to prejudiced statements from an authority figure. A board game, it seemed, could create a spontaneous atmosphere if it required fast-moving verbalizations. The excitement of competition reduces self-consciousness and consequent attempts to please. The game devised for the study was similar to Parchesi in its layout (see Figure 3.1). It pictures faces of eight American ethnic groups (black, Indian, Irish, Italian, Jewish, Mexican, Oriental, and Puerto Rican) around the edge of the board. The goal is for a man, representing one of the pictured ethnic groups, to overcome unspecified social obstacles and reach home, thereby becoming a complete American.

Before the game began, each of four players was asked to choose a particular group to represent, give reasons for that choice, and then discuss other possible choices in order of preference. When the game commenced, each child had to make a comment about one or another group whenever a throw of the dice caused landing on a color-coded space. The children were told that the point of the game was to find out their ideas on the problems these various groups had faced in becoming full Americans, so that either this game or another form of curriculum for social studies could be developed. They could either comment on problems they knew about or make any general comment so the game could proceed quickly.

The children tested were from public schools in the area around Boston. Forty-eight were city dwellers: 30 white, 13 black, and 5 Asian. The majority had workingclass backgrounds, although a few children of professionals and some from public housing projects were included. The city children came from two schools and a day camp representing 11 more schools. The suburban half of the short-term study, numbering 53,

FIGURE 3.1
The Game of Comments

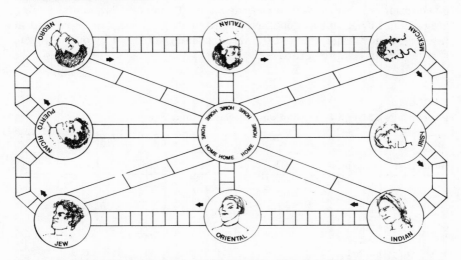

Source: F. H. Davidson, "Ability to Respect Persons Compared to Ethnic Prejudice in Childhood." *Journal of Personality and Social Psychology* 34 (1976): 1259. Copyright © A.P.A.

were from the same mostly workingclass school as the long-term group, but 10 of them were black children bused to the suburb from Boston. Both groups were roughly half boys and half girls. In addition, 53 sixth-grade boys from a wealthy suburb were tested, and 22 fourth-grade children had their prejudices tested as a part of checking the validity of the probes, gathered from local "prejudiced" children, against those in the familiar E Scale of Adorno, Frenkel-Brunswik, Levinson, and Sanford.

For most players, the comments were initially neutral: "Black people have dark skin"; "Italians eat spaghetti." However, after one or two rounds, the children began to express feelings. We found in pre-testing that many avoided commenting on blacks and Jews, so we painted 12 spaces blue that required a comment on blacks and 6 yellow that required a comment on Jews. Twenty-four spaces were painted red, allowing a comment on any group.

DECREASE IN PREJUDICE

When results were analyzed, a strong statistical correlation between lower moral stage and higher prejudice was shown for all groups (see Table 3.1). The lower-stage children, no matter what their ages, offered the most negative comments toward the various groups. The six- and seven-year-olds were all at the pre-moral stages, but the many older children at those stages also showed more prejudice, especially those with a stage one power orientation. Thirty-six percent of comments were negative at stage one, 19 percent at favor-trading stage two, 11 percent at goodness-oriented stage three, and 6 percent at law-and-order stage four (which was partially achieved by only a few of the suburban seventh graders).

TABLE 3.1
Percentage of Negative Comments at Each Moral Stage

Grade	Description	Stage			
		One	Two	Three	Four
2	City	45	26		
2	Suburb	30	19		
5	City	44	20		
5	Suburb	37	13		
7	City	47	25	12	
7	Suburb	(18)	13	6	8
5	Suburb, longitudinal study	35	18	(7)	
7	Suburb, longitudinal study	27	13	6	5
6	Affluent suburb	(11)	18	15	
	Totals	36%	19%	11%	6%

Note: For the numbers in parentheses, N = <5.
Source: Compiled by the author.

Studies of grade school children generally find prejudice declining with age, as did this study.[1] Between age 7 and age 13, prejudiced remarks decreased 10 percent in the city and 14 percent in the suburb (see Table 3.2). Someone might object that the decrease could have been simply the result of the children growing older, thus becoming better at observation and less cognitively confused, rather than the result of growth in moral judgment. Another problem is the presumed effect of intelligence on an ability to hide prejudice. However, when a statistical process was used to eliminate (partial out) both the effects of age and the effects of intelligence from the results of the long-term study, the overall inverse correlation between moral stage and prejudice turned out to be still highly significant (see Table 3.3). In other words, the results could not have occurred mostly from variations in intelligence or from the general intellectual development that comes with age.[2]

TABLE 3.2

Racial and Ethnic Attitudes of Three Age Groups of Children in Suburban Schools (by grade; in percent)

	By Whites			By Metco Blacks in Same Classes		
Attitude	Second (N = 13)	Fifth (N = 19)	Seventh (N = 21)	Second (N = 3)	Fifth (N = 2)	Seventh (N = 5)
Toward blacks						
Negative	23	21	18	51	38	30
Neutral	62	68	74	22	18	47
Positive	15	11	8	3	44	23
Toward whites[a]						
Negative	0	4	9	7	33	33
Neutral	91	84	80	93	47	50
Positive	9	12	11	0	20	17
Toward Jews						
Negative	12	6	12	0	3	10
Neutral	81	80	63	83	97	84
Positive	7	14	25	17	0	6
Toward others[b]						
Negative	21	19	9	35	31	15
Neutral	53	55	67	18	42	85
Positive	26	26	24	47	27	0

Table 3.2, continued

Racial and Ethnic Attitudes of Three Age Groups of Children in City Schools
(by grade; in percent)

Attitude	By Whites			By Blacks in Same Classes		
	Second (N = 8)	fifth (N = 15)	Seventh (N = 12)	Second (N = 3)	Fifth (N = 6)	Seventh (N = 4)
Toward blacks						
Negative	56	61	31	31	28	14
Neutral	15	19	53	27	53	54
Positive	29	20	16	42	19	32
Toward whites[a]						
Negative	6	0	23	71	74	57
Neutral	82	85	49	29	26	43
Positive	12	15	18	0	0	0
Toward Jews						
Negative	33	39	28	12	18	42
Neutral	67	55	72	83	82	58
Positive	0	6	0	5	0	0
Toward others[b]						
Negative	23	26	21	42	39	35
Neutral	38	53	61	37	45	42
Positive	39	21	18	21	10	23

[a]Irish, Italian, and so on.
[b]Oriental and Native American

Source: Compiled by the author.

TABLE 3.3
Correlations of Moral Stage and I.Q. with Other Variables
(longitudinal group; N = 22)

	Moral Stage in Fifth Grade	Moral Stage in Seventh Grade	Stanford Binet I.Q.
Moral stage			
Fifth	1.00	.79[a]	.60[a]
Seventh	.79[a]	1.00	.55[b]
Percent of ethnic negatives			
Fifth	−.73[a]	−.71[a]	−.46[b]
Seventh	−.64[a]	−.71[a]	−.41[b]
School achievement			
Fifth	.61[a]	.36[b]	.70[a]
Percent of directed thinking			
Fifth	.25	.39	.50[b]
Seventh	.44	.45	.49[b]
Percent of tolerant statements			
Fifth	.51[b]	.71[a]	.40[b]
Seventh	.15	.51[b]	.15

[a] $p = <.001$.
[b] $p = <.01$.

Source: Compiled by the author.

Environment affected prejudice, but it, too, had less effect than moral judgment upon the stage trend: Suburban second graders at low stages had more prejudices than older children at higher stages from the city, where the level of open prejudice was much higher overall. Additionally, there was a group exception to the downward age trend in prejudice, namely the black and white children from the abnormal environment of the city housing projects, where exposure to explicit hostility and violence requires defensive judgments. Negative statements and low moral stages prevailed among all these children, older as well as younger.

While stereotypic and negative comments lessened over the course of childhood, neutral comments were most frequent at all ages. Focusing only on positive and negative remarks may give the false impression that the subject of prejudice greatly occupied these playful children. On the contrary, the younger children seemed to be conscious of ethnic problems only for brief periods — as when asked to comment, or when teasing and tension levels rose between groups.

FORMS OF THOUGHT

To examine the mechanics of thinking at each age, the children's comments were divided into four categories: physical information-giving ("blacks have kinky hair"), social information-giving ("rats with little shining eyes scare those children"), personal remarks without supporting reasons ("blacks would get sick of so many blacks, if the schools weren't mixed"), and remarks showing social reasoning ("blacks get treated awful; they always get small toys, like Hot Wheels, so you can see how they must feel; they don't get big toys at Christmas"). Table 3.4 shows the percentages of each type of remark at age 7, age 9, and age 13. If the four categories are reduced to two, stereotypes and personal feelings — called stereotypic thinking and observations and social reasoning — called directed thinking — three-fourths of the comments at all ages were found to fall into one or the other of these dominant patterns.

TABLE 3.4
Types of Spontaneous Comments in City and Suburb
(in percent; N = 91)

Type of Comment	At Age 7		At Age 9		At Age 13	
	City	Suburb	City	Suburb	City	Suburb
Physical information	30	41	12	16	3	1
Social information	48	34	38	39	29	28
Stereotypes and feelings	7	9	26	18	37	12
Social reasoning	15	16	24	27	41	59

Source: Compiled by the author.

The seven-year-olds (and to a lesser extent the nine- and thirteen-year-olds) put particular emphasis upon physical information. "Mexicans live in dust, so I don't like them that much," said a suburban second grader. Her reasoning was based on a physical or sensual impression connected to a general category of disliked things. Three-quarters of the spontaneous expressions on ethnic groups from seven-year-olds contained relatively unprocessed sensory information. This physical information was usually about something obvious, unless it was quoted from someone else.

Very few of the seven-year-olds' comments were explicitly concerned with similarities between people. Differences are more interesting and challenging, and for the average seven-year-old, the basic physical differences between people are easily tied to their actions. Labeling ethnic groups as good or bad on the basis of appearance and unexamined actions is typical. Comments center on differences in face, hair texture, clothing, personal style, food, activity level, and fighting. Perceived power or size is an important influence on good-bad conclusions. Children in the city and suburbs find other groups to be "different," "funny," or perhaps "ugly." Being physically different is cause for suspicion, and for about half the suburban children, it is bad.

Negative behavior is noticed more when associated with ethnic differences in the minds of young children, as in a seven-year-old suburban boy's comment, "What do I think about black people? Black people are different. Some are mean. I saw some on TV, in the news, yelling." Of course, angry white people also make the news, but this went unremarked. The children see physical differences that cannot be denied, and because of immaturity, they come to associate these differences with psychological and social meanings.

The next step in thought advancement is anchoring perceptions of society's status differences in social, rather than physical, attributes. Accordingly, poverty and its physical stigmata are likely to become associated in middle childhood with social powerlessness and unimportance and also with visible racial and ethnic differences. "Their house smells like yechy food cooking, like cabbage, and they don't have styles, like clothes that cost more," said a city-dwelling, middle-class black fifth grader about her Irish neighbors. Perceiving social class differences often led to aesthetic condemnations and, even more often, to disdain for lack of economic power.

Around grade three, the children began spontaneously to notice similarities between people, and, during grade four, their statements changed in form from being predominantly concrete and information-giving to being predominantly explanatory. Both personal pronouncements and reasoned and directed thought became more prominent. The children seemed to assume more responsibility for what they said. They elaborated on their perceptions when given time in the individual interviews.[3] Piaget contrasted later childhood or adolescence with middle childhood as a period of theorizing and formally elaborating beliefs. However, more recent studies, like this one, have found that some younger children also theorize at length.[4]

By the fourth grade, the suburban children were beginning to abandon extreme, two-value categories (saying, for example, "I think Mexicans are dark like Negroes, or in-between") and were replacing them with more sympathetic, emotional expressions about blacks being "treated awful," having "no chance to be a boss," "a giant leak in their faucets," or "rats in the halls." The fourth-grade results are consistent with the mentality of that age group as described by Peel who said that such children are in a transitional period, shifting from lives of simple reaction to what is daily taught to a lively seeking for explanations.[5] In our study, about half the comments collected at age 9 were informational and half were the products of personal thought, illustrating neatly the transitional period.

As their thought matured in preadolescence, the children made less stereotypic and negative pronouncements. Between age 7 and age 13 negative statements were much reduced. As children begin to imagine the feelings of others, they also begin to articulate more complicated values. The values of goodness-oriented stage three were often expressed along with hedged prejudices. However, many seventh graders in both the city and suburbs who mentioned feelings accompanied them with positive ethnic remarks. Supraordinate categories, such as "most people, they will do the best they can," helped these higher stage children to see beyond ethnic differences and antagonisms to understand the more subtle differences and partial similarities of people. They also more readily spoke of value-based reasons to avoid prejudice. Decreasing prejudice seems to be the result of the increases in moral stage shown in Table 3.5. (It is possible that an attitude of indulging the most hostile type of prejudice could also hold back moral stage transition and, therefore, account for part of the high correlation between the two in some cases.)

TABLE 3.5
Moral Stages in Suburb and City
(N = 176)

Grade and Moral Stage	Percent in Suburb	Percent in City
Two		
One	29.5	82.4
Two	71.0	18.1
Five		
One	35.4	69.0
Two	40.2	12.5
Three	25.6	18.5
Seven		
One	6.6	12.5
Two	53.3	62.5
Three	26.6	25.0
Four	13.3	0.0
All grades totaled		
One	23.8	51.2
Two	50.0	32.6
Three	21.5	16.3
Four	4.8	0.0

Note: Average moral stages in grade two were 1.7 in the suburb and 1.0 in the city; in grade five, 1.9 in the suburb and 1.6 in the city; in grade seven, 2.5 in the suburb and 2.1 in the city; and for all grades, 2.1 in the suburb and 1.7 in the city.

Source: Compiled by the author.

CONTENTS OF THOUGHT

The objects of the children's negative remarks reflect society's attitude toward blacks because they received the largest number. The black children in the suburb also made more negative remarks about black people than the most negative group of white children. This might be because of the middle-class aspirations inherent in being bused to a suburban school as well as the contrast between behavior in that school and black children's behavior in the poorer city schools and neighborhoods. The remarks may also represent pervasive experiences with negative behavior that could cause more emotion-based prejudices and lower moral stages.

The white suburban children's negative remarks about blacks declined by almost half during the first 32 months of the long-term study as these children attained more understanding and desire to cooperate with the democratic professions of their culture. In contrast, the bused black children in the suburbs did not decline in their percentage of negative remarks until high school, and they were willing, in fifth grade, to accept the clearly prejudiced statements on a test used to validate our test, the E Scale.[6] Learning in this conflicted area could have been slowed by the challenges of biculturality. E Scale prejudices were gradually rejected by almost all the white children in the lower grades and were fully rejected in the seventh grade.

The black seventh graders rejected the obvious E Scale stereotypes of blacks provided by whites, but they persisted in maintaining other stereotypes about themselves. However, interview results at this age could have been affected by their dismissive verbal habits in which negative comments (including stereotypes) are made when they seem to be more interesting and provocative than a neutral remark. Many preadolescents think positive statements are "uncool."

Statements against blacks by children at all ages were frequently phrased as personal opinions or feelings. In contrast, statements about Jews, who received the second highest number of negative remarks, were mostly phrased as consenting to descriptions of attitudes by third parties. This may have resulted from the hesitation of some children to admit to inexplicable negative feelings. Because blacks seemed more different to them than Jews, and because racism is familiar, some children may have felt that black-white prejudice was understandable, whereas anti-Semitism was not.

The greatest drop in prejudiced remarks occurred in the group of white children who initially showed the most prejudice. A factor of cognitive maturation seems likely. The children making the highest number of prejudiced statements in the fifth grade expressed some negative feelings about blacks and Jews in one-third to one-half of their statements and about other groups in one-fifth of their comments. Except for comments about blacks, which remained about one-fourth negative, their total percentage of negative remarks dropped to one-sixth in seventh grade. The two less prejudiced groups and the bused black city children remained relatively unchanged. Their negativity toward blacks and Jews was more or less constant between fifth and seventh grades, although they did drop in their negative assessment of others, which represented all the groups other than Jews, gentile whites, and blacks.

"Others" was the least socially influenced or content-dependent category, because little peer interest was given to opinions about distant Mexicans, Puerto Ricans, Indians, and Orientals. As a result, cognitive and moral stage changes most affected gains in this area. The bused black children dropped their negative assessment of others by one-half during the study, in sharp contrast to their negative assessment of white groups, a percentage that remained unchanged. Here, they showed the same relative decline in the amount of negative prejudgments as the white children, which confirms the probability that there is a factor of cognitive development involved in all of these results.

A factor of social learning is also present. The current cultural climate of disapproval of prejudice is familiar to children, and that helps explain why expressions of prejudice generally declined from age 7 to age 13.

CITY VERSUS SUBURB

The city group was noticeably behind the suburban group in moral judgment from the earliest age but was ahead in apparent empathy. The city group was clearly less in the habit of analyzing. Almost three-fourths of the suburban second graders were at the favor-trading stage two (and the others at the power-oriented stage one), while all but 18 percent of the same-aged city children were still at stage one. The half-stage difference was not made up during childhood, but it did not widen, either. The average child of ten in the city sample resembled a seven-year-old from the suburban school both in moral reasoning and in being less able to describe the viewpoint of another person.

City second graders made nearly one-third negative comments about people, or twice as many as their suburban counterparts, omitting the African-American children. The average of negative comments made by these bused city children while in second grade (31 percent) was almost identical with their second-grade peers in the city. However, all was by no means worse in the city group. As can be seen in the following Comments game transcripts of second graders, the behavior of urban children as they made their comments was straightforward, direct, and honest. They seemed surer of what they felt, if not of what they thought. As they landed on the various squares eliciting comments on blacks, Irish, Jews, and so forth, they interacted warmly and without taint of hypocrisy. There was no reference to feelings, but like the one black and three white girls playing Comments quoted in the following transcript, they showed by their carefully calibrated behavior that they were intuitively aware of the feelings of each other and almost orchestrally responsive to them. Having fun and enjoying each other was more important than ethnic differences.

Sue (to interviewer, about Lynn):   That girl is a tomboy. She fools around like a boy. I wish you were all black because black people are more kind and not so selfish. (to Lynn) You and Mary write swears. I saw you.

Lynn: Mary did. Not me. I know one thing about black people. They were brought here to be slaves.

Sue: But we're not slaves to anybody now. My father told me that. I wish there were more blacks here than whites because I don't like white people. They make me more comfortable with black people. With whites, they don't make me so comfortable.

Pam: In a story we had, the blacks were always slaves. Harriet Tubman went down a secret path and helped them get away.

Sue: I don't know that story. Hurry up, you Ann, make a comment. You're always too slow. What's wrong with you?

Ann: You don't have to tell me what to do. Is Irish in Germany? Oh, no. Well, I like Indians. Where was I? They're nice.

Sue: You're a ding-a-ling, you know that?

Pam: I never met any Jewish people. But I know a lot of Finnish.

Sue: Chinese, let's see. We had Chinese New Year's a few days ago.

Pam: Blacks fight more than other people do. Do you know Mir is black?

Lynn: No she's not, she's white. I think she's Italian.

Ann: Mir's not black, you crazy. (slyly smiles) But she looks black.

These girls are clearly aware of gender, race, and skin color as factors in social status. The exchange about Mir exemplifies the subtlety with which ethnic awareness and racial negativity can be disseminated in a peer group.

The game-playing of four suburban children, two girls and two boys, was less spontaneous than that of the city children of the same age. Most remarks were guarded, even while being highly positive. Prejudice was either described or teased about, but it was not acted out. While awareness of the existence of prejudice is not the same as personal prejudice, the all-white suburban group seemed already conscious that the process of excluding disliked groups should be politely hidden. Judy and Frank agreed on the niceness of Jews even though no comment on Jews was required by the space landed upon. Frank corrected his statement on blacks to make it more positive, although later he revealed some negative feelings about blacks. Jane, the most expressive of the children, had some unrevealed thoughts behind her linking of Jews and blacks, as suggested by her application of the ugly-pretty and looking-acting contrasts to both groups.

Dave: My father is Jewish, my grandfather, my uncle, so I picked that. I think Irish is like being American.

Judy: Jews are nice.

Frank: I have a Jewish friend. Mexicans. They're the most interesting of all these. Their hats and all.

Dave: Blacks come on the bus.

Judy: Blacks have black hair.

Jane: I like Indians 'cause they do things I like.

Judy: Indians hunt, and they have no school, and all that.

Frank: Jews have nice houses.

Judy: Jews have funny candles, and they have statues with big ears that look like funny toys. I saw it at Matt's house.

David: One time Egypt stole the Jewish and they were there four years. They were hungry, but they escaped. Then they celebrated.

Jane: Jews are ugly acting. But they're pretty looking. Sometimes I kiss them, some boys I might. (kisses David, produces outcry and scuffle)

Frank: Puerto Ricans live in Puerto Rico. It's near Florida. Some people hate poor people. Their houses are dirty.

Jane: Blacks have ugly faces. Sometimes they act okay.

Frank: Some blacks are silly. (long pause) Just like regular people. They have the same humor as regular people.

Dave: Orientals have different kinds of faces. Indians are a little like that.

Judy: There are more white people than blacks.

Frank: Blacks are all black or brown, I don't know. I don't really like that.

Jane: I like Indian jewelry. And they have horses.

The differences in the types of comments offered by the city and suburban children were consistent. White city children in both the fourth and seventh grades kept about half their remarks on the stereotypic pronouncement or opinion level ("Irish only like green"), whereas only 18 percent of the remarks by suburban fourth graders were of this type, a number that dropped to 12 percent by seventh grade. While the seventh-grade city children offered about one-third social information and one-third reasoned comments, 37 percent of their comments were still in the form of either pronouncements or personal anecdotes, while the suburban seventh graders were now offering five times more social reasoning statements than stereotypes (see Table 3.4).

Interestingly, there were no significant correlations between moral stage and individual style (as shown by the percentage of analytic versus stereotypic comments) in any of the grade school groups. The development of moral judgment proceeded at about the same rate. Stereotyping, after all, was only one part of the empathic, friendly, overly personal teasing that went on in the city. The frankness and chiding warmth in the city children's involvement with each other apparently fostered moral development during the grade school years about as much as did the suburban child's analytic carefulness and curiosity. Later, in adolescence and adulthood, the development of an analytic type of thought process does have an essential influence on the ability to reach higher moral stages.

WHITE CHILDREN'S ATTITUDES

Developmental lags in overcoming prejudice were more likely to be made up among the children in the suburbs. By age 9, the white suburban children gave more sympathetic responses to the problems of ethnic minorities than the white city children did. However, a sentiment that costs almost nothing because it relates to far-away people holds the danger of a sterile moralism, which can also become a form of prejudice. The suburban children's ignorance of the range and intensity of their own ethnic feelings might well contribute to less caring attitudes later

The development of the suburban children's conscious empathy, which was relatively cool in feeling, was probably the result of the dissemination of knowledge on the harm of racism and prejudice. "My mother says, 'You should never say such things as Italians are better than Irish,'" said one boy. This raises the question of whether a kind of training for hypocrisy exists in the homes and in the schooling of white middle-class children as they learn to avoid negative remarks, and eventually most kinds of remarks, about blacks, Jews, and ethnics in general. If any suburban child had negative feelings about some ethnic group, or felt anxiety based upon knowledge that others have these feelings, the choice of an information-giving or an analytical comment could be an escape from vague feelings left unexamined.

In contrast, city children who are in constant contact with other ethnic groups, be they friendly, threatening, or actually abrasive, must deal directly with the people around them. They cultivate a style of half-joking toughness, which leads to either interethnic friendships or anger and fights. Lack of challenge to their ideas, or perhaps early personal contacts that were too stimulating, difficult, or neglectful, slowed moral development in the youngest group before age 7.

A further possibility is that low-stage values that all children at one time hold, such as "punish the bad" or "favor your own kind," are retained longer in city neighborhoods because those values are better adapted to coping with certain aspects of urban life. They serve as rationalizations for tough behavior that city children may have less freedom to experiment with and speculate about than did the suburban seventh-grade girl who decided, when newly confronted with louder peers, "to act real mean, to see if that will help." It seems likely that city and suburban children could each benefit from positive contacts with each other's cognitive styles and even more from guidance in how to respond to different kinds of peers.

BLACK CHILDREN'S ATTITUDES

The black children who were bused to the suburbs by Metco to some extent reflected the serious attitudes of parents who had gone to the effort and trouble of enrolling and sending them. Most joked around less than their counterparts in city schools, and they expressed slightly more liking of whites and no more rejecting of blacks than did typical black city-schooled children their age. Many Metco children, up until adolescence, contrasted suburban life with disruptions in the city that they attributed to the bad habits of their neighbors: "Lots of people just sit around and drink." "There's drugs." "It's amazing. Here dogs are nice, but where I come from, they bite. They teach them to bite!"

Being bused to the suburb for years had a disappointing effect as far as lessening the black children's apprehensive attitudes toward both blacks and whites. Prejudices remained as defenses. In fifth grade, they showed appreciation for the white community's sponsoring their schooling, but by the seventh grade, this kind of "grateful" comment was absent or scorned.

A major problem for black children bused to the suburbs lies in the intensified conflict in adolescence over how much to adhere to their own community as a "brother" or "sister" and how much it is all right to be as bicultural as they were in grade school. A social class issue exists here as well because the Metco children were relatively poor while their friends in grade school were clearly middle class. Even when quite able to think at stage three, their tendency was to turn away in practice from being an "Oreo," a cookie dark on the outside and white on the inside, in favor of the stage two ethic of fierce loyalty to friends similar to themselves.

At each new period in the formation of a child's identity, ethnicity has new significance, especially if it involves contrast with a dominant culture of another race. New sets of values must accommodate to a growing awareness of important aspects of oneself and how others see one. The bused blacks were challenged to make rapid advances later, even if they were unable to while accommodating feelings generated in their first years.

ATTITUDES TOWARD DESEGREGATION
IN CITY AND SUBURB

City children in this sample who attended desegregated schools became somewhat more favorable about their experience as they progressed. Approximately half (56 percent) claimed to be favorable to integration in the second grade and 62 percent in the fourth. There were no totally negative comments in the seventh grade. The number of black children who were favorable was close to the number of white children at all grade levels. All were asked: "Do you like your own school best, or an all-black (all-white) school?" A white second-grade boy responded: "It's better like this. Some fight, but some don't fight. You can invite kids over, and the whole world might get friends."

The subject of fairness was introduced spontaneously by a large portion of the children. When white children in second and fourth grades were asked if they would mind being born black or Indian, two-thirds replied that they would not. This seemed to be based on two typical assumptions of young children. First, there are no random events, and, second, people should try to be fair.

To the question about being born black or Indian, only one white city second grader replied with frank emotion: "I would mind, wouldn't you?" The typical answer, "they are the same as us," seemed more the result of an intent to be fair than of a willingness actually to compare the lives of blacks and Indians with their own. An additional 37 percent of the children were favorable toward blacks in their responses to this question, and many of those who preferred to be white appeared embarrassed by admitting it, as in: "Well, I want to be white, but just because I like my own family."

With the suburban children, this question succeeded as a prod to considerations of fairness, beginning with the fourth graders. The ability to respect others, associated by researchers with high socioeconomic status and other factors contributing to ego strength, had a clear effect on answers to the question: "Do you think Metco is a good idea?" Suburban responses were almost entirely positive, as when a white seventh-grade girl said:

It's a good program. Everybody gets over prejudice by the third or fifth grade, when they are fooling around with words, and might call names in a fight. They might not know what they mean. But in my parents' generation, you can't change their prejudices. I don't think so. We should give the black kids a chance to learn.

Although Metco clearly promotes considerations of fairness, there is no clear connection between the friendly idealism of grade school children and alteration of attitudes that would result in later individual friendships between blacks and whites. The whites reported that, beginning in the seventh grade, the black students separated themselves, which caused anger. A black girl in seventh grade said:

I think black people have to be allowed to do what they got to do, by the time they are our age. If we want to be with black people, it's okay, it's good for us. We know what we want better than the whites do, but I don't know if we are going to do it; but we know what it is. But it doesn't matter if whites are in the same school.

Depressed and confused about leaving the white friends she had associated with for years, this girl seemed to worry that her group's new and prideful attitude about future mainstream success might be mere hollow protest: "I don't know if we are going to do it, but we know what it is." However, she recognized the importance of asserting her racial identity, as well as her own ideas, in fighting off feelings of anger and depression.

When Useem studied partial desegregation throughout the Metco program in this and other suburbs at around this same time, she found that only 12 percent of the local students had invited a Metco student home during high school. Sixty-five percent in high school had no Metco students among their 15 best friends, 14 percent had 1, and 21 percent had 2 or more. At the same time, 82 percent had currently one or more classes with a Metco student, and many had shared extracurricular activities with several. Sixty-seven percent of the blacks, for their part, said that while the whites had mostly been friendly, they had had to put up with a significant number of racially prejudiced acts.[7]

At the time of this study, there were no black teachers in the suburban junior high school nor were there programs to make Metco more understandable to whites or to prolong its favorable implementation as experienced by the younger children. Few white students had any concept that African-American aggressiveness might result from African-Americans' severe minority status in the school, knowledge of prejudice, problems in home neighborhoods, or the attitudes of the host children. Therefore, the white students tended to take blacks separating themselves and any shows of aggression as personally insulting. In this context of ignorance, interracial contact did not promote lasting friendships.

To check further on the participating schools' assumption that Metco ought to have some effect toward reducing prejudice, we compared the attitudes of 53 sixth graders from an all-white school to those of children in the suburb that had a Metco program. The children in the all-white school were decidedly less interested in the subject of racial attitudes. One boy simply dismissed the question when he was asked if he would think it a kind of prejudice if he overheard a remark by an adult that black people are poor people. "How true, how true," replied the boy, airily. Both the lack of ethnic diversity in that school and the fact that its children came from wealthier families may have contributed to disinterest in racial problems. Higher socioeconomic status was associated with fewer negative remarks in all of the groups in the original suburb, but in the absence of any poor or black people, it seemed to insulate the children in the all-white school from the social concerns sixth graders often have.

CONCLUSIONS FOR EDUCATION

The correlation of prejudiced attitudes with moral stage indicates that attention to one will affect the other. Moral judgment is, of course, a product of cognitive development, but moral attitude is a larger concept because it includes attentional, imaginative, emotional, and behavioral aspects of life. The attitudes we measured as degrees of prejudice are closer to behavior than the children's responses to the hypothetical dilemmas of Kohlberg, but Kohlberg's test measures structures more fundamental than attitudes. It makes sense, then, to subsume attitude development under moral and character development, and at the same time to attend to the school's atmosphere as most important for motivation.

The main problem for stage theories such as Kohlberg's has been the inability to specify a set of processes by which a competence (or a stage of judgment) becomes a behavioral performance, or at least a very good predictor of a range of performances. The difficulty is that inner and outer contexts enter into whether a stage or level of moral judgment will lead to moral behavior. Contexts could include the preexisting relationships of the parties; how challenging, or, conversely, well-rewarded the act will be; how impulsive, lethargic, shy, or energetic the actor is; how important morality is to her or him, and so forth. Unless some of these factors are controlled, one can predict only loosely what behavior will result or what educational conditions will be likely to advance moral judgment. Among these, opportunity for identification with attractive and strong moral mentors is an intuitive first.

Some research by Kurt Fischer and Robert Wozniak backs their contention that human intelligence is always social. They imply that we ought to be speaking of the child not as possessing a stage but as being in process, or being at a range of stages, if we want to make predictions about behavior. They demonstrate that, without human support during testing, scores are lower than the child is capable of producing.[8] Similarly, behavior is likely to be lower than moral judgment would predict. Obviously, what they are saying has strong implications for other tests. It is even more important in explaining why a more supportive, caring kind of education is needed to make schools more productive.

The young child's interest in fairness to self has to be expanded not only through moral judgment exercises but also through social learning. A sense of mutuality results from growing up with loving and moral parents whose behaviors do not elicit excessive defensiveness in the child. For less fortunate children, schools with teachers who show caring behavior are all the more crucial for both moral and academic development.

While appreciating Fischer and Wozniak's point that children usually behave over a range of stages depending on environmental support, we will now consider in detail each of our individual moral stages in relation to prejudice. This should help to provide insight into why children think the way they do at each stage, why there are links with prejudice, and what helps bring about moral stage change. The following chapter is concerned with the pre-moral stages one and two, the stages at which most school children operate. Leah and Pat are two such children.

LEAH AND PAT: SERIOUS PROBLEMS PREVENT STAGE CHANGE

Leah's Story

Leah was the lively, smiling eldest of four children who lived with their mother in a dilapidated housing project. Their father was serving a prison term. Their mother protested his innocence to the children, perhaps hiding her doubts, just as she tried to hide her dislike of dependence on welfare. She set out to find a job on the same day she succeeded, through Metco, in getting her children into good suburban schools. However, the only job she could find extended late into the evening.

This job caused Leah's greatest trial. No adult greeted the children when their bus arrived back in the city, usually after dark. Leah, aged 10, would call her mother, then fix supper. She was paid $1.50 a week ("sometimes") to feed the others and wash the dishes. Her mother became upset when the children were disorderly and she was too far away to manage them. Leah described how she was alternately praised and scolded by telephone, whereupon she cried. "I cry every night, I get so mad. I cry to my mother, and I cry to myself."

Leah's suburban teachers, scandalized, wondered aloud if her mother cared about her children. However, this mother was far from indifferent. She soon worked at a second job, keeping the children beautifully dressed so they would be accepted and respected. She said she was happy during weekends at home, when she could be wholly focused on the children. However, when she came to the school for scheduled conferences, she presented herself, according to a teacher's written report, as "overwhelmed, passive, and unknowledgeable." The teachers at that time were ignorant of the threat that they and the white school posed through their superiority and unawareness of the problems of a lonely black mother. Leah's mother's ability to plan and to work at two jobs showed not passivity but quiet and resigned determination.

Her eldest daughter, on the other hand, was unable to be quiet. She hyperactively entertained the other children in school skits and plays as well as with her pranks. Her fifth-grade teacher described her:

Leah is an outgoing person with a wide smile, but uses crying spells and hysterics to get what she wants. She has the extremes from a dominant to a very weak personality. Often she withdraws into herself. It's just that she had a mind of her own and will do what she wants. She is very self-centered, but when she likes herself, she will go overboard to give really all she has to others. Often she feels outcast (and in many ways she is), but her naturally attractive qualities appeal to the children whenever she is happy enough to encourage it.

While Leah could take roles on the stage, she refrained rather strikingly from thinking about how the people around her felt (called role-taking by psychologists). Her I.Q. score was a normal 94 (brought down by the social items on the Stanford-Binet), but her contributions in social studies class, while full of curiosity, lacked common sense. She felt blocked and sometimes refused to do mathematics.

Leah's school problems were emotionally caused. They centered around her unsatisfied need to feel safe and cared for.[9] She spent her days, in winter from darkness to darkness, on a long bus ride and in an overly challenging new environment. Because of this, even though she was a warm child, she failed to be consistently interested in other people, including her friends, whenever she was not the center of attention. Defensiveness impeded her moral development.[10]

Card two of the T.E.D., which depicts a woman offering a cookie jar to a child, tests for trust. The T.E.D. authors write, "Trust is the primary task of emotional development. More than any other task, it has overriding significance to later development." Leah's story to this card was:

This, this — there is something fishy about this. This little girl's mother opens the can, and I think she's getting something to eat. She sticks her hand in. But, well. Well, it might be something hot to eat. There's something fishy. (long pause) It's the way the little girl sticks her hand in the hot pan. She almost got burnt. Then her mother took her to the hospital. She got some Band Aids put on.

Most notable was Leah's halting confusion in telling this story. Do mothers offer hot pans? Mother was not to be blamed, though. In fact, she was dutiful in taking her little girl to the hospital for the "almost" burn. Although the child could have been angry or hurt, she really cannot afford negative emotion toward the parent she needs so much. Leah finally decided that what was fishy is the way the little girl stuck her hand in the hot pan: that is, it was her own fault. There seems to be an intrapunitive process here. Leah's lack of clarity about the burn was evidence, too, that she mistrusted not only her mother or parents but also her own decision-making processes. She had to restrain and disguise her assertive self.

It was not surprising that Leah, with the sense of impending danger shown in the hot pan projection, had little energy for considering justice in society and what moral values might be needed. She progressed only slightly from her own low level at age 10 by age 13, remaining at stage one. This "can't move" syndrome was shown in another T.E.D. story, this one about a picture of girls about to play baseball in an open field.

The little girls are having a conversation, right? Another girl is standing in a corner, all alone, with nobody to play or talk with. She walks along, but they pay no attention. They must notice her, so they'll run away. She thinks she'll never have any friends. Just like me! Ever since third grade. But I do now. I had no friends in my other school. Should I tell why? Because I was a cry-baby. I think I'll never stop, and I'll have no husband when I grow up. No man will ever like that. I thought of it when I saw that scary show on TV.

Loneliness and scariness in both past and future were elicited by this ordinary picture. Having friends had not changed Leah's self-image; she mistrusted too much. At the expense of interest in her story, she began to speak of her own sad feelings and how she blamed herself for them. As the test is scored, this was a negative sign. Leah was low in ego-strength, although she was a high energy child and far from a quitter.

In the seventh grade, Leah looked at a card with a similar scene in which she proposed that one of the girls was black. She plunged in without introduction or stage-setting:

They don't see her coming. When she comes, they'll beat her up. It's four against one. They are against black kids. I don't know why. It's the way she acts. She is a nice girl, and she does act nice. It's the way she looks. Most white people judge by that. And blacks judge other blacks that way. The way they act. This is the black girl's backyard. So they walk off home. They run when they see her. She feels terrible. There's no use trying, they don't pay much attention to her. Some of the Metco girls don't like me. If I learned to play kickball they might like me. But I just can't. I can't kick. So, she goes to talk to somebody. But that doesn't help.

Next, Leah told a story with two beginnings and two endings, one angry and one nice "forever," symbolizing the two sides of her own personality. Because she was able to dramatize, she could somewhat enjoy herself, and so she seldom withdrew when depressed. She was fiercely bossy and then despondent, changing with a rapidity that infuriated her would-be friends.

Those two little girls are having a nice conversation. Kind of. Maybe a fuss. The one with the funny look won the fight. The big one went to the hospital for stitches in her eyes. She kicked her in the eyes. That's icky! The mothers yelled at each other. That's all. No. When the stitches got out, she was invited to her birthday. They made up forever. The end.

In fifth grade, Leah had asked the interviewer, "Don't you wish you was little like me, with a host-family to invite you over?" Leah gradually recognized that the prejudices of the other Metco children and of some whites would require that she separate from white friends. In sixth grade, she said: "Most white kids are enemies of blacks, but I didn't know this until last year. I was low in math, and the boys talked about me." On the E Scale test of prejudice, Leah, at age 10, marked as true, "All Negroes are about the same," "Most Negroes would become bossy and disagreeable if not kept down," and "It's natural and right for each one to think his family better than any other." In junior high, after blacks and whites formed separate groups, all these items were marked "NO!!!"

Nevertheless, Leah had trouble making friends with black classmates in junior high. "I used to think blacks and whites are both nice, but now it's the black kids that are mad because they want me to be with them. But they don't like me."

Both blacks and whites displeased Leah:

Definitely, whites act nicer than they are. I see a million of them pretending to be. Blacks are more honest. If they feel mean, they act mean. They sure act mean to me. But you should avoid people who make you feel that way. If you don't want to have anything to do with white people, I say, it's your life. The same for the others.

Here, we see how the limitations in Leah's social thinking dictated her response. Avoiding those persons who make you feel bad was generalized to avoiding their entire race. Then the justification was put in quasi-moral terms: everyone should decide his own case.

Retaining these constrictions on moral thought into adolescence served the anger in Leah. Without anger, she might have been overwhelmed by the need to cry. She limited her values to those of the low, egocentric moral stages because anger balanced her fears of white enemies, black indifference, and what she imagined to be her personal ugliness. ("It's no use trying to make friends if you don't look good. That's what you are.")[11] Studying others' motives, the usual means of introduction to higher moral stages, harbored too much risk.

Leah's case shows the fallacy of the idea that equality of opportunity through education alone is the solution for prejudice. Societal ignorance, racism and classism, parental choices, governmental priorities and consequent lack of money for job training, housing and child care so constrained Leah's freedom that she could not progress. Emotional turmoil blocked much of her ability to take advantage of the opportunities offered her. In this, she was like many other poor children, including those whose mothers struggle less to provide.

Pat's Story

Although he was a large, ruddy-faced and healthy looking boy, Pat was overprotected by his timid mother. She had brought her own mother to live in her home and still drew comfort and self-esteem mainly from her, seeking approval through perfect housekeeping. Pat was supposed to stay neat and under control, but he did his best to ignore both women, rather than defy or challenge them. The early pattern of avoidance continued. He saved his aggression for peers. His parents' marriage did not go well, and Pat's father took on extra work. The father than decided to work toward a college degree that would lead to a higher standard of living. He attended night courses and saw little of Pat.

When Pat was four, a sickly baby sister arrived, and she took more attention away from him. When, as a five- or six-year-old, he went outside to play, he was made to stay inside the chain-link fence that surrounded the house, even though the house was on a particularly safe dead-end street. The freely-roaming neighborhood children came over, but Pat would try to dominate them until they taunted him and ran away. His mother described this scene as formative of his later social difficulties at school and blamed the children rather than any adults. In a wan voice she described how a kindergarten teacher had cared about her son's development and told her to read with him, but no one could change Pat. He seemed to have an especially stubborn temperament.

In the fifth grade, Pat made unsuccessful efforts to become the class clown by making jokes as well as teasing and playfully tripping the other children. Friendship groups in the class had formed without him, so his joking hardly hid his sadness and hostility. Although he longed for friends, he said he saw no use in friendly gestures toward "brats and piggies. The piggies are the girls."

Although Pat had a high I.Q. (Stanford-Binet 126), the assumptions behind his social judgments showed little growth from fifth grade through high school. Greatest among these was that each person should decide issues in his own material favor or in favor of his own group. Then, if he cares enough, that person can go to battle for his side. So far, these were the typical assumptions of favor-trading stage two and normal enough. However, Pat was not sure he did care. "Prejudice doesn't matter," he said. "Be like Humphrey Bogart. Don't stick your neck out, then it won't get cut off."

Pat, at age 10, would only stick his foot out, getting attention from a few resulting titters aimed at stumbling classmates. Their school work and size did not measure up to his, a thought he used to rationalize his isolation. He avoided most emotional risks, as if he were still running behind the fence his parents had erected. He also avoided the physical risks of fistfights and sports. "Getting in a fight only gets you punished," he said.

The coolness that often characterized his household seemed to carry over into Pat's reaction to any kind of exhorting instruction or punishment put upon him. "He does not care," said his mother. "Nothing we do can change him. His father comes home and yells at him. I wish he didn't do it, but it's no difference to Pat. Still, he's a pretty good boy." His mother did not seem to sense Pat's underlying frustration and angry feelings, and she suffered with a smile his outer indifference: "Like his father, that's all." Lacking understanding of a child's need for play, frivolity, and cultivation of a sense of wonder, she blamed stoicism on maleness and mistaken genetics. "The boy inherits it from his father's side." Nevertheless, she felt proud of Pat as he got older, and she appreciated his not getting into trouble.

One of the most striking things about Pat as a child was that he disliked stories, both at school and on television.[12] Lack of interest in abstractions or fantasy caused him to give quick, somewhat aggressive, answers to most questions. He gained a sense of power through word games and conserving words. He would not have described himself as prejudiced because, "If you don't do anything to somebody, you're not prejudiced. You can be pro-white without being anti-black."

At age 10, Pat's thought had some elements of the lowest moral stage, that of power and coercion as the source of right answers. He thought that rioting of black people should be remedied by "putting them all in jail, to teach them a lesson. If they're not happy, we could give them some liquor." A doctor who opted for a mercy killing would be guilty of murder and should be punished. When asked why he should be punished, Pat gave an answer in terms of his own value of "toughness above all": "Because in all the courts I've seen, the guilty man tries to get out of it. So punish him!" Most of his ten-year-old thinking, however, represented not first-stage power plays, but second-stage reduction of moral issues to instruments of selfish expression and manipulation of others.

He thought himself clever and did not enter into others' views of him enough to feel sometimes corrected in that opinion. He held onto the importance of cleverness to resist his soft mother and identify with his father. But he would not appeal to his father for attention he would not get nor would he appeal to peers without an aggressive edge on the appeal. This defensive shutting out of people was a moral implosion, a collaps-ing inward of the usual means of moral and spiritual growth, and, for Pat, a personal tragedy.

Since role-taking abilities are generally correlated with intelligence as well as with emotional balance, Pat undoubtedly possessed skills he did not use to take others' viewpoints. He could shift, balance, recall, and evaluate social information, but, out of resentment left from previous failures, he chose to avoid a mutuality that would necessarily be based on appreciating others' capabilities, expectations, feelings, motives, and social judgments.

Asked whether Indians should be forced to become modern, Pat answered: "They wouldn't dance any more, but dancing isn't valuable. But if you make their ceremonies rare, it's good for the one who has it; it would be more valuable. Tourists would want to see it. It could get money. Then Indians could sell it to a museum." Pat understood tourists but projected his own ideas of value onto Indians, thus, losing sight of their enjoyment as well as of their separate identity.

Pat rationalized his isolation with such theories as "girls talk and like each other, but they blab their mouths off" and "boys remember fights, so they don't like each other." When Pat lost his taste for shared pleasures, not having had enough of them, he lost the usual childhood motives for sharing in others' viewpoints, and he did not progress to the next moral stage.

In fifth grade, Pat was shown a picture of a white and a black boy talking. The white boy has one arm raised. Asked to tell a story about the picture, Pat said: "He punches this black kid who's pretty quiet just because he doesn't like him. He punches him all the way home. Their parents are not prejudiced; that's not the reason. The kids just don't like him. There is no reason. He doesn't have to like him. He's too lazy to care."

In a similar vein, Pat also said, "It makes a difference if a slave is getting whipped. But I wouldn't help if I thought I might get caught. He's a stranger to me and I don't even know him." Pat's racial prejudices seemed closely allied with lack of any respect not rooted in fear. Pat did not hate girls or black people. He was simply motivated to be indifferent, which can be more opposite to loving than hating is. He was completely unaware of his own social stimulus value to others and, therefore, was unable to articulate why he felt so "turned off." Children who cannot pick up the feelings and intentions of playmates and lack the advantage of a smooth sense of timing in social interactions generally have no sense of these reasons for their unpopularity and need instruction. Pat's successful use of his intelligence to distance people from himself rather than to learn social skills predicted that he would not change much. He would, perhaps, be likely to grow more aggressive with adolescence, lacking both the ideas and the sentimental attachments that mitigate its pressures.

In junior high Pat was solemn as he offered the observation that the police ignore the little kids in the town's streets or think they are cute. "But just get to seventh grade and be in a store catching a look at a comic book, and it's 'move along now.'" Perhaps Pat did not really want to leave childhood, sensing he had not yet had a chance to enjoy it.

Pat seemed personally ambitious, but showed little sensitivity or creativity. By seventh grade this loss stood out in contrast to his brightness because he kept up his grades and gave no opening to being criticized by letting down his guard to show emotional needs. Minding his own business, he got no special help. Nevertheless, his persistent prejudices and moral judgments stand as an indictment of his education.

4

Power and Favor-Trading
(Stages One and Two)

Leah and Pat are typical of children who suffer from negative views of themselves. Rather than being able to take pride in the fact that she managed so well while her mother worked, Leah saw herself as "ugly" and as "a cry-baby." Feeling alone, she needed her teacher to encourage her to recognize and enjoy her considerable strengths. Pat, who rejected his insecure mother and identified with his absent father, also felt himself to be alone. The toughness he projected prevented the children he scorned in self-defense from reaching out to him. Loneliness and negative self-images kept both these children stuck in defensive thinking at low stages — Leah at stage one and Pat at stage two.

This chapter examines and amplifies the pre-moral stages one and two. To create Stages of Respect, respect being the psychological cause of morality, we have added some additional material from our study to Kohlberg's stages.[1] The purpose is to provide reasons for some ways in which typical children who speak in a prejudiced way actually do think. The more we can tune in to the child as an apprentice philosopher, not just an irrational kid or someone who says bad words, the more we are likely to model the behavior we want by offering him some appropriate respect and encouragement to progress.

Kohlberg made "a chart in a wasteland" to advance the study of moral judgment through scientific research, beyond where philosophy alone could take it. Had he not excluded attitudes and other content as much as possible from his structures and his scoring system, we would have less clarity about the confusing notion of structures of thinking and their role in moral judgment. Structures are confusing because they represent both fundamental ideas and rules for their own transformations. Because the rules for transformations are hard to identify and no very sudden shifts between stages occur, some cognitive psychologists now prefer to speak of general levels of development.[2] Kohlberg tried to help people's understanding by explaining that the structures of each stage are like the girders erected to hold up a building — they fit together and cannot be moved without a major shift taking place. Content is more like the non-weightbearing walls inside. Prejudices are attitudes and, thus, appear as mostly content, but they are also rooted in the structures that define each stage.

To the objection that structure and content should not be confounded after having been so carefully teased apart, the fact is that they inevitably overlap. As Kohlberg's critics pointed out, they cannot be totally separated. Accepting this "fuzziness around the edges" actually makes stage concepts more useful. If we consider that respect for other people is the basis of morality, it will seem less strange to add to Kohlberg's work in this chapter and the next some typical ideas taken from children's statements relating to respect for others and its opposite — prejudice.

EXAMINING STAGE ONE THINKING

In kindergarten and first grade, children are generally treated with indulgence because they are cute and are not expected to think coherently. However, when an early stage of judgment persists, as in Leah and Pat, people may listen to its expressions with a new harshness, unaware that there are involuntary psychological reasons for this persistence. An orientation to power to ward off exploitation may be unconsciously necessary to the child, even though conscious stage one thinking is troublesome at an older age because it is severely limited and limiting. The following ideas, from a list by Kohlberg, characterize stage one:

The worth of people depends most on their possessions, power, size, and numbers.

Obvious psychological characteristics are concretely rather than psychologically labeled.

Respect is defined as obedience to authority, not involving promoting the welfare of another, because only the powerful have that responsibility.

Consequences often determine whether choices are good or bad, because punishment is thought to automatically follow a disrespectful or bad act.

Only one person's perspective can be taken at a time, and often the perspective chosen is that of an authority.[3]

The study in Chapter 3 provides the following additional points related to prejudice and respect:

Coercion is considered important, because authority is needed for safety.

In reasoning, there is insufficient notion of individuality and a lack of differentiation of hypothetical individuals from the labeled groups to which they belong.

Intensified or continued prejudice may be based on poor processing (or misunderstanding) of fear or anger following bad experiences and unexamined stereotypes.

The power orientation of the stage one child seems reasonable because whether one's early and urgent needs are met depends on who has power and how it is used. The young child reads from the surface, not yet possessing the mental structures to imagine much about motives, connect perspectives, subtly persuade, or arrange values hierarchically. The cognitive problems described in Chapter 1 persist. The following quotation shows both interest in the subject of power and the characteristic faulty reasoning of stage one. A white suburban boy, age 10, said: "Indians always want wars. They like to attack people. They like to start trouble, like attack a wagon to get cheese and food. They're greedy. They send signals around the sky and make air pollution. You can't even read them."

The motives of Indians — greed and a liking for trouble — are read directly from a movie the child saw on television. Perspectives are inferred from behavior at one specified time; badness is defensively exaggerated. Because perspectives cannot yet be coordinated, it seems normal to the child to confound early Indian viewpoints with his modern concern for air pollution, and to assume that signals should be readable by all.

In response to Kohlberg's dilemma about whether a man should steal a drug to save his wife's life if she had cancer, even if he does not feel love for her, a black city boy, age 13, said: "If I didn't like my wife, I'd tell her to quit that smoking and leave the house. I'd find another girl. No one could stop me."

At this boy's stage, the man's wife deserves no sympathy or respect if she is not loved. Her perspective is not considered. Valuing love at the same time as focusing on smoking and cancer requires experience the child cannot yet attain by thinking about ambivalence or considering good and bad at the same time rather than who has the power to get his way.

The sources of human events and human behavior are little understood at this stage. The child's incipient capacity for respect is still fragile. Affection is certainly felt, but, in what was initially a surprise to Kohlberg's group, it is not mentioned as a reason for moral decisions at stage one, even by children from affectionate, nonpunitive families. Punishment, on the other hand, turns out to be highly relevant to decision making, even where punishments have seldom been given.

Older children who have been overpunished or experienced some other danger and have not progressed beyond stage one may find their feelings of respect for little known or unusual kinds of people overwhelmed by the idea that those people have some kind of power. A natural fear of punishment is exaggerated. The power of an absent parent may grow stronger in the child's imagination. Others may also be assumed to have the power of a truly fearsome parent.

At stage one there is no idea that respect is any sort of imperative, something owed to all others. A ten-year-old white suburban girl at this stage opined:

I think if everybody got together, it's better. The separate [college] dormitories the blacks want isn't right. And whites do wrong, too. But a riot could come from not letting them do what they want. Many buildings would be burned. Businesses will lose and be damaged. And about integration, let the black children come to white schools, but if any riot starts, split them apart again.

This child is focusing on one perspective that all parties should consider. She understands that others have different experiences and that these experiences can be given as reasons for action, but she does not have sufficient cognitive structures to relate reasons abstractly. When asked to respond to a moral dilemma, such a child chooses as right the perspective of the most salient or authoritative individual, ignoring the others.

There are advantages in this value system for a young child. The authorities she unthinkingly accepts will probably sponsor and protect her. In return, she may mirror their judgments uncritically. A nine-year-old remarked, "Black people are nice. My father said so." She may also ignore their statements absentmindedly.

Children at this stage do seem to sense, no matter their noisy protests, that their own judgments are inadequate. This may be a reason for some insecurity or particular fears. A frequent stage one preoccupation is that physical damage might result from a decision. Inconsistencies and half-formed opinions result in much mind-changing, even when dilemmas are more related to childhood than those in Kohlberg's test. Usually, an apparently dogmatic attitude is taken, but the content of the dogma can be abruptly altered. Values seem to follow labels, inexorably, as when a 13-year-old white city boy said, "If a slave owner mistreated his slave, and the slave came to me, I wouldn't feel sorry for him, because his owner had paid for him, so he was a slave."

Just as in this example, where slaves seem to have no rights, children at this stage make no clear distinction between the right of authority and being right. Respect for a powerful role may help create order in the mind of the child, who for the first time is confronting the world's confusing sociological puzzle. When asked about a husband putting to death a dying wife to end her pain (another Kohlberg dilemma), a white city girl, age 9, said, "The doctor has to make the decision. If you call in a doctor, your life belongs to him." Doctors are authorities, so there was nothing very strange for this girl about giving over one's life.

Exaggeration of danger also inhibits setting reasonable limits on the power of authorities. In the apprehensiveness that results from fragility of understanding, the source of the circularity and coherence of stage one reasoning may appear. In spite of its spurious basis, stage one has internal logic. The necessity of granting authorities power and respect turns attention away from any need to understand the worth and rights of other people or all people. This, in turn, fosters fear of retaliation and punitiveness because of awareness of the dangerous aspects of the stranger or, for that matter, of any member of humanity only slightly understood. However, most young children are happy and comfortable in the presence of their protectors.

Stage one children think that right and wrong exist in the same sense that the world exists, to be read from surface characteristics. He who does bad is bad, because a near-perfect correspondence between act and intention is assumed. In relation to prejudice, such a bad person probably belongs to a group automatically worthy of punishment.

A more serious danger to emerging personality lies in categorizing the self as bad. The frequently scolded child, well aware of not being pleasing, may fulfill her parents' secret fears that she will turn out badly. The child's stage one interest in the label "bad" may cause a continuation of displeasing behavior for that reason alone. "My parents always worry, so I know I am bad," said a first grader. Eventually, if a child is not organically retarded or extremely traumatized and fearful of the environment, increasing awareness of personal individuality becomes dominant over this closed circle of early assumptions. As self-confidence and both cognitive complexity and knowledge increase, the child is tempted to boast, "I think for myself."

The next step, imputation of the same right of decision-making to favored peers, heralds the beginning of favor-trading stage two. At that point respect for people based on their personhood rather than on their authority or power lessens prejudice, but such respect will be arbitrarily assigned. There is still no emphasis on caring about people beyond those the child chooses to favor.

WORKING WITH STAGE TWO

Each new stage of moral judgment is in better equilibrium than its predecessor, allowing an openness to new insights. At stage two, morality is no longer the simple product of the rules of an authority figure. Obligation to the powerful is diluted by a new sense of personhood. By age 7 or age 8, the child is usually aware of family and peer needs as well as some of the merits in the competing fairness claims of the world around him. His solutions are pragmatic, but there is movement in the direction of egalitarianism with the now obvious idea that at least the people within one's own group should be treated fairly.

Elements of stage one are transformed or elaborated in part because a new ability to take others' viewpoints has been achieved. Practicing this ability, the child considers new ways to handle the claims of others or understands them for the first time. Movement from stage one to stage two seems to be contingent not only on greater awareness of personal effectiveness, with perhaps a corresponding lessening of fear, but also on observations about the subjectivity of others. It becomes progressively more clear that their ends and goals may be personal rather than authoritative, do not coincide with one's own, and, yet, may not be bad. Still, stage two leaves plenty of room for pushing one's own advantage. The value judgments typical of Kohlberg's stage two can be summarized as:

Other people have individual goals that they have a right to pursue but so also does the self, which can oppose authority and instrumentally use others.

Trading favors means non-interference with others' subjective intentions, but "do to them as they do to you" and favor those who are chosen.

"All people are equal," (for lack of understanding of motives leads to a pseudo-liberality).

Fairness is balancing individual interests, perhaps trying to omit judgments of good and bad in favor of what seems smart, friendly to oneself, or pragmatic.[4]

Further elaborations from our research concerning respect for others are:

Evaluating other people remains egocentric, in that assumptions about them and whether they deserve respect tend to be illogical, highly changeable, and self-serving.

Subsuming human rights under the consensus of opinions of favored individuals results in acceptance of hostile stereotyping.

Insider-oriented egalitarianism leads to a kind of prejudice based on indifference to or avoidance of outsiders.

The child now realizes that all people are aware of each other's wanting different things. This startling new awareness appears to invoke the moral relevance of who gets what, along with a wrong answer to how to decide that question. The core notion is that a settlement will be fair because each person has had the option of pressing for what he or she wants. This idea avoids the necessity of doing what is still not cognitively possible at the beginning of stage two: considering individuals' motives and merits in working out a prescription for justice.

Although the need for mutual respect is not understood to be legitimate, the need for power is. Each person must arrange for his or her needs to be met. Respect owed to others can still be interpreted under the system of power relations, because while people are accepted as "all equal," it often comes down to "us" and "them." That this assumption has relevance for prejudice became clear in the answer given by a ten-year-old suburban girl when asked what she thought about a classmate saying that Mexicans sneak over to get jobs in this country. She replied, "Why sneak? We should let everyone in. But we should feed our poor people first. Then if the Mexicans came, it would be their own fault for coming here, if they starved and we ran out of money."

At this stage, respect generally means non-interference, as also illustrated by a 13-year-old black city girl discussing the problems of school integration. "I think," she said, "each case should be decided by what the people there would like. Whatever they feel like." Solutions such as this imply an obvious problem of what to do when "the people there" do not agree with each other. However, stage two children do not raise this problem spontaneously, nor do most enter into much discussion of it when it is raised to them.

Children at the favor-trading stage are usually sympathetic, despite the fact that they neither demonstrate very little role-taking of subtle feelings nor show much ability on role-taking tests.[5] They can also be cruel suddenly. Children tend to be inconsistent about connecting fairness with empathy, as if emotional reactions to others' pain were taking place on a level separate from their fairness judgments. Many stage two children are explicit in their indifference to others. A ten-year-old city boy said, "Segregation is not right, I guess. But I'd go along with the whites, because I know them better. I wouldn't worry about people I didn't know." Similarly, a 13-year-old black boy from the city said, "As far as helping a slave escape, it makes a difference if he's being whipped. But I wouldn't help him if I thought I might get caught. He's a stranger to me and I don't even know him. If I knew him, I might think he'd help me some day."

Although the stage two child is often manipulative, freedom from interference by others whenever possible is a central issue for this approach to morality. At the same time, links between a philospher's notion of freedom and effective freedoms, such as the necessity of equal opportunity, are generally not seen. Hence "all are equal" becomes an empty pronouncement. Cries of "no fair," however passionately felt, do not predict fair arguments or behavior on the part of the child at this stage.

Assumptions about others and the question of whether they deserve respect are based on very variable criteria. Not all favor traders think much about being egalitarian, and decisions by personal inclination are frequent. The less important person is easier to disregard, and favoring of one's own group leads easily to rationalization. When asked about how poor people should be helped, a nine-year-old city white boy replied, "Welfare, but I'd rather not have to pay for it when I'm grown up. I guess something has to be done. If some people want to, they can. Usually they do."

Positive affect is often attached to notions of kindness and goodness, even though the favor-trading children do not use these notions as final reasons for moral choices. Stage two children offer stereotypically pro-social responses, only to change them at the moment of decision-making. An example of this occurred when a ten-year-old suburban girl replied to the probe "Your classmate said, 'The blacks should like the whites, no matter what has happened.' What do you think of that?": "All should like all. If you are good friends, you should always make up. You should always try. The slums are not our fault! The people who live there can do what they want for themselves!"

A cliché or socially learned response, when used by someone who cannot explain it, is similar to a stereotype because it is not based on personal observations or deductions. Still, adult teaching of such exhortations as "be kind" and "you should always make up" eventually may cause a wedge of discontent with the circular reasoning of stage two that leads to further progress. These lessons are, therefore, valuable, but they need to come gently, with no implication that the child is not good enough to make the adult happy.[6]

The lessening importance of a good-bad dimension at stage two, as compared to being able to operate pragmatically, frees the young child from the responsibility for idealistic solutions. What is smart or dumb is usually cited in the place of what is good or bad. Instrumental hedonism espoused by children leads to conflicts of interest and a large amount of fighting over petty disagreements. Fighting becomes accepted, as when a ten-year-old suburban boy advocated a war and peace treaty as a simple and long-lasting means of settling the conflicts between blacks and whites in the inner city.

Unlike the outright denial practiced to maintain stage one, the psychological defenses associated with stage two are childish indifference, failure to take responsibility, and rationalization for prejudices and stereotypic responses. These defenses may be useful to protect the new assumptions about personal power that are needed to consolidate emergence from stage one's dependence on authorities. They consolidate a social identity different from others', a uniqueness more important than conforming to someone else's definition of a good child. These should be protected through the gentleness with which outside discipline is enforced, but without such discipline, there is danger that a sense of triumph at doing the minimum to get one's own way can lead to arrogance about the values of stage two. An unacceptably exaggerated feeling of self-importance and a habit of manipulating others grows when the child's demands too frequently succeed. When adult responses are inconsistent, children, adolescents, and even animals try especially hard to get what they want.

CONCLUSIONS FOR EDUCATION

Children at stage one do not yet have the cognitive structures to reason morally about rights and fairness. Nasty expressions of prejudice are common and should not be taken as a sure sign of how the child will think later. Instead of becoming angry or trying to reason with young children about naughtiness or prejudice before they are able to understand, adults must state their requirements while providing the emotional security out of which higher stages can be achieved. Teachers may have a role in offering insights about stage development to parents. Also, any neglect of the child's need for kind attention at home can be assuaged at school by careful attentions, thereby assuring more success and a possible transition to stage three.

Stage two children often incorrectly hear the Golden Rule as "do unto others as they do unto you," which expresses a part of their philosophy. Stage two begins as a childish mentality but can become a selfish one. Pre-moral stages are reinforced by the need to defend oneself, especially in a large junior high school. Some who have found no caring and direction find it in a gang. The resolve to be smart, get their way, and ignore outsiders may appear to pre-teens to work well defensively. Some adults also want to fit students for a harsh world where indepen-dence of thought helps. Pushy children may have high self-esteem and do well, but independence is better fostered after stage three, when a more empathic thoughtfulness becomes possible.

The usual problem for the young instrumental hedonist in moving toward stage three is not insisting on certain rights but, rather, becoming more able to connect judgments about rights with an only vaguely realized capacity for empathy. The inborn ability to share with others on an emotional level appears to atrophy when not made use of. The sympathy that should grow out of empathy does not develop. Because community feeling is a necessary engine of moral change, making empathy a conscious experience must be attempted in the classroom as well as at home. The goal of grade school moral education should be to bring about each child's transition to a caring stage three before the storms of adolescence hit. Tom and Jo, whose stories follow, were both at stage three when they entered junior high school in seventh grade.

JO AND TOM: CHILDREN WITHOUT PREJUDICE

Jo's Story

Jo had been an irritable, colicky baby who turned away from her numerous aunts, uncles, and cousins at about eight months. She remained much shyer than her confident sister, born four years later. When Jo was five, her family moved from a large city to the suburb, for both the better schools and a better job for her policeman father. The move was an uprooting for the girl, and Jo's teacher said she did not make friends in the early grades.

The changes brought by the move were mainly good. Jo's mother worked as a card store clerk to help meet new expenses. The family joined a Protestant church, being of Scotch-Irish descent. "We felt happier, except Jo, where we could see our family and old friends, too, whenever we wanted," Jo's mother said. However, a 17-year-old aunt/babysitter who had moved with them so that Jo's mother could work said that the girls fought more than they would have with a mother at home. The mother looked down as she described her own guilt about working. "Jo had nightmares almost weekly for a year after the move, and still does, once in awhile. I hope we weren't overly strict when she was little. . . . But I think it was more that her father has a dangerous job. She adores him. We're a very close family."

The school was asked for some special attention to Jo's shyness and emotionality, but, because she obeyed adults and learned well, not much resulted from the request until grade three. At that point a counselor started a weekly group meeting for Jo and three carefully chosen playmates. She wrote, "Jo is a high-I.Q. child who takes in too much, speaks rapidly in a high, chirping voice once she starts, but teacher says she blushes and withdraws. Needs friends. May have resentments. Referral from parents." The first phase of the counseling was successful in starting some seemingly spontaneous, playful relationships. A consulting psychiatrist had recommended setting the tone by using uncorked balloons as airships to fly around the room!

During the second phase of counseling the girls talked about self-conscious feelings, normal shyness, and fears. These included fear of punishment, but no unusual punishments were reported. Jo began to enjoy having an audience for expressing her imagination. She supplied the group with illustrated story booklets that she made at home. In the third phase, the girls told jokes to each other on play phones. They were then given assignments, such as telephoning their most popular and sociable classmates to come with their bicycles to a park, and a number of parents were brought in to support and encourage these classwide activities. Jo emerged as a sometime leader.

By grade five, Jo was voluble and lively, no longer shy. Jo had her own ideas of how things should be, and said she could not fit in with everyone. "City girls are pushy, and we can't be! Do you think I am?" The "can't be" presaged Jo's later remarkable insights. She also said:

I've lived in [the city] and I know how people act when things are too much for them. These kids here, they are selfish, but they can't help it. They are lucky, too, and easy to have fun with. Because we all, all of us, have all sorts of stuff, and we do share it. I also have black friends, so we hang out. I know they don't have stuff and it isn't fair. I really like their freshness. It makes me fresher, which I need, 'cause I'm still afraid of people, but they aren't afraid, so I copy them. They live where everyone has knives on them, at least knives, maybe guns, but they are just so relaxed and friendly. I can be friends with anybody I want, and I'm really so happy. Even when kids say I "act black." Who cares!

Although becoming popular seems to be one issue on Jo's mind, her statements illustrate a kind of bicultural consciousness she wanted to maintain, regardless of its cost to easily fitting in. Projective testing revealed a strong ego, partly rooted in being unique and partly in the averageness of her firm, kind parents. She described women who work as "lucky, although they might miss being with their daughters after school." She planned to become a doctor, "to help children who don't have much. They don't understand why they're sick."

By fifth grade, Jo did not have behavior problems at home. Her individually tested I.Q. was 128 and her Iowa achievement scores were in the ninetieth percentile range. Her moral judgments were unremarkably conventional. She showed no prejudice on several tests, nor any personality abnormalities.

Children without emotional blocks in the way of their progress not only reason better but also take in the sophisticated ideas of others. Jo's freedom from prejudice allowed her fifth grade concern about black children to widen the next year into a concern for their families as well and, finally, in seventh grade, to considering the relationship of individuals to the needs of the whole country. Her replies to the same probe evidence this progression.

Probe: Lots of blacks don't go to school, even though that's against the law.
Jo, age 10:   Their parents should train them, because it's good for you. Even though most kids hate it.
Jo, age 11:   You have to learn to get along in life, even though we hate school. It's for their own good to get up in the world, and support their families.
Jo, age 13:   The thing is to improve the slums, and the worst looking schools you ever saw. School shouldn't be a prison. Teachers shouldn't be yelling. They should put in art and music. Then they better have truant officers, or how will you be good for your country?

By grade seven Jo's tone of voice and style of dressing in old jeans attempted an age-appropriate cool image, but she maintained a warm and independent search for caring solutions to social problems. Her curiosity and achievements in learning formed some lively opinions about fairness and prejudice:

The Jews here are really smart; they figure it all out. But the blacks are fools to pull away from us, after all the trouble to get here. This year they stick together and make noise, like, "Look at us." I guess it's because there's too few of them. But it's so frustrating. I love the way they dress, like braids with ribbons. But you can't say it. They ignore us, so we do that to them. What can you do? Just get mad? Now I don't hang around with blacks; they wouldn't allow it. They are totally not the same as they were. I wish I could ask them why.

There was more at work than identification and caring in Jo's elaborate reasoning about what goodness is and what can produce it in people. She liked to reason, and she had found links between caring, thinking, and means of education:

My mother thinks if a kid gets busted [for drugs] it's a bad kid, but it's just one bad thing. I try to think how their mind works, how they are. But now my mother does let me out of going to church, because this year I hate it. Preaching. Going to church isn't religion. I think it isn't. Everybody should get equal chances to show who they are, to prove themselves. But they sure don't! And everybody should go to a great school like this. But there are teachers, like in Health, who don't know or care what kids feel like. Most teachers don't care what a kid might think. They have so much to do, they force it down you. You think they're your enemy, so I keep score if I'm bored and give points to the kids who won't listen and points to the teacher for shutting them up.

Jo was an engaging child who seemed to have gained many of the strengths that education can impart. For that reason, some of her observations were disturbing, especially those about teachers failing to consider how students are thinking, and those about the failure of school desegregation to result in integration.[7]

Tom's Story

Tom possessed a remarkable ability to think realistically about social problems, although he was less bright academically than several classmates. His maturity, poise, fairness, sports ability, and a deep-voiced, ruminative way of speaking made him the most popular of the boys. "My father told me to make all kinds of friends. If you don't get friends — it's the same with adults — you are always cranky and mad."

Tom's relaxed family included a brother in high school and a sister in college, both on such close terms with him as to influence his maturity. His mother, a third generation middle-European, had not worked outside the home and pleased her family with her happy conversation and her cooking. Tom's father, of Slavic origin, was one of the town's maintenance men. "He gets a lot of time to think. It's good. He made a love-match to a Catholic against his parents' will. My grandmother, she's still mad. My father is different from all his other brothers. Maybe it came from the time he went for my mother."

Bitterness and squabbles in the extended family were referred to by Tom as the source of his awareness and concern about ethnic intolerance:

My uncle thinks prejudice against Russians is unfair, but he makes my cousins prejudiced. My cousins keep talking against Jews, and Catholics, too. But my father tells them they should save up and be so smart. Once he made them scramble for pennies to tease them out of it! That's what kids do to Jews! Prejudice, it's really painful. People can really just hate. I can't believe how people hate others, and I don't understand it.

Tom consistently took the views of others to test his own. Some of his remarks at age 10 illustrate this. "A black kid from a bad ghetto would feel moody a lot. He'd assume all the whites feel good." "A slave owner should be captured and try out the work. Then he'd know, and really know, that all people deserve to be free!" "I think kids who are young now are growing up awfully sick of judgments made on skin colors."

At age 10 Tom's percentage of tolerance was 93, and his percentage of directed thinking was almost as high. Responses to two probes show his flexibility and awareness of others' viewpoints:

Interviewer: Should we try to change some primitive Indian beliefs?
Tom, age 10:   Indians had a real good thing going, and now they're poor and not living like Indians, with lots of buffalos, food, and the riches of whatever they need. We could at least give them a decent reservation, full of game, and not try to give them our ideas. They probably wouldn't want our help, even about medicine.
Interviewer: Should blacks in the city be made to go to school?
Tom: Well, it's basically the same question, but I feel different. They're not so slaughtered as Indians, though they were forced here. But they should go to school because they don't live the same as Indians. They will have to live the way we do, so they need education. In slave days that was different.

Tom was a very young incipient stage four at age 13. Yet, he knew he was not "a brain," and said, "I don't care if I get into college. It doesn't matter. The classes are too hard." His I.Q. of 115 was only four points above the school norm. His grades and achievement scores were also average (fifty-fourth percentile) except in social studies, where he excelled. All this illustrates that caring and paying attention to values are as important to moral judgment and good behavior as superior intelligence.[8]

At age 13 the question of prejudice still interested Tom:

Our friends' plumbing company was robbed by blacks, and now they're kind of prejudiced, but you can understand that. They live down South. If only we could understand this whole thing. I think the main problem causing racism is people just don't want to associate, anyway. They don't care that much. We put people together in the schools, and it's a lot better than white and black separate, but still nobody really tries. Especially in the high school; my brother tells me about that. I've seen here in junior high that more kids don't like black kids than before, and they don't try to make them feel better any more. They used to, in sixth grade. Now they go off, the blacks by themselves, so what can you do? Well, I get models and make them with Tim because we were friends in sixth. You got to care. Some Indians are starving, and people don't care. Even right here in the U.S. We gotta put money in that. I read the paper, and I see nobody knows what's going on. You gotta change the system of forgetting poor people, first of everything.

Tom was also aware that the rights of people transcend a national system. It occurred to him that people who share in setting up the standards of judgment must be prepared and that society has a general obligation to educate. At stage five, which Tom might one day achieve, such obligations are understood as not specific to roles and rules. Tom was already gaining a sense that duties are defined through shared perspectives and awareness of the rights of others. He also differentiated legal from conscientious obligations:

It's important to consider what laws should be made. It is laws that make a nation, because people would otherwise go by their own thoughts, and there could be no cooperation, no society, no progress. Cooperation makes progress. It would be better if the whole world could work on laws, but the way it is, nations do. If you don't have taxes, you can't have good education. You have to have money provided. If you put something in, you get something out. Then educated people can work on the laws, to make them more fair, and to see why they have to pay taxes. It's the main thing not to be rich, as an ideal, not to beat out the other guy, but just to live, and to preserve all life.

At age 13 he made good use of his popularity with age-mates to exercise the unselfish leadership he had already decided upon when interviewed earlier. His final remarks indicated activism and altruism:

After lunch I make models with this one black kid we don't really like. He's okay, but now nobody cares. It gets more selfish as you get older. Maybe you get a job and you're busy. Then you kind of forget the things you wanted to do for somebody. That's why I want to be a politician — to do all the projects I want to do, to change things.[9]

5

Goodness, Niceness, and Higher Ideals: (Stages Three, Four, Five, and Six)

Jo had been a very shy child, which could have hurt her moral development by cutting her off from others. She was fortunate to receive counseling that stimulated her playfulness and imagination. Being brought out of herself enabled Jo to look at the world from the perspective of others. Tom was encouraged to think morally by his older siblings and by observing the interaction of his extended family. His reaching out to unpopular peers showed a superior ability to extend himself for others. He was a natural leader. Both of these students were free of even the conventional, majority-held prejudices that are easily produced at stages three and four.

In this chapter, we will look at the characteristics of Stages of Respect three and four. Moral stages five and six will also be discussed briefly as goals in adulthood that moral education should foster eventually, although school children do not achieve these advanced stages. The chapter concludes with a fuller examination of what causes moral stage change.

THINKING AT STAGE THREE

At stage three, for the first time, social concepts such as friendship, trust, relationship, and society are fully understood as implying mutuality and agreement between persons. With increasing frequency and pleasure, the child is able to share the feelings, as well as the thoughts, of valued people. Relationships with a great deal of communication are enjoyed. Taking the perspective of another leads to understanding, which then leads to mutual desires to maintain shared expectations and approval.

The child now sees what could not be seen before — the limits of the selfish egoism of stage two for producing fairness. A more optimistic world view can be experienced as altruistic motives gain importance. It is possible to see what is good as what is natural and agreed upon by a majority, rather than by a particular group or gang. Prescriptive statements are, therefore, reorganized, including those taught earlier by parents, and the following interlocking stage three tenets are produced:

Respect, like praise and blame, should be based on motives behind others' acts, and not only on their effectiveness.

Golden Rule altruism, an ideal self, and an awareness of conscience make one good.

A model of dyadic and family relations should be substituted for objective human rights (because of a naive expectation of care and benevolence in society).

Universal collective norms and ideals are worth notice, partly because authorities need conforming cooperation.[1]

In addition to the above attributes of stage three, the study of prejudice and respect found:

Global sympathy and sentimentality produce a shallow and changeable evaluation of minority group members and continuing overvaluation of own group.

Ethnic and other stereotypes gain credence from being majority views, but caring mitigates them.

There is an obligation to display a concern for fairness to disadvantaged people.

Actual intergroup relations are based on the importance of feelings and majority views.

At stage three friendships deepen. Because it is possible to infer motives, children learn the effectiveness of "he didn't really mean to" for increasing trust. They may then feel more relaxed. Emergence from stage two might begin with awareness that the other person can be equally excusing and that this excusing can be traded like any other stage two favor. Then, the positive feelings generated by trusting the half-hidden motives of others provide a reason for further increasing the consideration of motives. The more reciprocity is contemplated and its implications logically extended, the more inadequate stage two values appear.

The obvious advantages of stage three niceness are a new understanding of motivation and a potential for social learning through taking the role of the other person. It is person-centered, not act-centered. Pleasure and ego-strength are the results of sharing feelings and thoughts in a non-judgmental atmosphere. By this sharing the child's future moral growth is also fostered, so that the beginning of stage three conventionality is a transition of major importance.

In addition to sometimes emerging from the inevitable maturation of the ability to take more perspectives, stage three can be socially engineered. Its exaggeration of cooperative niceness is more likely to be stressed by privileged parents, and stage three ideas are sometimes called "middle-class values." Lower class parents also desire trust and cooperativeness in their children, but, because a sense of trust and ease in all one's social surroundings can be important in moving children toward cooperative intentions, most of the city sample did not begin to achieve stage three before mid-adolescence.

Some disadvantages of this stage are its susceptibility to rationalization, so that idealism does not result in effective social reform, its lack of rationale in seeking goodness, and its idealizing of people. People still tend to be seen as all good or all bad: "Indians are so good, how could they be shot at like a moose?" Governmental policies are often judged less for their merits than for having sprung from the psychology of stereotyped individuals. Complex political, economic, institutional, and psychological causes of social problems are ignored or not understood, and useless ideal or panacea solutions may be propounded.

Enjoyment of friends and family seems to solve personal problems when people are not too contentious, which leads to the idea that conforming to simple prescriptions for virtue and niceness will also solve social problems. It is thought to be enough simply to fulfill the good expectations of others. If that is insufficient, and problems persist, the stage three value system falls back upon subjectivity. The in-group must be maintained, and there is collusion in covering up each other's weaknesses.

Not violating the expectations of those toward whom one is most oriented leads to extensive rationalization. Typical of the kind of "good person niceness" that African Americans recognize as adding to patronizing prejudice is the response by a stage three suburban 13-year-old girl to a story about a woman who runs a rooming house with some current vacancies and whose boarders threaten to move out if she accepts blacks, which she is required by law to do: "I think it's not a good law, because each situation can be different. If she likes blacks, but she is just worried about getting the money from the other renters who were there first, then I guess it's all right to be mean to blacks. She'd have to. The main thing is, she really likes them."

Because meanness is disliked, stage three children usually show a fear of jeopardizing the positive relations of their own group. Perhaps there is a dimly-sensed awareness that if agreement on what is nice should break down, the internal logic of stage three would collapse. This introduces a new coerciveness. Social pressure is often assumed to be automatically beneficial.

Durkheim described how a *sui generis* feeling of respect grows out of group life. Groups impose pressure on individuals within them by surrouding themselves with a certain sanctifying halo. As conforming children accept the stereotypes of their culture, they attach a moral significance to those stereotypes simply because their own "good" group or their culture has espoused them. If pressed for an explanation of their correctness, they may say it is because everybody or most people say so.[2]

Because stereotypes are components of shared expectations, they are still prominent at stage three. However, they are less negative, and there is also less stereotypic or pronouncement-oriented thinking than at stage two (only about one-third of statements, as opposed to about half, in our results). Concern about niceness versus prejudice often does not mean that personal negative prejudgments are eliminated. Prejudice may go underground. Rationalization may be used to resolve hardly-recognized contradictions, as in the following statement by a white city girl, age 13:

There's this girl, this black girl in our class, May. She's a nice kid. But she's so tough; unbelievable. She has a good personality. She likes everybody, and she is a real good athlete. But her father's all for blacks. That's just not right. All it says is "we want rights," when they got them already. Her father should be like May, then things would come out very well; no problems of race and all.

Certain children impatiently disdain a democratic process and believe that group pressures should be applied to induce a narrow conformity to their own simplistic standards of niceness. This leads to conservatism, lack of progress, in-groupism, and prejudice. Idealism about people can cause shock at human aberrations, which in turn justifies conventional notions of blame and punishment. At this stage, there often is no firm perspective on what makes strength of character. The psychological insight and the principles needed to maintain a more consistent and unshockable trust in human potential are lacking.

Out-groups are easily ignored, and the result is that unhappy children, including those who try to become tough, are allowed to go their own way with no reaching out to them on the part of many of their stage three peers. The rougher stage two children may be either looked down upon or given up as beyond the reach of teachers.

When the social group's opinions, rather than a logical rationale, are cited as the justification for values, the content and structures of this stage can fuse into a somewhat impenetrable ideology. Mutual approval involving flattery, optimism, and the sense of possessing shared hopes tends to stifle doubts and foster a patronizing approach to people less fortunate. However, prejudice is less apparent than at earlier stages, and may be reduced still further through successful integration of different ethnic groups. The warmth and enjoyment of people that is a part of the value system of this stage creates opportunities for anti-prejudice education.

REASONING AT STAGE FOUR

Before stage three, young children do not formulate hypotheses so much as they classify descriptions of events. At stage three, speculations and conclusions about causality are often based on only one or two experiences. By stage four, hypotheses are used to make a more precise and extended construction of reality. Role-taking ability has progressed so that the child can now imagine the point of view of a generalized other, a neutral observer.

This view of an outside observer brings a whole new awareness of society as a structured whole, possessing even more right to make demands on individuals. Ideals at stage four are no longer transparently related to personal feelings, so what is correct seems all the more definite. Correctness is usually said to be carried out by the established system of justice.

Some particular items that characterize the stage four respect for people are:

People are not to be treated arbitrarily, because laws must apply to all, but merit and friendship should derive from esteem for the same values.

The neutral or third person perspective means others should be valued as highly as the self; exchanges should be reciprocal and of value to each party.

Obligation is to one's moral code, not individual personal relations, so concern should be about dishonor more than about disapproval.

Responsibility can be painful and demand discipline; the socially productive results of a sense of duty (hard work, education) are respected, and authorities should merit respect.

Conflicts between moral laws and the legal system cannot be clearly resolved, but the legal system usually predominates.[3]

In addition to these items from Kohlberg, our study developed the following stage four characteristics related to prejudice:

Prejudices and sentiments of anti-prejudice are based on plausible role definitions.

Emphasis on roles and categories permits conventional prejudices and may foster moralism.

Interest in the thoughts and feelings of others and careful neutrality lead to fewer prejudgments.

The ability to take the point of view of a neutral observer has its analogue in the ability to formulate criteria for respect, as shown in a

13-year-old white city boy's answer to a moral dilemma:

A slave? He needs to run his own life. You do want to run your own life. A fat rich guy owns you like a dog; that could get you down, no matter at all how you were actually treated. You'd be an object. Not really a human being. Not feel equal to that person. All people have to give respect to all people. Otherwise, you'd be more like a dog.

Kohlberg's well-known Heinz dilemma — whether to steal to save a wife's life when a druggist priced life-saving medication too high for purchase — brought a possible stage four answer from a white suburban 13-year-old girl:

I think Heinz did the right thing. I think the druggist was wrong to take someone's life in his own hands. Somebody was dying! He was too much business and not enough human. That is the moral problem, to see that everybody is human, to feel they deserve certain things because they are human — all.

Stage four adolescents are also concerned about merit as a basis of respect. They recognize the socially productive results of a sense of duty and begin to give more esteem to those who possess this. As the partly stage four girl who spoke in the last example continues speaking, she amends her statement on all people deserving life:

We don't have a moral right to capital punishment, but we have a legal right, because there are too many people in the world, practically speaking, and so you have to earn the right to live. If you kill, you don't have the right to live. What can you do? They're each making five pounds of garbage a day, and taking up space, and the money to keep them should go to a worthwhile cause; there are those who need it. We're not killing to teach a lesson, and we know it's morally wrong, and it is not up to any man to judge another in that absolute way. But laws are meaningless if not enforced.

This girl makes a real effort at careful reasoning, although she assumes that societal rules take precedence over moral law. Murderers must face our just and fair "legal right" to kill them, even though "we don't have the moral right to kill them." The necessity of maintaining a reliable order predominates.

The moralistic emphasis of stage four lends itself to a hidden and patronizing prejudice, as in, "We need a rule that everyone has to take home a Metco kid once a week, so they would get used to seeing nice things and hearing our stereo, and start thinking straight about how to work to get things." The lack of principled thought and the typical reference to majority views at this stage means that there is no defense against the subtler levels of conventional prejudice.

A white city boy, age 13, answered the question, "Should poor Mexicans be allowed to come here to work in our fields?" with: "If they couldn't get a job there, we could show we care, but our President's job is to take care of the U.S. citizens. We have to take care of jobs for our poor." When asked, "What if our poor are better off than their poor?" the boy replied, "The President has to go by our laws and by the definition of his job."

This boy found no difficulty in distinguishing between "us" and "them" as he exaggerated the virtues of loyalty and reliance on law to the point where "we care" became mostly rhetorical. Love of the virtue of loyalty easily enhances the importance of categories that separate people.

Stage four is a clear advance over stage three because, for the first time, there is correspondence between the individual and the societal points of view. A more sincere sense of justice can be the result of simultaneously taking many viewpoints. Stage four is fundamentally conventional because interest in duty and loyalty to others leads to its sense of obligation. Truth becomes more important, a legitimate perspective, at this ideal-seeking stage. The wider culture and its truth take on new interest, as does deviance. Broadened awareness has the effect of softening stereotypes.

A disadvantage of stage four is the tendency to isolate problems so that they can be dealt with by legal and moralistic solutions, when it might have been possible to initially prevent the problems through a more inspirational, trust-maintaining morality. A stage four view of people that defines them by their dutiful place in the social system may ignore the importance of trusting others' ability to grow and change or their ability to negotiate differences of viewpoint if the atmosphere of the particular social system becomes less blaming and legalistic.

A problem especially relevant to prejudice is that at the ideal-seeking stage four, virtues and traits are often isolated and become labels for judging others, which can make people uncomfortable. Thus, there is a bias toward making dispositional attributions rather than situational ones. If this evolves into blaming, it can destroy a sense of community. Relationships are threatened when states of mind are called traits of mind. In fact, the present state of mind of one group or person may be temporary and caused by the aggressive or overly submissive behavior of the other.

STAGES FIVE AND SIX

Principled people cannot rationalize bigotry. Although children and adolescents are too young to achieve stages five and six, descriptions of these stages illumine the goals of moral education. Goals like eliminating prejudice should be conscious. They can be presented through personal example and the kind of enjoyable, heroic literature that challenges young people. The U.S. Constitution is full of stage five ideas.

Stages five and six are said by many to be indistinguishable because all principled persons, even as they abide by most conventions, strive for a rational perspective not based on being a member of a particular society. They see themselves as autonomous moral agents and their principles as valid apart from any social or psychological ties to others who share the same principles. They go beyond not only their own self-interest but also their group's. Human dignity partly rests upon conceptions of individual and group rights, but mutual respect requires that principles beyond the law must be sought in an atmosphere of caring.

Kohlberg believed that human rights are derived from natural law and are those agreed on after critical examination by a whole society, the same society that also agrees on procedural rules. However, human rights are more fundamental than society's laws, which are not so fixed as they have seemed to be at conventional stages.[4] Stages five and six are incompatible with prejudice. People at principled stages recognize that the right to be respected actually applies to everyone; it cannot be a matter of custom or agreement. Rights to power are less basic than people's rights to be respected and cared about.

It is imperative to follow these principles in order to provide dignity to the oppressed, even when the majority-oriented (stage four) legal system is aiding in oppression. Maintenance of the basic rights of individuals is more important than the letter of the law, property rights, or even collective property rights. Deviation from the law is justified, however, only when there is violation of moral law.

Keeping a widespread mutual trust is the goal of human relations, superseding, but not denying, maintenance of limited loyalties. For this, there must be a general sense of respect for human life. There must also be a morally ordered hierarchy of values. Even so, other peoples' values cannot be judged wholly by one's own, because they are relative to circumstances, times, and cultures. A lack of desire to judge when judgment is unnecessary contributes to trust and to the pride that others need to take in their own identities. Because there is an awareness that all circumstances cannot be known, more value is given to the free choices of other individuals than to the notion of absolutely correct choices. Freedom, or equal rights, also means the right to equal opportunity within the governmental system of the society. Human dignity requires that no one be punished or used as a vehicle of punishment simply for teaching a lesson to others.

Indeed, people must never be treated as means, but only as ends in themselves. The focus at stage five is on the rights of people in general, while stage six includes more emphasis on growth of awareness and the rights and reciprocal obligations of individuals. Agreements for reaching consensus are stressed in order to decide upon the greatest good for the greatest number. While at stage five, there is increasing appreciation of the decision-making mechanism of the social contract, which balances individual and societal points of view, at stage six, its limitations for individuals are evident. Kohlberg stressed universal rules of valid inference and respect for personality. Hartman, like Buber and many religious writers, descried the highest morality as the complete involvement of one person with another in a community that is so empathically related as to form a unit.[5]

Stage five has been criticized as too mechanical, too based on "you cut the cake and I get to choose the first piece" as a guarantor of justice not necessarily based on caring. Lively students discussing its principles might agree with Weiskopf that it puts too high a value on formal analysis, measuring, and being technical "at the expense of ends, goals, purposes and ultimate meanings."[6] Kohlberg described John Rawls' philosophical system as an expression of principled morality,[7] but it, too, favors the autonomy of the systematic judge and underappreciates the confusion that results from many caring human ties. For example, Rawls says that basic freedoms take priority over welfare considerations, which seems to indicate a preference for a formal statement over a deeply felt social understanding. Respect at stage five seems to result from a somewhat impersonal judgment based on high standards that are also imposed on the self.

At stage six, one becomes more aware of unavoidable paradoxes and contradictions in moral life, and the need to accept the pain that comes with awareness of irreconcilable differences. A person who believes he or she is responsible for his or her own inaction when there is injustice to any individual is vulnerable to a shared pain. There is a duty to protest evil, and considerations of prudence should interfere with those of justice as little as possible. Yet, the self is limited by its loyalties as well as by its need for rest and care before taking action. The certainty of disappointment because of frequent human failure to do right may be somewhat tempered by a guilt-lifting awareness of the inevitability of intersubjectivity and reciprocity in the causes of human events.

SOURCES OF MORAL STAGE CHANGE

Kohlberg's starkly described stages of judgment do not measure — and were not intended to measure — the complex emotional, motivational, and behavioral factors that influence the development of each moral stage. Therefore, it is still necessary to look at what there is in children's lives that keeps thinking and judgments the way they are and what seems to bring about change. The difficulty of finding formal mechanisms of stage transition has left the moral stage theory incomplete and open to revision. Piaget spent his last years trying to refine his influential suggestions about stage change. He had long held that a variety of thought-imbalances from challenges to previous conclusions lead to seeking and finding a new equilibrium or balance of ideas at a higher, qualitatively different level.

Following Piaget, Kohlberg argued that stage change could be brought about through cognitive means, such as thinking about and discussing hypothetical moral dilemmas. However, purely formal or cognitive explanations seem to be insufficient whenever one must examine why change did not take place. For example, while young children cannot put themselves in another's place, this imaginative incapacity is not retained after age 8 or age 9 even for stage one children, and cannot explain the poor judgments of some adolescents. The question of why most people fail to progress morally as rapidly as they progress cognitively remains.

As a theorist of conscious thought, Kohlberg discounted the role of emotion and empathy in stage change. He confounded the latter with merely imagining oneself in another role — a cognitive activity. R. S. Peters joined others in objecting to the intellectual bias in this, and E. V. Sullivan charged that the whole Kohlberg system has a major problem in latching onto cognitive answers "thus immunizing itself from the pain in empathic social understanding."[8] Eventually, Kohlberg thought this likely.

In contrast, altruistic emotion, empathy, and compassion are major interests in the feminist work of Kohlberg's colleague, Carol Gilligan. Her assumption is that empathy and the desire to help others lead to a kind of personal responsibility fundamentally different from the "no fair" justice orientation that develops in children along with their potential for empathy. She points out that many males continue to overlook the fundamental importance to human development of ongoing relationships of care and response, and there is a masculine bias in society that predisposed Kohlberg to define morality as justice alone and to test only boys during the period when he was devising his instrument.[9]

Although many studies — including ours — have failed to find significant gender differences in moral development, Gilligan's point about the importance of caring can be applied to the question of what causes stage change. A summary theory of stage change being developed by Kurt Fischer cited "emotional and motivational adequacy" as one determinant. This he went on to interpret as caring that necessarily merges with supportiveness in the environment. Fischer's five determinants of movement to a higher stage are: current stage, rules of transition (being researched), tasks that organize steps to goals, supports in the environment, and emotional and motivational adequacy.[10]

The life stories of classmates we have included show how crucial these last two elements are to moral development. Children must be able to respect and like themselves before they can offer the same to others. A child whose ways of judging self and others as good or bad are misunderstood, or who is looking inward at unmet emotional needs, often pays little attention to what others need. Therefore, warmth of environment — having enough of one's own needs met — is prior to moral growth. People who do not warmly experience their connections with each other lack a context for social responsibilities. Leah and Pat could not grow morally because they lacked emotional and motivational support; their schools and families did not know how to give the support to them. Jo and Tom, on the other hand, were fortunate in their families and schooling. Now we must ask: Is not moral growth too important to leave to fortune?

CONCLUSIONS FOR EDUCATION

The stage concepts discussed in this and the previous chapter are intended to help teachers and parents understand where children stand in relation to fairness. It would be immoral to use the stages to judge children as more or less worthy. Rather, they are presented as benchmarks at which to apply different styles of education at appropriate ages. In high school, only skills of independent reasoning can bring young people to stage four, thus allowing some insightful appreciation of classic authors who are principled.

A developmental sequence in planning teaching activities for moral development would have more effect on prejudice than multicultural information as now taught. At stage one, to maximize caring and self-esteem, children should have their attention drawn to pride in success, caring, politeness, observing, obeying, and contributing to those in need. To make progress through stage two, they should learn to negotiate, broaden their other social skills and friendships, and recognize similarities among people as well as the multiple forms of human diversity that lead them to stereotype. At stage three, while still young and relatively safe, children's awareness of social stratification and human oppression should be increased in a non-threatening manner by careful teaching. Focusing on and rewarding caring acts in their own environments is as essential to their lives as academic learning. Stage four implies a caring form of consciously dutiful respect and a desire to serve in some form of social action. Mobilization for human rights might lead to local actions or starting a chapter of Amnesty International in the school. Adolescents at this level could study classism and racism with less discouragement if they are themselves acting morally, perhaps volunteering in the community. They should be pointed toward a higher stage philosophy that goes beyond needing personal freedom, recognizing that others have the same need that will not be realized without commitment to action.

Students entering high school should be intellectually prepared to appreciate at some time during those years the differences between stages three and four. Moving toward four, seeing the necessity of law and order, dreaming about solving problems, and being dutiful about keeping their own lives clean and on track allows a more equilibrated view of a world disrupted by prejudice and evil acts. Elevation of moral stage gives young people the tools they need to respect themselves and others, make good choices, and, not incidentally, become less prejudiced.

The following chapters elaborate somewhat on what schools and parents can do to provide Fischer's environmental supports for stage changes through his "tasks that organize steps to goals." We will look at specific ways to apply an understanding of the needs of the low moral stages. Many of these strategies focus on helping the child to feel secure and cared for so as to reduce defensiveness and prejudice. To illustrate their application, we will first visit a successful elementary school, one of several following the reformist regimen of black psychiatrist James Comer. Comer has gained essential insights into what teachers and parents need in terms of school governance and what young children need for avoiding prejudice, growing in caring, and learning the discipline to master academics.

STRUCTURE, SECURITY, AND DISCIPLINE: THE LINCOLN-BASSETT COMMUNITY SCHOOL

Verdell Roberts walked briskly down the hall of her school, talking about plans for the day — the older students were visiting a local community college and CNN was coming to film the young black children meeting with mostly white veterans from the VA hospital. As she walked down the hall, Roberts' brown eyes took in the passing children and staff members, and she stopped and spoke to each one.

She saw a teacher coming toward her with two small boys. The boys wore identical white shirts and blue slacks and ties, as if they were in church. The shorter boy —not older than five or six— lit up at the sight of Roberts. "There he is!" she cried out, stopping and holding her arms open for a hug. The boy ran up to her, wrapped his arms around Roberts' knees, and buried his face in her dress. "I just love this boy," she said. "We go running together." Then Roberts noticed that the other boy had started to back away.

"Where are you going? Come here and get your hug!" she said. The boy grinned and came up for his hug.

Roberts released the children, said goodbye, and moved down the hall. She spied an older boy, perhaps eight years old, sitting on the floor. He jumped up when he saw her coming.

"You better get up!" she said, half playfully. The boy dusted off the seat of his pants.

Near the stairwell, Roberts met up with the school security guard, a heavy-set woman in a windbreaker carrying a walkie-talkie. "There's some teenagers outside the door," Roberts told her, and the guard went to investigate.

Downstairs, Roberts got a report on how the school vaccination program was going from the nurse. The nurse, with a stethoscope draped around her neck, then discussed with Roberts the week's schedule for the mobile van that the school helps promote, which provides health care to young mothers in the community. The nurse added that she had collected several bags of clothes to distribute from the van as well.

Leaving the nurse's office, Roberts passed the kitchen and noticed several cafeteria workers sitting around a table, having their morning cigarettes and coffee. She banged on the glass door with an open palm.

"You think it's going to be a calm day?" she shouted. They all laughed.

Outside the school walls, New Haven, Connecticut's, Lincoln-Bassett Elementary School is surrounded by abandoned houses with smashed windows, decrepit houses with peeling paint and broken front steps, empty lots strewn with trash and overgrown with weeds, and street corners where the unemployed and drug-addicted loiter. However, inside these red brick walls, Lincoln-Bassett is a sanctuary of joy and quiet discipline that surrounds children, teachers, and parents with an aura of success and hope.

For the past nine years, Lincoln-Bassett has participated in the School Development Program developed by Yale University psychiatrist James Comer. Comer began his program 26 years ago in two New Haven elementary schools that, like Lincoln-Bassett, served an almost entirely poor, urban, and minority student population. Test scores of these children were among the lowest in the city, and discipline and truancy problems were widespread. Comer believed that these schools were failing because they were trying to pour knowledge into children who were not prepared — mentally or emotionally — to receive it. Economic and social stress interferes with parents on their own giving needed kinds of background experiences. Comer wanted to develop a system by which the entire school would be centered around caring for the needs of the parents and their children in such a way that they would become ready and able to learn. Parents and teachers were also to enjoy the school's atmosphere in a circle of mutual support that would respond to problems of low self-esteem, whether from racism or other experiences, with no need to label such causes. If adults were not initially defensive and demanding their due, they would not meet defensiveness in return.

Comer based his understanding of what the children needed in large part on his own childhood. In his book, *Maggie's American Dream*, he described how his mother, the stepdaughter of a cruel Mississippi sharecropper, managed to raise her five children in East Chicago, Indiana, with a combination of grit, determination, and love.[11] Comer and his brothers and sisters now hold among them a total of 13 college degrees. In addition to his mother, Comer also credited a third-grade teacher who took a liking to him and walked him to school every day, holding hands. He wrote that he was a happy child that people responded to with warmth. He felt that the difference between himself and his many black classmates who did not go on to lead happy or productive lives was that his parents, rather than being rejecting or fearful of the white-dominated world, urged him to learn the skills he would need in order to survive and succeed in it.[12]

Thus, bridging the social and cultural gap between the school and children's home lives is a major aspect of the Comer program. The school begins with the parents. All parents must come to orientation before school begins, to learn how the system works and to get to know the staff and other parents. Teachers work tirelessly over the next few weeks at welcoming, to get them engaged. "You have to get everyone connected emotionally." Parents do volunteer work in the school, organize fundraisers, babysit, and hold parties and potluck dinners for other parents. "The first thing we do is help people feel good about themselves," said Verdell Roberts. The school organized a beauty parlor event in which parents gave each other haircuts and makeovers and later held classes in social graces, such as how to write thank-you notes and how to have a pleasant telephone manner.

The parents, like the children, learn that the school culture is very different from the street culture. "Out there, on the streets, when someone yells at you, you yell back," said Roberts. "In here, when someone yells, we say, 'When you calm down, I will respond to you.' And it works." The entire school community models a positive, calm constancy — no anger or fighting are allowed in front of the children. "In here, we all respond the same way — we all sing from the same hymn book," said Roberts, in one of her favorite phrases.

Roberts described how, once, a parent criticized a white student teacher in front of a class. The student teacher reacted defensively, and angry words were exchanged. Roberts called both the teacher and the parent to tell them how disappointed she was in them. "The teacher should have said, 'If you need to speak to me, let's go outside the classroom,'" Roberts explained.

In the initial, experimental year of the School Development Program, Comer and his team from Yale — an institution traditionally feared and distrusted by the poor in New Haven — battled with the parents and had trouble getting the support of the school staffs. After that, he determined that his program, like the schools themselves, needed structure. He also realized that any changes would need the prior support of everyone who had a stake in the school.

Comer and his team then developed the model that has been in place, virtually unchanged, since 1969. It consists of three mechanisms, three operations, and three guidelines. The mechanisms are the governance team, the mental health team, and the parents' program. The operations are planning, staff development, and periodic assessment. The guidelines are actually goals to live by, vital to the warm school climate that makes all the difference: consensus, collaboration, and avoiding finding fault.[13]

By 1974, test scores in the two schools participating in the program had risen to a tie for third in the city, and absenteeism and discipline problems dropped to almost nothing. Similar results have occurred in the other schools and towns where the program has been instituted. Results are lasting, as well: A recent study of Comer school graduates found that their test scores, attendance records, and self-esteem measures continued to be above secondary school averages, even when they went on to non-Comer middle and high schools.

The primary component of the School Development Program is the governance and management team, which consists of representatives of the administration, teachers, parents, and the support staff (such as clerical and janitorial workers). In Comer middle and high schools, students are represented on the governance and management team as well. This team meets frequently during the year to develop and carry out a comprehensive school plan that contains specific academic and social goals.

"The team is a big piece of what we're doing," said Roberts. "Everyone is involved in deciding what the yearly objectives will be. That way, no one can say they weren't part of the decision making." At Lincoln-Bassett, the governance and management team meets once or twice a month.

In addition to the governance and management team, the School Development Program includes the mental health team, which is made up of any available guidance counselors, psychologists, social workers, special needs teachers, and other mental health professionals (one of whom also serves on the governance and management team). This team works with teachers to help them address individual students' problems as well as ways to prevent problems in the school as a whole. The mental health team helps the school apply child psychology and a developmental understanding of how children think to all its activities. The third component of the program is the parents' team, which works with the other teams to involve parents in the social and academic life of the school.

Comer's system contains several guiding principles to help the teams work together for the benefit of children. These are: team participants cannot paralyze the leader; but decisions must be made by consensus to avoid the "winner-loser feelings and behavior" that might come from voting; and a no-fault, no-blame, problem-solving approach must be used at all times. These guidelines have worked not only to empower teachers, parents, and staff members but also to give the schools the strong, dynamic leadership they need as well. A principal like Roberts embodies the caring, hard work, and commitment that is required of everyone.

"I'm working on balancing high expectations with a sensitive, caring leadership style," Roberts said. She added that she is also working on helping her staff to internalize what they're doing. "It has to be a part of them. Otherwise, when I leave, it goes with me."

Roberts cares for her staff, as well as for the children. They need her counsel and support, especially to model a quiet, non-reactive style. "It's almost a spiritual thing," Roberts said. "Sometimes, I need to meditate and calm myself in order to come in here and deal."

Despite the severe family problems that many of the students have, Roberts emphasized that the attention and concern for personal problems does not get in the way of learning. On the contrary, the problem in most city schools is that the teachers have firmly learned that poor children cannot master the material, yet current reforms are deemphasizing the interpersonal.[14] "We'll spend some time discussing what a kid brings to school, but we're not going to disrupt a whole math class with one kid's problems." The structure and orderliness of the school day helps the children make sense of their chaotic lives and to put aside, if only for these few hours, their home problems. "We're dealing with a lot of deaths this year. We talk and listen. Every kid can learn something," Roberts said.

In the hallways at Lincoln-Bassett, the children march, single-file or in boy-girl pairs, behind their teacher. They wear uniforms of blue jumpers and white blouses for the girls and blue slacks and white shirts for the boys, except on their gym days, when it is not practical for them to change. The uniforms were instituted five or six years ago, at the parents' request. (Uniforms have worked in many poor, urban schools to minimize the sometimes intense competition among children to wear expensive clothes and sneakers.) Despite the neatness and order, the children seem as cheerful and spontaneous as at any school, and Roberts said there are actually very few rules: "Speak when spoken to, no hats, saying excuse me, keeping your hands to yourself." Roberts emphasized that the school has few rules in order to make it easier for the children to know what is expected of them. "All our rules are based on a school-wide theory of having respect for one another," she said.

Lincoln-Bassett takes a pro-active approach to discipline. Through their social skills curriculum, the children practice responding to situations that may tempt them to misbehave. The school also tries to respond to discipline situations with nonpunitive measures; for example, when a number of students were found to argue repeatedly, the school nurse and social worker started an after-school cooking class. The children practiced conversation and cooperation while they made snacks, set the table, and cleaned up. If discipline problems are serious and parents have to be called, Roberts is forthright but keeps the emphasis on the child's strengths and positive qualities. Focusing on the positive "is as natural to us as walking," Roberts said. "We always find the good in people."

Lincoln-Bassett has 550 students in kindergarten through fourth grade. Many teachers keep the same students for several grades, which is encouraged. Like the teacher who held Comer's hand on the way to school, they develop lasting relationships with their students. When it comes time for them to move on to Jackie Robinson Middle School (also a Comer school), "the parents don't want their kids to leave here," Roberts said. She added one fifth-grade class in 1991–92 and another in 1992–93. Funding is tight; Comer schools in New Haven get no more money than any other school. The extra time, attention, and dedication comes from parents, teachers, and staff. Although student turnover is a problem, because of many moves, divorces, and family disruptions in the community, staff turnover at Lincoln-Bassett is low.

In a second-grade classroom, three girls and two boys were getting ready for their television debut. CNN had come to film these students' encounter with several Vietnam vets, who are being treated for post-traumatic stress disorder at the VA hospital. The veterans visit once a week to work on projects and talk with the children. The older students had already left for their visit to the community college, which they do several times a year, in order to make the campus and the idea of higher education familiar to them.

The CNN crew set up its lights and cameras around the five children seated on the floor. Around them was a circle of adults — teachers, veterans, social workers, reporters, and the camera crew. Another teacher stood at the back of the room, amused by all the fuss. "For years, no one paid any attention to what we were doing," said this 14-year veteran of Lincoln-Bassett. "Now, it seems like there are visitors every day."

Indeed, Comer's program is catching on. With a multimillion-dollar grant from the Rockefeller Corporation, it is now being instituted in 154 schools in 14 states. Prince Georges County, Maryland, schools have been Comer schools for several years with great success. The superintendent of schools in New Haven recently ordered that every elementary school in town be a Comer school. Several middle schools and one high school are also participating.

This was Earth Week, and the veterans and children were talking about the environmental consequences of war. A vet sat beside a board and wrote:

> How Does War Affect the Earth?
>   Sherman's March to the Sea
>   Hiroshima
>   Defoliants in Vietnam
>   Kuwait

"What kinds of things can we do to help clean up the world?" the veteran asked.

"Recycle," said one boy.

"We could put out literature to tell people what to do," said a girl.

The conversation moved from the environment to a more general discussion of war.

"What are ways to prevent a war?" a teacher asked.

The children were silent, thinking.

"Well," the teacher pressed, "what do you do when somebody wants to fight with you?"

Several hands shot up.

"When someone hits you, you can stand up for your rights, but you don't have to hit them back," said a little girl.

"If someone's trying to fight, even a grown-up, you have to stop them from fighting and talk to them," added a boy.

"After they've been through a war, why do you think the veterans want to come and talk to us about it?" the teacher asked.

"So we can spend time together, and share stuff," suggested the boy. Everyone smiled.

"You know," the veteran said, "we went through some pretty awful things over there. And for 20 years, we never talked about it. We never talked about our feelings."

"You can talk about it," a girl reassured him. "It feels good to talk about things." She waited awhile for him to reply, but he did not. So she added, "If you feel bad, and you never talk about it, you feel worse."

6

Creating Character in Early School Years

James Comer's fundamental insight is that motivation for learning depends on human relationships. At Lincoln-Bassett and other Comer schools, teachers, parents, administrators, and staff members work cooperatively. Although breakdowns in communication within and between groups have occurred from time to time, training teachers to focus on the feelings that spring up in individual relationships has paid off. The children's need for security is supported by the structures and quiet restraints of the school, including the lines and the uniforms that get no undue attention, the respect and politeness adults give each other and expect from children, and, most importantly, the affection and positive means of discipline.

In New Haven in the 1980s, the dropout rate plummeted from 42 percent to 15.5 percent, and in Comer's school in Landover, Maryland, in the same period, average achievement scores rose from the fiftieth to the eightieth percentile. Comer says these results "are entirely from building community . . . because much of learning is unconscious and related to the surrounding environment."[1] The person-related conception of morality springing from care, as opposed to Kohlberg's higher stage aim of impartiality while judging rules and principles, creates the intellectual space for a true community to develop. Comer's schools demonstrate that children feel important, pay attention, and learn well when adults work closely with each other to promote supportive attitudes and treat children as needing both love and limits.

The implications of the lower moral stages for pedagogy need to be grasped as clearly as those of stage three now are. However, many Americans stilltend to bristle at the idea, of grown people forcing children to be quiet, walk in lines, and sit still. Since the Nazi atrocities of the 1940s, this kind of discipline has been thought of as a source of prejudice not its cure. Many psychologists adopted a theory of permissiveness, mistakenly presuming that childhood anxieties cannot grow where restraint and punishment are minimized. Instead, gently teaching at the appropriate stage such foundations of success as dependability, honesty, and perseverance creates security and breeds far less childish resentment than trying to change the adolescent.

Neither should creativity be linked with unruliness in children. Howard Gardner's report of his recent research among Asian children compels that conclusion, especially because he is well known as an advocate of allowing freedom for all kinds of intelligences to flourish. No single kind of intelligence is intrinsically creative, he writes, because creativity comes from honing one or more areas to a high degree. Visiting China, he found elementary schools stressing traditional teaching of the basics, "in the most rigorous — and often rigid — way imaginable. . . . Yet these practices do not prevent spectacular performances by the youngest children in art and other subject areas." The Chinese wanted no part of the non-directive means of fostering creativity he advocated to them, ways of allowing the child to explore and discover an elusive, inner problem-solving capability in a progressive atmosphere.[2]

If the idea that Asian children are overtrained and, therefore, uncreative has any truth it may relate more to the numbing pressures that increase with age than to overattention in the first years of education. On the contrary, it appears that not learning the value of following rules early in life impedes creativity and productivity. Fear and failure that leads to more failure undermine spontaneity and creative expression much more than quiet discipline and learning pleasing means of expression do. Children seem to need enclosure, security, and trusting relationships that include their good behavior to shift from stage one to stage two. They need authority, as distinct from authoritarianism with its assumption that goodness is mere obedience. Success in school, in the child's mind allied with goodness, is almost as essential to self-esteem as belonging.

As Comer schools show, no-fault discipline works. Using resource rooms where children under pressure could be sent, his schools in New Haven were able to eliminate serious behavior problems among students. When children understand that others really care, punishment can lose its negative context by becoming cooperative. Its sting, rooted in fear, becomes less necessary as a positive atmosphere relieves adults of their need to assert power too forcefully. Teachers share this insight with parents who have become part of the school community.

Because some of the most important moral education in children's lives happens at home and begins before schooling, we will describe a detailed system to promote behavior change that co-author Florence Davidson developed as a family therapist. The "quiet family" method has been successful in promoting the kind of relationships that foster moral development at home and cooperation at school. This chapter also addresses ways to make young children's natural empathy lead to progress in moral judgment. Empathy is innate, but the delight young children take in sharing feelings and helping can be lost if not frequently encouraged and rewarded.[3]

THE QUIET FAMILY METHOD

Most psychologists have neither emphasized the different approaches to discipline needed for children at different stages nor, until recently, focused on ease and regularity in early child-management and the ways habits shape the kind of character that will follow. Instead, they have stressed talking it out with children of all ages. Parents do not intuitively know that any kind of attention, even the kind they would hate, can be welcomed by children feeling bad. Children unconsciously learn that misbehavior is a path to attention. Too much talk leads to becoming manipulative, not because children are born bad but because of the underlying structures of the low moral stages.

Special education teachers have found that, even for disturbed children, the basic principles of quietly modifying behavior work well enough for them to avoid insistent scolding. These same principles can be used at home. The chief thing to remember is that attention, either positive or negative, leads to a repeat of the behavior that is attended to. Therefore, much pleasure-giving attention should be given for positive acts, and very little excitement or even talk should be the response to the child's negativity.

A parent becoming upset, hitting, yelling, or even discussing at length makes some children feel a surge of power and a secret "I won." Talking it out in the middle of the confusion should be done only with older, higher stage children but even that risks rewarding malfeasance and prolongs feeling bad. It is better accomplished the next day.

Misbehavior is not to be ignored, however. The trick is to administer limits in near silence and move the child briefly to a lonely space, over and over, if necessary. A truly secured time-out room and a soft voice with few words sometimes brings about "a whole new child," to quote one mother. Being banished for five minutes should be described beforehand as "not a punishment, but a reminder that each of us can stop, think, and choose behavior. Would you like your parents to also hold back, and not get mad? We're going to try."[4] Time is doubled to ten minutes for arguing or being unable to go quietly, and tripled for a tantrum, especially one outside the home (to be paid for upon return). Success usually comes quickly as children understand what is sought, while newly empowered and less frustrated parents feel a genuine warmth toward the yielding child. It is important to remain consistent; to cease all nagging, labeling, and picking at the child; and to reward good behavior with delight and closeness. Other rewards may also be added, such as stars for a day without a time-out, several of which can be traded for a prize as long as the child understands the cooperative goal.

Only one behavior (not an attitude or feeling) needing improvement should first be cheerfully chosen by the parent. Cheer is necessary because raised voices, threats, slaps, spanks, or blanket criticisms distract the child from the offense and lead, instead, to personality defenses. Parents who have been at all out of control themselves can confess to stress and offer to stop being discouraging. This "stage two trade" should be in return for the child's agreeing in the future to go quietly to a bedroom after offending. In our experience, children change easily with this method when they have agreed in advance to the need for the family to change. The hardest part is for adults to cover their own sometimes legitimate anger, even for the few weeks or months that it takes for the child to gain a new sense of self. Parents are more likely to be the source of a child's values the more they seem strong, give the child emotional warmth, and supply attention for the behaviors they have chosen to reward. Benevolent parents protect children by trying for quiet consistency.

EARLY EMPATHY, ALTRUISM, AND POSITIVE SELF-IMAGE

Nel Noddings writes, and experience confirms, that commitment to ethics basically grows out of being given respect and being cared for early in life.[5] Leon Blum has a felicitous phrase: "the responsiveness to connection released in early childhood."[6] The term "released" implies a kind of rush of joy between child and caretaker that, repeated often, powerfully shapes personality. Happiness then becomes a source of trust and of future unprejudiced development. Having affiliative needs met lowers some of the walls of self-defense that, while necessary and normal on both sides of any relationship, lead to misunderstandings. We have seen in the case-study children how defensiveness learned in family settings affects stage change and prejudice. The child who becomes used to enjoying others and sharing with them is more likely to gradually abandon labels and stereotypes that are otherwise beginning to serve the typical personality defense of seeking spurious superiority to compensate for feeling inferior. In reviewing the large number of studies that demonstrate a strong relationship between negative attitudes to self and rejection of others, it becomes clear that experiencing mostly positive emotions as a young child offers freedom to advance.

Jerome Kagan noted that a sad feeling is often shown in the second year of life when an ideal is not met or the child comes upon something broken. "I am bad" begins around three.[7] Self-liking or self-condemnation is not always from agreement with parents' condemnations; it is also the result of reflection. Comparing the actual self with parallel inner standards for behavior dictates a relatively positive or negative identity, following the young child's split, good-bad way of thinking.

Identity seeks its confirmation in present and future choices among possible behaviors. There are strong correlations between showing social responsibility and altrusitic sharing in nursery school and comparable behavior five or six years later.[8] Correlations between feeling successful and acting generously have also been demonstrated.[9]

Tests of whether and to what extent empathy is trainable are still primitive but have promise. In one experiment, a group of kindergarteners took turns pretending to fall down and get hurt while others pretended to be helpers. Roles were then reversed. Another group received no training. The next day the trained children were more responsive to recorded crying sounds in the next room than were the untrained children.[10]

Results of similar trials with older children showed that it was important to ask them to notice their own feelings. Being asked to describe how they felt while acting out various human situations during ten previous days increased some apparently unrelated sharing of candy on an eleventh day. Switching roles in playlets about problems, especially roles of aggressor and victim, and describing the feelings experienced in the old and new roles had even more effect on the sharing afterward. Priming children to arouse their feelings of sympathy before the experiment brought on still more helping behavior.[11]

Emotional arousal is, thus, a critical element in causing helpful behavior. William Damon pointed out that the early moral emotions provide a ready-made structure for the education of deep and abiding concerns, which then may develop in the light of the moral reactions of others.[12] Attitudes are formed by frequent repetitions of the same orientations. Admiring one's mentors, sharing toys, taking turns, being labeled as kind and generous, and doing favors within friendships keep the feeling of being a good person going.

Children who are victims of poverty and racism may be neglected, crowded and scolded, feel discouraged, have neither mentor nor parent with knowledge of child development, and recognize disrespect in most of their families' transactions with the dominant culture. If they behave badly they may be simply confirming the self-image that began in a survival mode. When teachers view them as losers these children's life possibilities may well be over. If the children are poor, they will remain not only in material want but also in poverty of hope for the kindness and gentleness that maintain beauty of spirit.

The support they lack can be offered by affectionate teachers who understand that a whole range of performances become more probable from their own understanding of childhood prejudice and the need to create an atmosphere that counters it. Children require management.

Negative attitudes among children hurt isolated or low status children as much as adult attitudes may.

The slim book, *You Can't Say You Can't Play*, describes young children's responses during discussions of the school rule named in its title. Many shared the depth of their feelings of rejection from some of each other's earlier behaviors. Over time, they listened to and made up stories, mostly involving animals, that called attention to the teacher's interest in empathy as she insisted upon the playground rule not to exclude anyone. Classroom climate greatly improved.[13]

Thus, there are ways to discuss rules without implying blame. Adults' wariness of indoctrination or of seeming too blaming and moralistic leads children, and especially adolescents, to downplay moral issues. They begin to mentally file them as others' issues of power or obedience and then to overvalue their own feelings. If empathy and sympathy are to be active emotions in middle and late childhood, moral judgments on both the children's and the teacher's part must be shared.

Between the ages of six and nine children become cognitively ready to understand injustice as a function of differences in people's situations. Oppression, illness, and handicaps are understood as not just situation-specific, but as general and protracted states.[14] Children can be made conscious of the many human beings who are needy, so as to achieve a more heartfelt understanding (like Tom's). Their increasing maturity brings responsibility to study and learn so that they can help others.

Parents' roles are similar to the schools'. Diana Baumrind studied the effects of what she called "maturity demands," whereby parents maintain high standards in accordance with children's abilities by assigning responsibilities. Making maturity demands while talking clearly to children about cooperativeness was associated with friendly and nurturing behavior in nursery schoolers.[15] This finding agrees with anthropologists' observations that in cultures where there is considerable early assignment of responsibility, the children become especially helpful and supportive of peers.[16] Reasoning with children old enough to appreciate the respect implied, especially during a "teachable moment," also leads to helpful behavior.

Opportunities to reason with children at such a moment in school, when an unfair incident or disagreement has just occurred, are typically lost when the group is too big or too unaware of the importance of supportiveness. Hawlemont Regional Elementary, a tiny rural school tucked into the hills of western Massachusetts, has "a spirit of caring that is almost palpable," according to a reporter, R. Matthews.[17] This emanates from its nine full-time teachers' obvious respect for each other as well as their dependence on the constant help and fundraising of parents for the educational excellence that won a national citation in 1986. The community has little money (the school's desks were salvaged from another community's dumpster), but because the parents as well as the children regard the school as a second home, caring is both taught and experienced.

Another experiment in prosocial education shows the extra effect enough money can have. Funded for many years by the Hewlett-Packard Foundation, teachers in several elementary schools in California's San Ramon Valley are studying how to create an atmosphere of mutual caring through the organization and tone of classrooms, the content of new lessons, and the time-out approach to discipline. Shared decisions, such as what children can do together about a bully, have been found to create better learning experiences than calling on a teacher to end an incident. Parents are given homework assignments to do with these children, such as literature-based reading, oriented toward values. Chores, charity, school governance, and community responsibility are viewed as natural and daily activities.

The ethical mission of this Child Development Project includes reaching out to parents to persuade them that both inconsistency in discipline and too much external control may induce some children to decide that manipulation of the system is a goal of life. With team teaching, several teachers exchange information about what helps a certain student and pass this on to parents. Cooperative learning is a hallmark of these schools. One of the teachers, a former military man, commented in a report about their early successes: "It's a wonderful thing to see. These kids are helping each other, caring for each other. . . . Holy mackerel, this actually works!"[18] Children are taught about other cultures and how to sort out other people's differences in perceptions, backgrounds, and cultures from their own ideas about good and bad motives. The project has recently been expanded to include two schools with multiethnic populations. They will be carefully measured before and after to help other schools learn what does or does not work.[19]

Although moral stage progress is not included in the measures used by the Child Development Project, caring behavior has been linked with higher moral stage in other studies. The moral maturity of fifth-grade boys in one of Kohlberg's first studies was significantly positively correlated with sociometric assessments by their peers of each one's cooperation, sharing, being considerate of and defending victims, and, especially, helping others.[20] In another experiment, higher stage seven-year-olds, given a chance to be altruistic, took more opportunities to donate candy to poor children and to help a younger child than lower stage seven-year-olds. This correlation was statistically significant with mental age partialed out.[21]

CREATING CHARACTER AT SCHOOL

Some critics maintain that the "therapy model" of education (but not that practiced by Comer) has brought test scores down since the 1960s. They describe the model as one in which "too much understanding" has produced forgiveness of failure, and, consequently a lack of resolute-ness toward setting firmly any standards that make those who do not meet them feel bad. These critics prefer to see self-mastery rather than self-expression.[22]

There is no reason that mastery and expression cannot exist in the same child if we view the timetable of the moral stages as showing the importance of early achievement of self-mastery. Cleaning the room and the class pet's cage with pleasure and without complaint is as im-portant as working through fewer grammar, writing, and math prob-lems slowly, so as not to seize upon short-cuts while misunderstanding critical steps. In the first three grades, a curriculum of playful affect can run parallel to a curriculum that indoctrinates standards and cele-brates human achievements. Frequent short, vigorous recesses could alternate with memorizing inspired quotations from storied leaders.

A well-known African-American teacher, Marva Collins, has achieved success by alternately teasing, enjoying, and pressuring her inner-city pupils to emotionally invest in such statements as "A future president doesn't keep a messy desk." She demands that children mem-orize some simple moral truths that summarize profundities. "Every time you say 'That's not fair' or you wonder why something is the way it is you are questioning life, just as Mr. Emerson did. He believed that every person has a free will and can choose to make his life what he wants it to be." The poorest, most depressed and disturbed children, on whom others have given up, apparently achieve with her as well or better than more affluent children given less intense teaching.[23] Collins abhors the common belief that less able students cannot do quality work, a belief that is fatalistic, class-ridden, and racially prejudiced.

Teachers and principals who are like Collins personalize everything they do, tailoring and varying its content according to the competence of each child and rewarding any successes at once. They raise expecta-tions by measured increments at the same time that they lead the child, other teachers, and parents to see competence and achievement potential as connected with current progress, however small. What this child could become seems to be always first in their minds, not how the child looks now.

The affective curriculum is, thus, integrated with the cognitive one. In this regard, it is vital that children feel academically successful before they have much opportunity to compare themselves unfavorably with others. However, for children already behind, enhancing the teachers' affective skills and training parents to help has been shown to be more successful and cost-effective than providing remedial educators.[24] Difficult children should be seen as sources of energy, able to share in finding out what their own particular talents are. Those most "impossible" may be the very ones whose drive takes them farthest. Getting them to believe in their potential for the future by making a positive evaluation of current capacity can be accomplished by love, which, again, is humanly restricted by group size and not only by teacher incapacity. Making children do work over, learn in depth, and compete with themselves to create papers and projects they are proud to display works best. New "hooks," reasons for work that make the relevant personal connection for each learner, need to be found, with the teacher then serving as coach. Once some success is achieved, the regular curriculum should be frequently interpreted to children as giving them the tools needed for manifesting their talents and reaping specific rewards in the future.

Henry Levin, a professor at Stanford University, has devised a dramatic means of helping those children who have already concluded that they are in some way not as good as others. Termed "accelerated learning" to express the depth of emotional penetration to which its prescribed curriculum responds, it denies the entrenched notion that the best means of teaching children from impoverished backgrounds is to track them or to dismiss them from class for remedial help. His system responds to the damage done to future learning by self-labels such as dumb, unimportant, uncool, and unacceptable. Children are given accelerated lessons with special help along with roles in the regular class that lead to pride of accomplishment.[25] While some educators worry about grade inflation, in Levin's experience, young children, especially minority children, learn more when they are given high marks, with learning so paced that no more than 10 percent of answers will be checked wrong. A key factor is to make clear the expected steps in learning and not to dismiss the wonder of them once accomplished.

While a child's personality depends on family interactions in the earliest years, once school begins, high self-esteem depends to a degree much more than is generally realized on the simple ability to work and an enhanced pride and sense of belonging. This has not been obvious, although movement in the other direction is well-known: Low self-esteem leads to poor work and giving up. Recent evidence comes from Ohio, where those in the lowest 10 to 20 percent of first graders who were tutored in reading early in the year for half an hour a day during only 12 to 16 weeks continued to improve at the classroom rate three years later, unlike those whose remedial work was more typical in beginning later, remaining ongoing, and being less intense.[26] It seems likely that the successful group of children kept sharpening their attentiveness in order to perpetuate a self-image strengthened by early achievement. The others may have thought themselves dumb.

MORAL EDUCATION IN GRADE SCHOOL

The fact that self-esteem leads to enhanced cognitive skills, current coping, and future job opportunities does not lessen the importance of training the power of reason for family responsibility as well as responsibility for a democratic society and its world relationships. Clear thought is especially important in the moral realm. Moral judgment should be emphasized as soon as children are old enough to create their own reasons.

Eliot Turiel found that development of better judgment can be induced by presenting children seven and older with moral thinking one stage beyond their present level. In a free discussion of story dilemmas among peers, this tends to occur automatically, with the teacher interpreting childish comments and facilitating conclusions.[27] Moral education in this context means actively wrestling with ambiguous but age-appropriate issues, such as whether to fight a nasty younger child or whether to rescue a kitten from a tree that a safety-conscious father has forbidden climbing. However, dilemmas beyond the current experiences and interests of the children should usually be avoided, because inconclusive outcomes of discussions teach moral relativity (that there are no certain answers) before children can consider its unsettling implications.

An essential element in moral education is for a teacher to challenge children to defend their reasoning, asking why they think as they do. "To save a cat stuck in a tree, why did you say disobeying Dad saying 'don't climb' is wrong?" The children should be asked to describe their ideas of fairness in such a way as to give them a more universal applicability as in: "I think you should love your father even more than your cat." If the teacher is neither too approving nor too disapproving of the answers, the children will listen to other children's justifications. Adult answers ought to be added at the end (perhaps that cats don't mind waiting, or fathers will be understanding, or thinking for yourself is important). Blatt, Turiel, and colleagues have shown that children prefer reasoning one stage above their own, and that this peer-prompting technique, used repeatedly, causes stage movement.[28]

Still, there may be no carry-over into actual behavior unless there is additional coaching by adults. Part of the effectiveness of an overall supportive environment is that it promotes contacts with parents who might want to know how typical children think about human relationships and might also welcome suggestions for more actively supervising fairness in peer play. A small, caring school empowers teachers who know how vital friendships are and how distracted from learning children may be by peer and sibling rejections. Empowered teachers reach out to parents, sharing responsibility for social development.

The consequences of low peer acceptance are so severe as to be worth considerable attention all through schooling. How others treat a child tells her who she is, and consequently how she feels about herself. Cliques leave those outside alone in the social isolation that is all children's nightmare. Heterogeneous friendships, on the other hand, make children focus on more than one idea at a time as a means of attempting to understand the others' points of view, which brings on decentration. Moral stage progress would likely be even more facilitated if these friendships crossed ethnic lines. How to resist the peer pressure to reject nonfavored others, as well as the idea that some children are better and more valuable than others, should be a topic for writing. Most children are aware that in our society there is a clear relationship between visible ethnicity and low social status, and many wonder why.

Some other topics for classroom discussion in higher grades are why most rules of courtesy are not arbitrary; why some seem to be and are, therefore, often disobeyed; and why children (and also grown-ups) are sometimes rude to people they love. Children could be asked to consider and tell about what promotes courtesy and friendliness on their street, in their club, or among some adults they know, describing cultural differences. Stories read aloud and activities that teach about others' lives should deal not only with how the characters live and work but also with their attitudes, beliefs, hopes, and fears and how these contribute to future possibilities. To move the children toward stage three, they should be asked to infer reasons for the motives and emotions described in stories.

Grade school children can be taught early to manage their friendships and not be simply reactive. Managing means trading phone calls, trying for equality and generosity, giving in when it does not matter, or, perhaps, telling your friend when you have been giving in too much. It means listening when your friend has a problem, sharing your ideas and your things, being honest, and being polite. For those needing special coaching, stars could be given for favorable recess and lunchroom activity, for mentioning any of these skills in a "play diary," or for following directed assignments to create supportiveness and equal treatment.

Keeping a "play diary" or a "happiness diary," with comments about enjoyment of sharing, is an idea that preserves memories and allows a parent, teacher, or counselor to suggest and organize weekly goals and rewards for appropriate socializing. This could evolve in later grades into a record of self-investigation and private arguments with oneself, perhaps expressing positive and negative feelings about media extremes, the youth culture, or the differences between one's own and one's friends' professed ideals and actual behavior.

Positive moral words can be kept on the board for use in spelling and writing lessons and to emphasize to mostly stage two favor-trading children what community is about. Words such as love, care, fair, just, respect, moral, equal, loyal, ideals, health, integrity, personality, character, compassion, community, courage, nurture, gratitude, virtue, and excellence are worth dwelling on. A way to keep the children involved is to have them use these words in sentences about real or imaginary disputes. They might later trade a word they value for one already listed and then compare the new word's importance with that of the one dropped. This introduces concrete thinkers to the debatability of many ethical abstractions.

Such a discussion is most useful when tied to examples of moral issues in children's lives. Who should get various kinds of care or rewards leads to different answers at different cognitive stages. Children in the early grades tend to say everyone should share equally. However, when they are given actual food treats to share, it turns out that they really believe in entitlement, not deservedness, so they may suddenly take back candy that they had begun to distribute. They are likely to say it is theirs, so they have the right to change their minds and share only with friends. Distributing treats and then pointing out contradictions between ideas and behavior has been shown to increase generosity.[29]

Even subjects that would seem to have nothing to do with morality can be jumping-off points for discussion. A science class might weigh moral issues in health care and biotechnology, simply stated. A mathematics class studying fractions could cut cookies in exact parts to reward several winners on a test of merit in math skills, then discuss whether various kinds of merit should, in the wider world, determine who gets to eat enough.

At lunch, the lesson could be expanded to who gets to eat well, with 60 percent of the class given rice to eat with their fingers, 30 percent tortillas and beans, and 10 percent an appealing school lunch. These fractions illustrate world averages.[30] As an introduction to economics and what might be good about industrialization and people living close together, the social studies teacher might ask why world averages are this way. The goal of such lessons is not only to raise issues of fairness and caring but also to emphasize their complexity, as opposed to mere nostalgia about earlier times (Sal's Indians with a deer), and moralistic oversimplifications that move typical preadolescents toward confused mistrust.

If such lessons cause children to feel frustrated, the teacher might point out the friendliness of mathematical exactitude as compared to issues where correct answers do not appear in the back of a book. If is important for children to give frequent thought to why some people gain the experience to appreciate mathematics and know more beauty than others, why economic inequities exist, and why they should take neither a passive nor an overly aggressive (thieving) attitude toward not having money. This is essential background for understanding much about ethnic prejudice and why "tolerance" and "benign neglect" are not enough to satisfy an ethical thinker.

STRATEGIES TO REDUCE ETHNIC PREJUDICE

Managing friendly contacts with minority children can reduce status differences. Glock and colleagues noted that with children "cognitive understanding is as important as interacting, in shaping ethnic attitudes and behavior . . . [hence we need] educational materials on self-understanding and prejudice, particularly in the lower grades."[31] A grade-by-grade curriculum on some current and historical effects of prejudice could be devised by a faculty, taking story-dilemmas about prejudice from the actions of conquerors and from children's literature.

Supervised opportunities to reach out to help others, such as bringing a holiday party or a performance to a nursing home, also produce gains in children's awareness. After expressing satisfaction with generous actions, a teacher could call attention to all the trouble the children have taken for the elderly while there are children right there in the school who feel ignored. Discussions after practicing altruism are very useful, because children who consciously decide that being kind is important for them have proven to be more consistent later in expressing kindness.[32]

Dramatizations of dilemmas improvised by the children about their own problems are another way for a group to become more oriented toward people's feelings and motives.[33] The teacher need compose only some opening lines and position the actors. "You be me, your teacher, trying to help Sara, who, as you know, was just insulted on the playground. And Bill can be the big kid who did it, and Mary can start by telling what happened. Afterward we will switch roles, then see how everyone felt." After one such playlet, a sixth grader said, "It isn't the power that matters, it's the way you treat people." It is only a short step to relate such an insight to the uses of power in the history lessons and stories of the regular curriculum.

Personalizing the social studies is emotionally effective. A typical how-to article suggests pretending to be a diarist or a newspaper reporter present at some moving event, or during some period of social history that appeals to children. The role of an Indian pursued by the cavalry, a cavalryman's son at home on the frontier who is worried about danger to his father or himself, an immigrant arriving in a new culture writing a descriptive letter to a friend, or a Jewish child hiding from Nazis are some of the possibilities suggested. Briefly dramatizing what a child has written is especially enjoyable. Switching roles in order to look at the situation from the participant's various viewpoints and going back in history aids moral development, even when the play's issue is not serious enough to be called a moral dilemma. That empathic feelings lessen prejudice could be explained to children, many of whom see no reason to learn "dead history."

Typical multicultural plug-ins are less effective than lessons that address children's questions and their need to expand their imaginations.[34] The following are playful and creative elaborations of traditional ways to combat racism and ethnocentrism. Discussing these activities while doing them helps prevent stereotyping:

1. have an ethnic holiday or birthday celebration for each child in the class, along with a world map with pins for each family's origins;
2. teach words from several languages and cultures, along with their literature, poems, and songs;
3. describe social practices and the similar values they imply (clean homes and tulip growing in Holland; African fresh huts, house-plants in cans, and river baths);
4. sponsor celebrations with ethnic foods cooked by parents, possibly with costumes for role-playing, brief dramas, or statue tableaux with music;
5. present foreign clothespin dolls in settings, all made by children (perhaps for a grandparents' day);
6. create homemade booklets of either family history or handed-down stories, with photos or drawings;
7. bring tape recordings of an older relative being interviewed by a child and transcribe its essentials;
8. arrange visits and stories from immigrants or ethnic helpers in the school and representatives of major ethnic groups, especially blacks and Latinos;
9. make posters and plan trips, real or imaginary, to ethnic areas and sister-schools, helped by parents;
10. give privileges for a day to those with brown or blue eyes only, to make discrimination upsetting; and
11. use the school building for cultural events, parties, cross-age tutoring with invitations to the elderly to gain a child-friend and to parents to learn mentoring of the other people's children.

CONCLUSIONS FOR EDUCATION

A brute fact about moral education, as R. S. Peters put it, is that "do as you are told" is a non-moral edict that gives the wrong message to an older child but is absolutely essential for a young one to absorb. Our culture currently neglects the fact that discipline is the basis of all future success. Parents must conquer the guilt they feel about having to work away from home and ignore such confusing advice from psychologists as "let your angry child draw your picture and stamp on it" in favor of restricting anger by the quiet family method. Untroubled children lessen parental guilt and allow teachers to teach. By the same token, teaching to the stage one mentality is not a sign that the educational community has taken up ancient habits of subsuming ethics under a grim rubric of authority and conformity. On the contrary, it can be seen that when young children obey those they trust, they experience a needed security, a surprising lessening of anxiety about outcomes, and more readiness for the next stage.

A child with stage one structures of thinking inevitably senses the dictates of authority as validly moral. Rules are assumed to have a sacred, unchangeable quality. This may become frightening, which is a strong reason that parents and schools not emphasize fear in relation to punishment, no matter how effectively they recall being trained themselves. Adults should assume that the worst-behaving child is all too aware of his badness and does not need repeated education on what it is. Instead, limits need to be set and gently, but inexorably, enforced. All children will predict their own natures based on current behavior, long before they understand why they do what they do.

The great majority of grade school children come to think at a premoral stage two level but then remain there. This does not mean they cannot recognize the superiority of stage three ideas, as research shows. The problem of stage transition lies in the lack of helpfulness of the culture around them. Sometime during grade school, all students need to recognize the importance for morality of understanding intentions, reasons, motives, choices, and being able to act upon choices. They must then base their actions on the discipline and habit-training given earlier.

As adolescence approaches, children require a different set of techniques to foster moral growth than have been discussed in this chapter. Middle school is increasingly being recognized as a crucial period in children's lives. The next section describes a school that has devised a way to give middle schoolers the adult support they need while they are making conscious choices about values and behavior — choices that will in large part determine their futures.

SMALL GROUPS AND AN ADVISORY SYSTEM: SHOREHAM-WADING RIVER MIDDLE SCHOOL

"I have to do my Spanish homework."

"Hey, can I have a basement in my solar house?"

"What movie are we going to see?"

"Where are we going for lunch? I want Chinese."

"Nah, it's too greasy."

"Can I put the radio on?"

"I've got a new tape. I'll go get it."

It was 8:30 in the morning, and the students in Chris Cummo's eighth-grade advisory were piling into the room, each with something to say. They congregated in a corner of Cummo's large science classroom, next to a picture window. Outside, the sun was starting to warm the trees and fields surrounding Shoreham-Wading River Middle

School on Long Island's northeast shore. Some students lounged on the two old sofas in the corner, while others sat on table tops or milled about, fiddling with the radio and chating about the coming day. Cummo, a 23-year-old who was recently hired, was talking with one student about the solar house models his science class was building. Baseball pennants and old Rolling Stone magazine covers decorated the walls above his head.

Education at Shoreham-Wading River is built around the advisory system, which is designed to give middle schoolers a close and motivating relationship with an adult other than their parents and to foster a sense of community through small group meetings and shared activities.[35] Every morning, the advisor meets with his or her ten advisees for 12 minutes to take attendance, discuss plans, make announcements, collect milk money, and conduct the Pledge. The whole advisory also eats lunch together every day. They brown-bag in the advisor's classroom (the school has no cafeteria), go out to eat, or make lunch in the home economics room. The advisor is the school's liaison with the student's parents and her advocate with other teachers. Advisory groups go on field trips to New York City or Montauk, go to the movies, go running, study, do art projects, have picnics, go camping or boating — in short, they do everything together.

Once a month or so, each student meets individually with his or her advisor for 45 minutes in the early morning. These one-on-one meetings enable the advisor and student to talk more personally about the student's schoolwork, interests, and problems. "First period makes advisory what it is," said a sixth-grade teacher. "Without the first period option, the 12-minute advisory would be just like homeroom in the old days." Shoreham-Wading River has two bus runs to ensure that students with advisory meetings can get to school early. If they're nervous about meeting with a teacher alone, they're welcome to bring a friend. Some advisors also encourage students to communicate with them through journal writing. Advisors are also available for meetings at other times with any student who has a need.

Students and teachers rave about the advisory system. "It's the best way I've ever seen a school set up," said an eighth-grade girl.

"You learn to talk to adults," said another student. "It's easier to talk to friends, but since sixth, I've learned to talk to adults better."

"The teachers become more like friends," added an eighth-grade boy. "Especially Mr. Cummo. You can talk to him, tell him things you can't tell your parents."

Another advantage of the advisory system, as this same boy pointed out, is that "You get to be friends with kids you otherwise wouldn't be friends with."

Cummo said: "All the kids in my advisory are very different, and in the beginning of the year, not one hung out with each other. Now they look to each other for support. They see the value of a relationship with someone who's not like them. They try to work it out, even if they don't get along."

The heterogeneous advisory groups usually have a mixture of male and female, outgoing and shy, athletic and academically-inclined students. Their intimate size gives students a sense of belonging to each other and to the school. An adult who is on their side, willing to listen and go to bat for them, is comforting during the trials of early adolescence.

"Like one time I was failing," said an eighth-grade boy, "and I couldn't tell my dad. I told my advisor, and he told my dad. He told him I was trying to bring my grades up. That helped a lot."

Missy, a chubby eighth grader, said: "My advisor told me not to let kids get to me. They would always tease me and make fun of me and pick on me. I always felt left out and hated. She said, 'I want to help you build up your self-esteem this year.'"

In general, the school tries to match the personality and interests of students and advisors. Students are allowed to switch advisors if they cannot get along with them, although they are encouraged to "live with it" as a training for similar experiences later in life.

One girl admitted that last year she did not like her advisor. Although disappointed, she decided not to change. "This year," she said, "it's more personal. I have Mrs. Snow, and her advisory is just girls."

New advisors for the following year are chosen by the current ones. Incoming sixth graders are placed with care, after they have been at the school a few weeks, by an administrator, guidance counselor, reading teacher, and social worker in consultation with their counterparts in the child's elementary school. The advisors include all the members of the faculty — music and art teachers, coaches, librarians, and administrators.

Shoreham-Wading River is located in a semi-rural, predominantly Catholic, middle-class community. The school district is quite wealthy, thanks to the tax revenue generated by the nearby Shoreham nuclear power plant. The middle school has 50 faculty and administrators and 50 support staff to serve the approximately 450 students in grades 6–8. It occupies a single-story brick structure surrounded by a 12-acre campus that includes a track, a baseball field, tennis courts, a greenhouse, and a barn where students keep chickens, rabbits, sheep, and goats. It has extensive art, music, and shop facilities. The carpeted hallways are lined with glass trophy cases; the school has two large gyms. Students have the latest computers and video equipment available.

After an extensive legal battle, the nuclear power plant was recently deemed unsafe and ordered closed. Its payments to the school district will be reduced at the rate of 10 percent per year until they are completely phased out. The loss of revenue will force the school to scale back a lot of its programs and facilities, and some teachers and students will be leaving. However, the faculty is confident that the essential component of the school's success — the advisory system — will not be affected.

"When we started out, in 1972, we didn't have the money we have now," said media and theater teacher Jerry Silverstein. Silverstein is among the 30 to 40 percent of the faculty who have been with the school since the beginning. The middle school was founded by innovative educator Dennis "Doc" Littky, who was then 26 years old. He how heads Thayer High School in Winchester, New Hampshire. "We were all in our twenties, and we had limitless energy and enthusiasm," said Silverstein. The school had an image then — which it still somewhat retains — as a "hippie-sandal" school, in the words of current principal Cary Bell. Littky had a strong philosophy of what middle schoolers needed that included the then-unknown advisory system. He hired people who were also committed to the idea of dealing directly with all aspects of children's lives at a school. Parents at first were wary.

"Some felt that the advisors were too personal," said Bell, who has been principal for 14 years. Bell and others acknowledge that advisors have a delicate role; they have to develop rapport with the students, yet not delve too deeply into a student's private life nor try to usurp the parents' role. "It's not an advisor's place to ask, 'How's your mother treating you?' or that kind of thing," said Joanne Urgese, the community service coordinator. Serious personal or discipline problems are referred to the school's counseling staff. Advisors do meet frequently to help each other do their jobs better, and they take a once-a-year workshop conducted by a guidance counselor and psychologist. The topic for 1991–92 was how to develop trust; the previous year's was drug and alcohol abuse in families.

Shoreham-Wading River's progressive image also stems from the fact that the day is not rigidly structured. There are no bells, and students can be found sitting in the halls, talking and studying, when they are not in class. The school is organized into four teams, each of which contains students from all three grades. Students stay in their team for the whole three years, unless there is a compelling reason to change. Four advisor-teachers share the approximately 45 students who are in the same grade and team. The team concept was developed to stop the older students from intimidating younger ones as well as to improve communication between faculty members and advisors.

In keeping with the cooperative spirit, academic competition is discouraged at Shoreham-Wading River. There is no honor roll, and no prizes or awards are given at eighth-grade graduation. The school tries to recognize each student through the teams and advisories. Students are encouraged to work together, and teachers practice team teaching and cooperative learning in their classrooms. Students rarely fail and never have to repeat a grade. Athletic teams do not cut students; the number of teams is expanded to allow everyone to participate. There is some ability grouping in Spanish and math and a small gifted and talented program, but the overall tone is one of mutual support and encouragement.

The philosophy seems to be working. While some high school teachers have complained that the middle schoolers are not as prepared as they could be (especially in Spanish), in 1990, seventh-grade students exceeded national averages by two years in math and three years in reading on the Stanford Achievement Test. Students go on to high school with an enthusiasm for school and a willingness to take risks. They enjoy their work, unlike the students in Grant and Sleeter's survey of junior high schools, where the word most often used to describe instruction was "boring."[36] It is also unlike Goodlad's description of the vast majority of classrooms as "emotionally flat."[37] Shoreham-Wading River High School, which gets its entire enrollment from this middle school, has had only three students drop out in 20 years. Ninety-three percent of its graduates go to college.

With a student body as homogeneous as that in this town — according to Principal Bell, the families are 80 percent Roman Catholic and 95 percent white — the question of racial and cultural sensitivity arises. This issue is of particular concern to Bell, who is black. He said his three children were at one time or another called "niggers" when they attended the school, but he shrugged this off as a typical experience for a black child growing up anywhere in America. Bell said he has recruited minority faculty members, and the school has several race and cultural awareness programs, including an exchange program with a 50 percent black middle school in Queens. Sixth graders trade letters with students from the city school, and then the two classes visit each other's schools for two days each year. Teachers say the program has worked to dispel a lot of stereotypes that city kids and country kids (who are suburban) have about each other. "Kids here were scared to death of the city," remarked one teacher. Presumably, the exchange program helps them to get over at least some of that fear. The school's peer mediation and community service programs also help students develop awareness of the needs and rights of different groups. They learn that their social class background has prepared them to be more independent about controlling what happens in their lives, and that they should not harshly judge those whose backgrounds give them much less freedom.[38]

As an example of the school's attitude toward minorities, Bell told the story of a white boy who recently moved with his family from the city. The boy was placed in an advisory with a black teacher. He then wrote "niger" [sic] on the teacher's door, apparently in an effort to impress his new peers. According to Bell, the boy said it would be normal graffiti in his other school. When Bell called the boy's parents in to discuss the matter, they defiantly said they had moved out of the city to get away from black people. Bell showed his father, a fireman, what his son had written, and the man said, "Goddamn, he didn't even spell it right."

Peer influence was stronger than that of the older generation. The other students at Shoreham-Wading River told the boy that what he had done was "uncool." The boy regretted it, and wrote a note to the teacher, whom he now knew and admired. He apologized and asked to remain in his advisory.

Despite the lack of minorities, the atmosphere and values promulgated at Shoreham-Wading River Middle School appear to foster tolerance and respect. This is done not only through the race and cultural awareness programs, as important as they are, but also through the underlying emphasis on the advisory system. The advisory program demands that students learn to live and work together. It encourages the values of trust, cooperation, and honest communication.

Recently, three students and three teachers from the middle school were invited to talk to representatives from another school district about the advisory program. The other school district was looking for a way to cut down on discipline and vandalism problems. When the meeting was over, one of the Shoreham-Wading River students commented, "Their teachers said there was no time for an advisory system. No time to talk with kids! Isn't that the main thing about being a teacher?"

7

Making Choices in Middle School

The path to maturity, having taken a sharp and critical upward turn during grade school, does not continue straight up. Surges of aggressive energy, new powers of abstraction, and greater self-consciousness set middle schoolers apart from their younger selves. Typical adolescent behavioral changes include more open expression of casual prejudices, even though hatred of inequality and unfairness is also verbalized. Equally incongruous moral lapses in try-outs of misbehavior are also likely, allowing pre-teenagers a chance to learn from mistakes while they are still close to adults. Much talk and self-evaluation needs to happen before they assume the stronger convictions of adulthood in relation to a wider world.

Some psychologists believe the early adolescent mind's sorting processes cannot keep up with the avalanche of new impressions and ideas resulting from the stop-and-go start of formal operational thinking or thinking by way of abstractions. This thinking process can be further undermined by feelings of insecurity as they begin to doubt every aspect of reliance on adults. Fischer and Pipp, for example, found that some 12-year-olds could not coordinate an experience of a mother's kindness with their discovery of her lying, even white lying, for the sake of being kind. The young teenagers not only reacted emotionally but also could not accept or understand rational explanations for the lie.[1]

A similar phenomenon is the baffling, moralistic choice of one parent and shutting out the other when family problems — especially divorce and separation — strike early adolescents. Middle schoolers are aware of feeling confused, but many cover their confusion with the largely false veneer of cool indifference that puts off adults. Too often they also cover the tender side of their interest in the opposite sex and a desperate desire for group acceptance by becoming rivals in out-spoken toughness. A masculine or brave state of mind is supposedly achieved by early acceptance of traumatic tests, including family break-up. Street talk, violence, drugs, sex, and access to older friends with cars challenge the inadequate reasoning of brash or neglected adolescents still more.

The need for guidance in the transition from childhood dependence to adult independence is met in few of our current middle schools and junior highs. *Turning Points*, the 1989 report of the Carnegie Council on Middle Schools, describes the volatile mismatch of student needs with the organization and curriculum of schools that are at once much larger than the child's elementary school, farther from home, more impersonal, and with classes and teachers changing six or seven times a day. These ways of organizing do nothing about feelings of alienation and depression that may lead to poor work, drug use, and absenteeism. There is typically no chance for students to get to know people outside their cliques, including teachers, no time to ask serious questions, consider others' perspectives, think about values, deal with fears, or plan a life-course in which education has a determined purpose. The Carnegie report cites Shoreham-Wading River Middle School's ideas as prefer-able alternatives — education in a small learning community where stable, close, and mutually respectful relationships with adults and different kinds of peers are considered fundamental.[2]

Adults who want to reach middle schoolers must take into account not only their desire to mock established ways of behaving and explore life anew but also their desire — perhaps hidden — to speak up intelligently, have ideals, and imitate someone admirable. These needs can and should be mobilized for social actions as they are through the mentoring and the community service initiatives at Shoreham-Wading River.

This chapter will focus on programs and policies to shape the goals and values of early adolescents in a positive way. As before, some of these suggestions may not appear to be directly related to raising stage of judgment or lessening prejudice, but they emphasize warm relationships with other people, the primary mover of moral growth.

TRAINING VOLUNTEERS TO BE MENTORS

Mentors might be described as admired people who listen, nod, nudge, coach, and set up contexts for achieving a group's or an individual's goals. Most schools do not have enough adults to arrange the focus on small groups that is said to allow none of Shoreham-Wading River's students to be lost. The importance of individual attention for all types of learning means that, until the schools are downsized, teachers must work together in new ways and with more outside helpers.

There are many partially trained volunteers already at work in the schools. Some 52,000 nationwide have been recruited by way of links between schools and businesses, universities, and churches, but few are given training as tutors or teacher-aides.[3] Too many of these willing adults are assigned to clerical tasks or playground and lunchroom supervision. What now blocks change in classrooms is not the unwillingness of outsiders to help, but many insiders' narrow definition of their jobs, their shortage of time, closed doors, lack of broad imagination, and irrational fear of losing their unique professional power.

Teachers, tutors, and mentors need considerable training in order to share their roles and learn from each other. Mental health personnel already in the schools can help. In one report, they were asked to create several courses that trained teachers, volunteers, parents, and even some adolescent tutors of younger children in how to listen. For the short spell that mentoring lasts, the helpers learned to listen as if the young person were the most important one met all day.[4] Volunteers from each group would ideally join in the further training of another group to facilitate sharing or roles. School counselors, psychologists, and social workers who now fill locked filing cabinets with reports on children's problems could multiply their influence by passing on the major elements of their expensive training. Counselors should be allowed to give up their clerking and scheduling duties so as to have time to teach community members the creative effect of forming a warm and respectful relationship with a child before tutoring or advising.

Good mentors foster dreams that grow out of whatever real possibilities and talents the child possesses. Because listening ability is exceedingly useful in personal life, volunteers appreciate the training.[5] With the inducement of a certificate attesting to skill as a "Therapeutic Tutor," they might be found among college students, young workers, mothers at home with babies (requiring a volunteer sitter), people whose children have grown up, and, especially, retired people. Adults who had a hard time in adolescence or a hard life in general might be the most effective mentor or tutor for a troubled youth.

Tape-recording a tutor's initial session with a child for a later supervision session is the best way to note a new helper's typically dominative style. Effective communication means hearing what is intended (rare); exploring and understanding the child's views without a trace of judging them (rarer); and using the shared emotion that develops to persuade, not preach or coerce (rarer still). It means using silence for reflection on what is being spoken, clarifying the feelings that seem to hang in the air, and checking on them. Causes for feelings may then come out, and responsibility for what may happen be absorbed, long before any options are laid out or advice proffered. Skills of genuineness, candor, and sometimes gentle or humorous confrontation are required. Later, there must be follow-up, or the child's suspicion that he or she is not really all that important is confirmed. The tutors should continue to meet as they work, for mutual support and learning from their taped sessions.

Who the teachers are is the critical element in school change. Both teachers and tutors are excited by learning to show unconditional acceptance and seeing its effect upon education. Early and sustained outside attention certainly overcomes the disabling effects of poverty to some extent, but what is not known is the amount of attention a damaged pre-teen needs. Hawaiian psychologists involved in a large and long-term research project wondered why one-third of a very high risk group of babies (none drug-addicted) developed a resiliency that allowed them to flourish all through school, unlike the other two-thirds, who suffered pronounced failures. Two explanations were uncovered. From the beginning, the successful one-third were especially active and alert. Then, being attractive, they were fortunate enough to find unconditional acceptance, which was documented, from at least one adult. As they grew older, this group continued to attract mentors who taught and encouraged them. Probably because of the support they received, they successfully negotiated adolescence.[6]

The organizational skills a child needs for future jobs can be emphasized once a mentoring relationship is solid. Working one-on-one for a reward of uncomplicated affection and seeing the mentor's excitement is not boring in the way that a classroom exhortation to pay attention to detail is. Although social skills and the importance of character and commitment in the job world should be taught in a middle school course that explores the nuances of available careers, most early adolescents are so much in need of some emotional connection to their future life that they have no idea what they might do or how their schooling will connect with their adult life. To be interested in college, they require prior recognition of their strengths. Younger adolescents are even more sensitive to praise and approval than older ones, especially where self-damaging comparisons to others have been felt.[7]

Peer counseling, using the same listening skills provided to train mentors, is powerful. In San Antonio, Texas, the Valued Youth Partnership Program has older students who are at risk, mainly Hispanics, tutoring younger "street boys." To become a Valued Youth, a mentor must be declining in marks, held back two or more grades, reading two years below average, or suffering from behavior problems and absenteeism. Caring about and helping others, then listening to local speakers about career options and participating in recognition ceremonies with rewards, has caused a rise in self-esteem, soaring attendance, improved grades, and fewer discipline problems. Tutoring offers an excuse to review the basics without being insulted by beginner books and assigned elementary arithmetic. The program has reduced the dropout rate among these tutors from 45 percent to 2 percent.[8]

STRATEGIES TO REDUCE PREJUDICE

Slavin and Madden have shown that task-oriented interaction among the students in integrated small groups during their regular classes was even better than a multiethnic curriculum for bringing students from different ethnic groups together.[9] Friendships, discussions of prejudice near and far, role-playing, and learning games, including those in which students tutor each other, are especially effective desegregators.

Although teaching about prejudice is challenging, around age 10 or age 11 may be the best time for students to make rapid progress in intergroup education. At this time, stage three niceness holds appeal. Moral outrage often dominates discussions of prejudice, but anger is less likely to be destructive than with older students. Parents may also be more comfortable participating in planning for children not yet fully adolescent. For a program stating clearly "prejudice is wrong" either a popular teacher or a counselor could be designated to join with parents in collecting such items for class discussion as stories and strategies to role-play, rented videotapes on anger management, cartoons mocking snobbery, and audiotapes or movies on prejudice. The Southern Poverty Law Center offers videos free to schools along with its attractive magazine *Teaching Tolerance*.[10]

Most research has shown that teaching black history to white children, or giving any group ethnic information about another group without personalized discussion, fails to reduce prejudice. Just as H. E. Kagan found that information about Jews did not decrease anti-Semitism by itself, a summary of available research by Phyllis Katz uncovered no evidence that education about prejudice without emotional involvement actually influences attitudes.[11]

Broad-based "thought curricula" are inductive means of changing students where passive listening to an exhortation would not. They must be well planned and have official and parental support. Concrete symbols are useful for condensing middle schoolers' diffuse feelings and assimilating them to new ideas. A photograph of a slave's scarred back moves anyone to abhor slavery, and discussion of the topic leads to despising the prejudice that is its efficient cause. However, the course should also point out such examples of idealism in American history as Lincoln's abolition of slavery, Truman's desegregation of the armed forces, the lawsuit *Brown* vs. *Board of Education*, Johnson's Civil Rights legislation, the Elementary and Secondary Education Act of 1965, and the recent attention to the rights of the handicapped. Insistence upon awareness of these is needed to counter youthful cynicism over failures to implement laws and some very prejudiced acts of government: genocide against Indians; taking land from Mexico; excluding Asians; the Dred Scott decision; and the lynching, segregation, and underpayment of black people that preceded our modern expressions of prejudice.

The meaningful beliefs, myths, and rituals of another culture or an earlier U.S. culture have strong motivational energy only when studied in depth. Unless some attempt is made to organize and contextualize teaching about other cultures in relation to the questions and the more local types of prejudices the children have in mind, an effort to celebrate a culture can lead to a static view of it and more stereotyping. However, because some human needs, such as recognition for coming of age, are universal, one way to get middle schoolers emotionally involved is to explain how cultural celebrations and stories are concrete symbols of people's underlying needs. Coming of age and other rituals that celebrate toughness or militarism could lead to a discussion or an assignment to write about why the students think they must be tough, or feign that they are. In this country, must boys attain masculinity by traumatic testing with weapons, like knights of old, or is it a local and regressive idea? Is it important to prove readiness for such testing by fighting, sexual bragging, wearing insignia, or earrings and nose rings, rather than by productivity? Does aggression lead to ethnic groups separating from each other within the school out of fear? Are girls here imitating boys, reacting to them, or developing their own culture? Why do some want babies, which tie them to home? Do you think out your values or accept them from your group as a mark of membership? In what ways do students oppose those in their own group who are prejudiced, and how do they resist knuckling under to the prejudices of other groups?

Classmates could poll each other, then present subjects for discussion such as whether differences in styles and music preferences among them represent differences in basic wants or beliefs; whether tolerance and benign neglect are good policy or affirmative action is needed; what symbolic racism, tokenism, and reverse discrimination are; what to do about violence and real threats caused by prejudice; and whether society is sexist and in trouble when 24 percent of a recent large sample of middle school boys agreed that it is acceptable for a man to force a woman to have sex if he has spent money on her.[12]

In some schools, poor or lower-class children in small groups may find a brave teacher or counselor to initiate some chiding and joking talk about the prevalent stereotype of "weak minds and shaky morals," which these children are in danger of unconsciously adopting.[13] Is there a relationship between these stereotypes and the statistics about weapons in schools or early and unmarried pregnancies? Why are more urban teens HIV positive? What about drugs, which are also prevalent in suburbs?

By pre-adolescence, class prejudice is already well known to these children. They need to have support while fighting it with their own hard work and loud voices and have opportunities to be creatively visible in their own right at school. They are typically proud of their assertiveness and enjoy practicing it when asked to simulate resistance to peer pressure concerning drugs, or intimidation about being born with the wrong skin shade. Making up skits and videotaping their stories helps distance embarrassingly close problems. However, students who refuse to reveal any vulnerabilities, or who socialize with older friends in their neighborhoods, need adults who counsel them specifically against becoming dropouts or drug burnouts.[14]

Middle schoolers need to become clear that in the United States both racial and class barriers are high, but they can climb them by intently seeking the right mentor, working hard to fill gaps in previous learning, and refusing to become discouraged. Hitting the lottery or throwing a basketball well enough for a scholarship to college are in no way likely to make this work unnecessary, as many who fear academic inadequacy say they hope. If, in anger, adolescents later lament loss of opportunities and blame school and society for their predicaments, they may convince themselves of a right to revenge, which can come to mean crime. The equation "revenge equals self-destruction" needs to be made explicit. So, too, does the temptation of laziness and drug money. To the 11-year-old, but perhaps not again until the mid-twenties, crime is clearly a self-defeating choice.

To turn them toward positive values, younger students could be asked to recognize and constantly report on any sharing and generosity they find around them, getting extra credit for such reports. In contrast, they can acknowledge a lack of generosity among angry and prejudiced people, people whom they one day will need to educate, not attack. Teaching the history of religious contributions to world cultures and to their own cultures may suggest that help for a positive outlook is still locally available. So, too, are voluntary associations of ethical people interested in learning the needs of youth, which the youths should report on and perhaps join. A financial sponsor for some short-term recreational needs could be sought, but only after considerable training in how to make sincere requests with fully elaborated plans.

Media awareness courses are popular because the manipulations in advertisements and music videos are easy to recognize. Teenagers like to search for signs of sexism and stereotyping. In a curriculum developed by James Gabelko, teachers bring in controversies described in magazines for students to pick out the slanted or emotion-laden words in the reporting, any peculiar selection of evidence, special accentuation of some facts, and the author's particular interpretations. Letters to the magazines' editors then express the students' views. Research showed these activities reducing prejudice.[15]

MORAL EDUCATION IN MIDDLE SCHOOL

In early adolescence, fitting in and belonging to the peer culture in a carefully conventional manner seems to be the only way to avoid being ostracized and shunned. The price should become more conscious. The teacher could ask whether students agree that boys seek power in sports rather than care about relationships, while the sports they are in often leave all but the best athletes to sit out the game. And is it not so that girls who focus mainly on popularity may fail to further explore the detailed knowledge of people and relationships they had earlier?[16] What is a real self and what is a false self?

Upsetting questions must not be pursued with fervor but with a wise wink. Moral education in middle school is to be approached lightly. Behaving honestly and honorably is still the issue, but students must recognize it on their own in each context of their newly discovered and exciting independence, with only the slightest fear that the teacher wants to indoctrinate them or pull them back to childhood. One teacher tried asking a class of sixth graders: "What would you do if you found three dollars' worth of quarters in the return-slot of a public phone?" Hoots of derision let him know that they thought this silly, believing in "finders keepers." Further questioning turned up: "You could send the money to Africa for hunger." This won the most votes, after discussions of "give it to your parents, you owe them a lot," "share it with a friend," "give it to a bag lady," and "return it to the phone company or the police; it belongs to someone who might be asking." Recognition of personal feelings (such as greed or lack of concern about morality) and sensitivity to those of others plus a change in behavior were the goals of this prolonged discussion. Several years later, a student reported that the simplicity of the discussion and the big word ME on the blackboard remaining undiscussed had caused a turning point in her thinking. "Little things aren't little at all," she said. "A week later I told a teacher I had cheated on a test. And, boy, that was hard!"

Moral education ought to have an upbeat, positive caste and deal with abstractions such as commitment, not just information on drugs or the human body. Students could be asked whether there are principles of ethical conduct that are true everywhere. Are Aesop's fables still relevant? These principles will be easier to develop if the children have, from their early years, known, written about, and believed that their schools stand for certain truths perhaps proclaimed on posters they were required to discuss. Now student-made engravings on scrap wood could enscribe such notions as: affection is needed for life; compassion and courage make community; drugs destroy the young; respect for people is the basis of civilization; you're not perfect, either; honesty is the best policy for both talk and action; beauty conquers suffering; I'm special because I'm different; love is a verb; and love is the best.

Moral education must also deal with negative images — those that are tempting or frightening. Children are deeply disturbed by environmental pollution, by local evidence of weapons and drugs, and by the minefields in boy-girl relationships. The prevalence of teen depression and suicide and the breakdown of families require some recognition of these threatening topics at school, enough so that those most menaced will seek out an adult to trust with the burden of possibly unbearable sadness.

Knowledge of the world's moral sleepiness can be highly motivating at this still somewhat safe time of life. It is a time when children should be tentatively deciding what job or cause could make their adult life meaningful and how to avoid the pitfalls — discouragement, drugs, violence, and early parenthood — that would ruin their dreams. Discussing, reading, and writing are the three means by which children can be made to confront threatening issues and overcome pessimism or fear. The National Writing Project at Berkeley, California, is training 80,000 teachers yearly to use writing as a means of making material psychologically one's own, which is possible in many kinds of classes.[17] Pairing suburban or private schools with nearby city schools for group visits and exchanges of telephone numbers affords material for writing, including writing about prejudice and a wide variety of fairness issues.

COOPERATIVE LEARNING

Children like to learn from each other, especially during middle childhood, when peer culture thoroughly captures their attention. Cooperative learning can help students progress without mindless exercises, show them the difference between competitiveness and excellence, apply peer pressure to prevent laziness, and produce good work from each, because no one is finished until everyone has mastered the material. Claims have also been made that cooperating groups help individuals to overcome tendencies to selfishness, prejudice, and even incipient violence.[18] Where bright students resent being slowed down to help others, their value priorities need education.

"Everyone usually seems to do at least as well (and low and average students usually do better) when placed in mixed groups," concludes Jenny Oakes from her large study of various school systems. She found that low-achieving students perform better in mixed classes and have better morale and interpersonal relations than when taught separately. While top students and teachers do enjoy each other more and are more comfortable in a segregated upper track, the high and low achieving students, when mixed, are able to help each other to articulate their different points of view and become more understanding.[19]

"Invariably the smarter kids help the slower kids . . . and the smarter kids get something out of it because they are helping their classmates improve," said Rafael Valdivieso, who promotes cooperative education as especially agreeable to children from his Hispanic culture.[20] There is evidence that both black and Hispanic children learn particularly well in cooperative groups and that many children become more accepting of classmates who are different when they have worked closely with them. Gains in self-esteem also come from children in the group offering one another explanations and not just answers.[21]

A problem is that it is not easy for the teacher to make sure the group is initially friendly and remains efficient. There is a need for ongoing and supportive teacher workshops. Just the right choice of children, appropriate assignments of sections of work, and watching over the groups to bring out supportiveness in members' interactions are crucial. For this reason, claims that such groups can do away with all tracking and reduce social strife may be exaggerated. However, one report of a class where severe prejudice was evident says two months of cooperative grouping showed students thoroughly surprising observers with their new friendliness to each other.[22]

In one variant of cooperative learning, Aronson's "Jigsaw" program, the same parts of a report are assigned to an individual in each of several small groups, while selected other parts are given to each of the other members. After making friends, each leaves the first group to share information with those from other groups similarly assigned. When the information is thoroughly explored and learned, they return to teach their original group's members in a final phase. All teach each other what they were initially assigned and work out conclusions. Grades depend in part on one's own work but also on the total of the original group's efforts. This promotes an inclusive attitude and a new sense of responsibility to raise another person's level, while lessening exposure to embarrassment. New roles can be assigned for the final phase to correct each child's psychological leanings, such as giving to the biggest talker the role of "silent observer" of how the group operates, to a quiet but talented child the role of "leader," and to a child needing prestige the role of "final summarizer." The "checker," assigned to see whether everyone understands, should be a bright child who is told to let others do the leading until the very end, then describe honestly, but in positive terms ("John and Mary socialized" not "they ruined it"), what kinds of behaviors moved the work forward and what interruptions and confusions held it back.[23]

STUDENT-ADMINISTERED DISCIPLINE

Behavior problems at all ages exert a continuing drag on the community's atmosphere and awareness of being a special place. Uncorrected, the acting-out of youthful problems can initiate a downward spiral that turns teachers into burned-out authoritarians. The school's discipline system is an important part of reducing tensions. Student government, with "Big Rules," or broad guidelines, initiated by the teacher, and "Kid Rules," voted as interpretations, can begin in younger classrooms as the legislative preparation for a democratic court system.[24]

In middle school, adults may begin to share authority for discipline with students, some appointed and some elected. The more aware students, as well as those elected for other reasons, should agree to accept responsibility for making the school environment more friendly. Adults need to make them fully cognizant that the school cannot change without their efforts to go beyond their prejudices or self-interests. Otherwise, the circular reasoning of the children at low moral stages will be strengthened, and any primitive assumptions about people in general will be reinforced. (Also, when non-cooperators like Pat are ignored, they are convinced that no one cares about them.)

Rules legislated by students and backed by a student court can provide a forum for negotiations and small punishments of the unruly, including those who refuse all cooperation in improving the school. Student-administered discipline exerts peer pressure and diffuses a democratic awareness through the whole community. Negotiations should ideally be accompanied by teachers prepared to make debate orderly and to address whatever some children are likely to allege to be unfair about school, such as more adult than student authority; teachers' impatience; too much homework; favoring the girls, the boys, the blacks, or the whites; and feeling singled out when everybody's doing it.

In front of her class, a teacher who cannot explain away these errors or admits to having shown impatience might volunteer to pay a playful forfeit, such as joining in a sport or bringing a treat to distribute on a day when the class cooperates well. Teachers and principals with authority over people who have no choice about being in their care must concentrate on their own fairness once their authority has been psychologically established. Students who observe them admitting to faults and trying to be caring would likely become more insightful and perhaps more able to cope with aspects of their own lives that are not fair.

Because the role of the adult authority is sometimes uncomfortable, training and backing student mediators is another way of handling negativity. Mediators learn how and when to introduce to people who disagree a range of options to choose from. First, fights are stopped by each side stating just the facts. Second, the personal meanings of these facts are explored. Understandings are clarified by repeating what one has just heard. Finally, each side states the outcome desired, considers the options presented by the mediator, and commits to one or another option after the mediator summarizes the situation. Studies have shown that after an initial period trained students wearing T-shirts that say "Mediator" are able to break up fights between combatants by demonstrating that they want to hear both sides. Hundreds of schools across the country employing peer mediation have found that it emphasizes fairness and reduces playground incidents and trips to the principal's office.[25]

Several additional techniques exist for helping students avoid fighting. Classroom isolation leading to aggressiveness is treatable with an intervention that Robert Selman calls peer therapy. He paired bullies to attempt together some enjoyable building tasks, gave some materials to each, observed them being antagonistic, and eventually helped them understand that lack of success was an unfortunate result of not having shared. At some point, they developed a little trust and began to experience mild pleasure in the results. Having a friend came to mean more to them than to less isolated children. Selman has now expanded his technique to include children who have been painfully scapegoated.[26] Integrating these children into friendship groups is an important goal for a school dedicated to community.

Comer schools do this through relieving a relaxed and talented faculty person of normal teaching duties to maintain a room where needy or disruptive students may be sent for time-out, extra help, and individual attention. Disruptive children often have hidden leadership potential that can emerge when they believe they are being mildly punished and simultaneously given self-understanding and social skills. The room should be viewed as a haven from routine and perhaps an after-school hangout for anyone, not a place tainted with a judgmental reputation. Misunderstandings from prejudice and fights need to be talked out, not judged, but this depends on setting up a special place and finding a teacher more interested in help than punishment. When punishment is needed, the in-school detention room should be in another area. Out-of-school detentions should be abolished as uncaring and unproductive.

A core group of disruptive students probably ought to be the private responsibility of not just one teacher but a faculty committee dedicated to their welfare. Jobs in the building that confer status could be surreptitiously awarded to these disruptive students as a result of any new ability to fit in and help. Jobs could include friend-tutor, peer counselor, fight negotiator, hall decorator, group leader, class senator, teachers' messenger, parliamentarian, and so forth. Out of school jobs, providing training and perhaps opportunities to imagine a productive role in adulthood, might also be solicited from businesses, local musicians, hobbyists, and so forth. While workers this young are bound to be a nuisance to supervisors, the immense value of on-the-job mentoring for an age group that has not yet firmed an antisocial identity should be pointed out. For many, it could be a last chance.

CONCLUSIONS FOR EDUCATION

In middle school, 95 percent of children say they believe the statement: "My chances of success are as good or better than most."[27] This is the time of life, while children are still idealistic and optimistic about their futures, that they most need guidance from a close, caring relationship with a parent, teacher, or mentor. Adolescents need to avoid overwhelming temptations and the often unconscious pangs of guilt that add to aggressiveness while taking pride in asserting a quest for a special identity. For this identity not to narrow into a toughness that allows cynical put-downs of others and for empathy and sympathy to continue to be part of it, generous qualities must be modeled by adults and encouraged by the school's curriculum and broader agendas.

Education against prejudice should add to the school's clear goal of establishing connections between people. Melding the increased aggression of this age group with their capacity for concern can be accomplished through discussion, drama, and literature and by finding volunteer jobs outside school, such As pushing book carts and wheelchairs at a hospital. The emotional component in many children's prejudices is countered by progress in understanding what others experience and feel. Considering the implications of feelings and resisting impulses to show prejudice are both aided by maturity gained in outside work. The next section describes a famously successful high school in New York City that has integrated a wide-ranging community service program into its curriculum.

EMPHASIZING COMMUNITY SERVICE: CENTRAL PARK EAST SECONDARY SCHOOL

It was May 6, 1992, less than a week after the worst riots in this century turned much of central Los Angeles into smoldering ruins. At the 92nd Street "Y" on Manhattan's upper-east side, the riots were very much on the minds of a group of students and senior citizens gathered to discuss and act out issues of race, class, gender, and generation.

"Those people," declared one elderly woman in heavily accented English, "don't belong here." Referring to the looters and rioters, she went on: "They don't appreciate what it means to live in America."

The woman was quickly, but gently, told to hush by Rose, another senior sitting next to her. It seemed that all the other members of this intergenerational theater workshop — the senior citizens from the "Y" and the students from Central Park East Secondary School (CPESS) — disagreed with her. There was a moment of awkward silence. Then Miki, a 13-year-old Dominican-American girl with dark, curly hair and freckles, spoke.

"You don't understand the pressures on kids — who has better sneakers. It's hard on poor families. They don't teach you how to deal with anger, except with violence, in those very bad neighborhoods."

"There's so much underlying anger," added Brownwyn Rucker, the social work graduate student at Hunter College who ran the workshop. "Because it's unequal. There no housing, no jobs."

"I would have felt just as bad," said another elderly woman. "I would have done something, too. Maybe."

Gradually, the first woman who spoke made it clear that she was referring to the large number of illegal aliens who had supposedly participated in the riots.

"Maybe some were illegal aliens," responded Miki, "but you got to understand, it doesn't matter where you come from — if my parents didn't have money, and we were living in one of those little houses with nothing to eat, we might go take food, too."

Rose then told the story of the laundromat she ran in East Harlem during the 1960s. "The police weren't around during the riots here," she said. "Gangs were directing traffic and protecting stores." Rose explained that she had conflict with the locals at first. She, like all the other seniors present, is from a Jewish immigrant background, but she tried to speak Spanish and be friendly, and after a while, they came to like her. During the riots, her shop was the only one on the block that wasn't destroyed. "One of those gang members later went on to become a news commentator," she said proudly. "RFK came to interview him."

Sarah, a chubby, white student with short blond hair and glasses, wanted to talk about the media response to a protest of the Rodney King verdict staged the day before by several dozen CPESS students. They had walked out of classes and marched down the street to City Hall.

"The press made us look like savages," said Miki. "Like we had come to fight."

"I know people who came just to get out of school, but I didn't," Sarah added. "I did it to make a statement. Most did, I think."

"You young people are wonderful," one of the seniors said to Sarah and Miki, beaming. "We need more like you."

The theater workshop had changed members throughout the semester, but a core group of six or seven — including Miki, Sarah, and Rose — remained. They held monologues, dialogues, skits, and poetry readings on such issues as racism, sexism, anti-Semitism, violence, sex, and intergenerational conflicts. This was the next-to-last meeting of the year, and it was a performance of sorts for Anne Purdy, the community service coordinator at CPESS. Attending the workshop fulfilled these students' community service requirement. They would be graded on it by their advisor and Rucker, with either S (for satisfactory) or D (for distinguished). All the classes at CPESS are graded the same way. "I get all Ds," said Miki, proudly.

Students at CPESS, a new, progressive public school in Spanish East Harlem, are not allowed to fail. If they get an incomplete, "the teachers bug you until you finish your work," as one student said. "We all know that if you don't do your work, it'll come back to you." Students are also encouraged to re-do assignments as many times as they like.

The results of CPESS's personal approach have been nothing short of spectacular. The school has been in operation since 1985, and by 1991, only 2 of the 61 members of the first graduating class had dropped out. Nine more voluntarily returned to CPESS for a fifth year. This compares to an average graduation rate for a New York City public high school of 50 percent. Even more impressive, 48 of the first 50 graduates went on to college. These students are no different from those at any other city school — they are 80 percent black and Hispanic, from predominantly poor families in the surrounding neighborhoods. The school budget is city-prescribed. The differences are the teachers, methods, and attitudes at CPESS.

CPESS was founded by Deborah Meier, a white woman in her early sixties known nationally for her innovative ideas on education reform. Meier was a kindergarten teacher. She started the first wave of current reform in 1974 with 100 children in K–3, all of whose parents wanted a small school-within-a-school. Starting small allows organic growth, minimizes initial problems, and leads to spinning off clones to keep the benefits of smallness.

Meier is also a founding member of the Center for Collaborative Education, the New York City affiliate of the Coalition of Essential Schools. The coalition, headed by Brown University professor Theodore Sizer, began in 1984 as a support organization for schools wishing to reform and simplify their structure.[28] It offers no specific rules to plug in; rather, it emphasizes certain principles such as "less is more," or deepening basic studies rather than skimming over everything, personalizing education, giving students and teachers more flexibility through fewer requirements, insisting that students demonstrate mastery over their work, and offering the right incentives, such as producing elaborate projects and portfolios rather than taking tests. The coalition now has 125 member schools — public, private, and parochial — in all regions of the country.[29] At CPESS, Meier has refined the general principles of the coalition into five "habits of mind" that underpin education at the school by helping students to learn to critically examine evidence, be able to see the world through multiple viewpoints (step into others' shoes), make connections and see patterns, imagine alternatives ("What if?" and "What else?"), and ask "What difference does it make? Who cares?" The overall purpose of the school is to turn students into productive, critically-thinking citizens.

CPESS is one of three schools in a three-story, concrete building on the corner of Madison Avenue and 106th Street. The other schools are the Center for Creative Learning, an elementary school that, like CPESS, belongs to the Center for Collaborative Education, and an unaffiliated middle school. The building houses about 1,000 students; CPESS has 550 students in grades 7–12. Half of these students come from all over the city. The rest are from local elementaries with similar philosophies.[30]

Jacques, a tenth grader, explained how he got into CPESS as a transfer student: "My mother came here every other week. She talked to the principal. They looked at my scores — but that's not why I got in. The teachers interviewed me, and I had to stay in class one day to see how I reacted, how I answered questions."

As in the Comer schools, parents at CPESS must take an active role in their children's educations. They cannot get their children into CPESS with phone calls. They must come and spend time there, observing classes and meeting with the teachers and administrators. They must demonstrate their commitment to the school's philosophy before their children are admitted.

The school also has similarities to Shoreham-Wading River Middle School. The advisory system is key at CPESS as well. Every faculty member and administrator, including Meier, has 12 to 15 students to advise. The advisory is part of the daily curriculum. Advisors teach health and sex education, have frequent individual meetings with students, and serve as the liaison between school and home. "Your advisor is always on the phone to your parents," one student complained, with a laugh. Students and teachers agree that it is hard to be anonymous at CPESS. One teacher said that several students have transferred to bigger high schools to get away from the scrutiny, only to find that they missed the personal attention of CPESS and, therefore, transferred back.

The drab, green walls of the building housing CPESS are decorated with gaily colored, finger-painted drawings and fabric collages from the younger students, and with the maps, essays, photo collages, wood cuts, tile mosaics, brooding portraits and educational boards of the older ones. A board on the life of Martin Luther King offered a pouch of information sheets with the words "Take One." Although the elementary, middle, and high schools are on separate floors, the presence of all ages adds to the family atmosphere. School rules state that the elementary students must always be looked out for and deferred to, especially on the stairs.

There are no 45-minute periods at CPESS. For students in grades 7–10, the day is divided into two extended blocks of math/science and humanities/social studies. Students in those grades also take Spanish in the early morning (unless excused for excellence), advisory, and community service. After graduating from tenth grade, students enter the Senior Institute, which is designed to prepare them for life after high school. In order to graduate, students in the Senior Institute must work 100 hours at an internship or apprenticeship in the career field of their choice, take at least two college courses in addition to their course work at CPESS, and complete 14 portfolios. The portfolios include postgraduation plans, autobiography, community service and intern-ship, ethics and social issues, fine arts, practical skills, media, geography, second language, science, math, history, literature, and physical challenge. Students present these portfolios in a variety of ways: writing, speaking, video, drama, art, and music, for example, or a combination of these. They are encouraged to work collaboratively with other students and to make presentations combining several disciplines. Students must also complete a senior project — usually an expansion of one of the portfolios — as well as several standardized, state-required tests.

Teachers at CPESS enjoy more time with fewer students, yet, in keeping with the guidelines of the coalition, the school must spend no more than 10 percent above what a traditional school spends. Extracurricular activities are, therefore, limited. There are few art and laboratory classes and, as yet, no music. There are no gifted and talented programs, which administrators recognize could hurt morale.

Jill Herman, who wears her brown hair long and straight and her keys on a chain around her neck, runs a relaxed resource room for students who need special help. On one afternoon in the spring of 1992, four older teens were sitting at a table in a corner, talking quietly. Others were studying, scattered around the room, which contained an old sofa and an overstuffed chair, as well as the traditional school desks and chairs. One girl took out her Walkman, put it on, and started dancing around the room.

"Hey, put that away," Herman said. Walkmans are not allowed in school. Herman seems to know every student, as well as their friends, teachers, and problems. "You can't teach someone you don't know," she said. "Learning is risky, and you have to feel safe and comfortable to take risks. The whole tone is, we're role models, but we work together."

Herman also runs the conflict-mediation program at CPESS, and she said that, while the races tend to separate, she had heard of only a couple of racial incidents, directed against the school's few Asian students. "I chaperone the school dances, and they may say, 'Are you going to play *their* music?' But by and large, kids are treated with more respect here, and therefore they treat each other with more respect."

Herman added that a faculty "race/class/gender committee" has convened to look at its own awareness. "Teachers in progressive schools have just as many prejudices as those in traditional schools," she said. Still, Herman stressed how different the tone and atmosphere is at CPESS. The unique vision of Deborah Meier empowers the teachers to keep them focused on the goal of empowering children. "She says we should all see ourselves as principals of this school, and we do look at it that way," Herman said. The school is self-governed, and parents are welcome participants at the staff's weekly meetings.

A Hispanic boy came into the resource room and sat across from Herman, his face about two feet from hers. He was chewing gum and looking at the floor.

"I got up at 6:00, to help you with your Spanish," Herman said sternly. "And you weren't here. If you don't do it, you're not going to graduate. I'm willing to help you, but only if you make the effort."

"Okay," the boy said, glancing up at her. "I'll do it."

Teachers at CPESS voluntarily put in a lot of extra hours, including nights and weekends. Instead of griping in the faculty room, they share enthusiasms and serve as role models for one another. "It's our baby, it's our school," said librarian Mark Gordon. "It's like having your own business. You don't see it as taking on an extra burden."

Because CPESS serves a mostly poor, minority student population, its goals and focus are different from that of Shoreham-Wading. "Most kids who come here think education belongs to other people," said Gordon. "Our goal is to make them take ownership of their education and make it part of their lives. We make them think about going to college from the moment they come here. We take them on overnight college trips, so they can see the dorms, the library, and fill in a picture that doesn't exist in their lives. We open options for them."

Preparing these children to contribute to society is the overall goal at CPESS, and so community service is an integral part of the curriculum. All students from seventh to tenth grade must perform at least three hours a week of community service. They can choose from a long list of placements, including local museums, hospitals, schools, day care and community centers, nursing homes, and city offices. The city provides 2,100 subway tokens a month for students to travel to and from their placements. By the end of tenth grade, they are expected to have worked in at least six different places. The school expects that the community service work teaches the children not only valuable workplace skills but also how to relate to adults other than teachers and parents, how to adapt to a variety of situations and institutions, how to apply their social and academic training, and how to understand that they are able to make a difference in people's lives.

Until recently, CPESS students may not have gotten as much out of community service as they could, because it lacked a formal reflection component. Anne Purdy, the community service coordinator, had her hands full just getting some 260 students to almost 100 different placements every week. She had little time to respond to the teenagers' thoughts about their work. Nevertheless, some students did get a reflection and writing session during their Friday morning advisories. Purdy also produced a self-evaluation form for students to fill out after working at a placement. It included such questions as: "How would you define service learning?" and "What incident provided you with learning that you consider to be significant?" In response to the second question, a Hispanic tenth grader who worked at a day care center wrote: "There is this kid in my class who has dark skin, and one of the white kids said that he was a black person. When the dark-skinned boy heard this, he said he had dirt on his face." Presumably, the boy described the incident because it had prompted him to think about issues of race and prejudice in a new way. Other students' evaluations were more routine. "The little kids don't listen to me." "My muscles hurt after carrying cement." "My placement is boring and I want a different one." In 1993, Purdy expanded and deepened the reflection component, and students' in-depth evaluations of their placements and themselves have become an integral part of community service at CPESS.

In the Senior Institute, the internship/apprenticeship program is more directly related to a student's future career choice and does not necessarily have to be for a nonprofit organization. One student worked at a veterinarian's office only to discover she was a "people person," according to Purdy. Others have worked at banks and businesses. The program is still being developed and does not yet include a formal reflection process, except for the required portfolio evaluations.

At the 92nd street "Y," the students and seniors put on their final presentation for the assembled guests. Miki read two monologues she'd written, both about girls who became mothers at an early age. Sarah and Rose performed a skit about a student who wanted to drop out, with Rose playing the role of a counselor trying to understand the student's point of view. Another senior citizen read a short story she had written about racism. Afterward, the group talked about how much they had learned over the course of the semester. They thanked Brownwyn Rucker for teaching them about acting, as well as leading their lively discussions of serious issues. They were disappointed she wouldn't be coming back to conduct the workshop the following year. Rucker's supervisor at the "Y," who also attended the presentation, said he would find another graduate student to fill her place.

"Good, because this has definitely not been boring," said Miki. "We've learned about other peoples' cultures, different generations, about life."

"We've had good and bad experiences, but we've learned about how to compromise, how to talk things out," said Sarah. "That's how we've solved a lot of our problems."

"It's been a wonderful experience for me," said Rose. "It's been a pleasure meeting young people. I've come to understand you better, and I hope you understand us better, too."

Miki smiled at her. "I've learned my grandmother is not the only cool old person!" she said.

8

Fostering Ideals in High School

Central Park East Secondary School has been successful with some of the most disadvantaged students in America. The combination of ideas, methods, and people that Deborah Meier has put together motivates these teenagers to do well in high school and gives them the sense that their lives have a purpose that may be fulfilled through higher education. Teachers at Central Park East Secondary School insist their school is not a paradigm for others: "It works in this community with this group of teachers and these resources," said librarian Mark Gordon. Yet, the school has several approaches in common with other successful schools we have looked at. It is organized in an intimate, relational way so no one is ignored or lost. Friendship and supportiveness are fostered. It features school-based management for less bureaucracy and higher teacher morale. And it fulfills the school's optimal role as a community center, not only through a charismatic principal who enjoys involving parents but also through teachers and the students' service activities in the surrounding neighborhoods.

Despite the calls for smaller, more focused schools by such experts as Theodore Sizer, John Goodlad, and Ernest Boyer, most high schools are still huge, impersonal institutions filled with discouraged teachers and self-centered students who frequently must attend to defending themselves from the negative attitudes of another group. Caring and moral maturity are not just neglected, they are undermined. Without serious reflection on values, students can only join what Bellah, in *Habits of the Heart*, calls the American culture of narcissism in which rationalization allows individual preferences to be elevated into transcendent principles.[1]

Adolescent capacity for idealism is allowed to sleep. In the early 1980s, Getzels found no significant differences between the values held by freshmen and those held by seniors in each one of several high schools, then noted the same result from another researcher who waited four years to retest the same pupils. "Whatever values children brought with them when they entered a particular school, they also took away with them when they left."[2] These schools had failed to foster the moral development of students, even though academic learning took place. No overarching purpose, such as a core commitment to human rights or to the local community's needs, inspired students or reminded teachers of the hope to make a difference that they had when they chose their profession.

In this chapter, we will look at specific ways to encourage and sustain adolescents' interest in ideals that require opportunities for expression. Antagonisms between groups must be dealt with, which means ending violence and facing up to prejudice. Researchers in the 1970s described "the consistent finding that the most effective armor against prejudice is cognitive sophistication."[3] However, 20 years later, a national survey of teenagers by Louis Harris and Associates found more than half the students having witnessed racist acts, one-fourth having been victims, and 30 percent saying they would be likely to commit racist attacks. "Intolerance," the study said, is "seeping into every corner of the nation, in urban, suburban and rural communities and among every ethnic group . . . a crisis by any measurable means . . . auguring a bleak future for an increasingly diverse nation."[4]

Something must be done, however frightening for teachers dealing with the large segment of students who fear neither acting on their violent feelings nor facing those who do. For those youths as for others, gains in cognitive sophistication must be joined to community service or a job cooperating with the school to coax more academic work out of the student. Embattled secondary school teachers need the help of parents and other adults determined to find support for each student's graduation and transition to a better job than bagging burgers. The topic of ethnic and racial relations can then be repeatedly connected with morality. "Community service changes you. It really inspires you," said a high school dropout in a Boston program for blacks and whites. "I love this work."

REDUCING PREJUDICE IN HIGH SCHOOL

Prominent researchers, including Willis Hawley, Janet Schofield, and many others who studied the effects of desegregation in the 1980s found its success varied with the amount of opportunity people had to get to know and work with each other as individuals. They summarized their findings by listing six requisites of programs that work: changes planned and effected locally, school by school; cooperative interracial contacts planned for both classroom and extracurricular activities; intercultural and human relations programs made a part of the regular curriculum; continuous teacher training with incentives for successes; school and district officials making clear their support; and involving the parent in changes.[5]

Even in the best of situations, some self-segregation by ethnicity is natural in adolescence. Teenagers need to seek like-minded friends to help them work out their conflicts and make the choices necessary for each one's particular variation on a common identity. Studies have shown that specific programs must promote interracial association or it will not occur, either in social groups or in typically resegregated classrooms.[6]

The worst of this resegregation has resulted from tracking students according to their presumed levels of interest and ability. Such levels are so easily misjudged because of the influence of a poor early environment that the long-standing practice of tracking is being reconsidered. Goodlad points out that it often has the perverse effect of suppressing attention to individual variability and learning problems, rather than taking care of them.[7] Beck, citing research, finds no leveling down of standards in mixed classes, which he says are generally geared to the highest level students.[8] Working teachers may disagree about the value to students of abolishing all tracking in high schools, and many think it would be a disaster, but there is general appreciation of the unfairness and harm of labeling and tracking too early. Certainly, no benefit results from the students farthest behind the others being judged as not fit for the normal curriculum and then being given the least work to do.

The practice of tracking is most psychologically damaging to minority students. In the low tracks, the scarcity of rewards, reduced expectations, lack of recognition for small successes in the uphill fight to learn, disruptions by bored and angry youths who may have failed several grades, and lack of special training for the teacher to handle all of this ends, predictably, with resegregated black and Hispanic students mired in failure, low self-image, and bad behavior. Others — including parents — harass these students for their failures, blaming the victims and completing the cycle of oppression.

On the other hand, a highly competitive situation works a special hardship on ethnic children who have fallen behind. Those with low academic self-esteem, as well as low racial or ethnic self-esteem because of the prejudice around them, should not be constantly experiencing failure from the presence of aggressively bright students, including those in a cooperative group. This requires that students in heterogeneous groups be previously trained to show thoughtfulness and recognition of each other. Unless teachers, too, know every student's mind and heart, they will be unable to vigorously encourage adolescents' struggles to voice their thoughts and feelings.

The best overall solutions to problems resulting from tracking and discouragement about study are said to be parent education for raising self-esteem and getting homework done, school-to-job apprenticeships, and training teachers to be supportive and do cooperative grouping. This means providing parents with specific instructions as to how long the student should sit in the same supervised area and, when his work is done, read something valuable until the time is up, with no argument accepted. It means recognizing that schools are not sovereign, cure-all institutions, but rather part of a community in which a lack of jobs and apprenticeships causes students to feel that the school's program is irrelevant to their major concerns. It means providing students with new concerns and providing teachers with fewer students and more time to individualize and carefully correct many more written assignments. Another, more quickly available and partial solution might be to imitate the Cambridge, Massachusetts, school committee's recent directive that every tracked student also take accelerated classes in at least one area, whatever the cost in necessary extra help.

Armor, advocating magnet schools as a more rational solution for desegregation than busing based on numbers, agreed particularly with the importance of involving parents.[9] He emphasized the value of magnet schools, which heighten parental interest as they offer specialized programs to bring together a variety of students from all over the city, even when deliberately situated in minority areas. Students can choose from among paired concentrations, such as science and health care skills, drama and literature, world history and business, each applying a classical background to currently applicable skills.

On the other hand, critics argue that magnets are often too unfamiliar and far away for parents to get involved. Money spent on the transportation of students could fund smaller, closer schools with wide-ranging extracurricular activities that bring together sister-school groups of teens. A sister school might be in a totally different community or might be nearby, so as to share athletic events, proms, school plays, and ceremonies. However, the magnet school advocates point out that sharing such events is unlikely to initiate interracial or interethnic friendships in the current urban scene and might even enhance unfriendly competition.

Some ideas for improving school integration suggested by Pettigrew are based on classic contact theory, which says working toward shared goals increases friendliness, while competitive contact increases stereotypes wherever there is no strong institutional support for positive relationships.[10] Cook described the importance of individuals associating so that personal information that contradicts group stereotypes can emerge.[11] Tajfel and Katz both succeeded in reducing prejudice by reinforcing the importance of differences between individuals rather than between groups and then supporting individuality within the group.[12]

An approach to a more caring education at Brookline High School in Massachusetts, now run with student leaders as a representative democracy, began with small pilot programs in which counselors guided social studies and English teachers to address prejudice and other moral issues. These programs were successful in raising students' moral stage scores as compared to those of the students not in the program. Moral dilemmas were provided, but some teachers devised their own. One Brookline counselor had Jewish, black, Hispanic, and Asian counselees sit on cushions on the floor to exchange anecdotes involving ethnic customs and then "customs used in our homes to discipline us." They explored what stood in the way of intergroup friendships, including their own prejudices. These educators were able to circumvent what usually happens in schools — the official attempt to be color-blind in order to manage large groups. For example, in another urban high school, the principal had the art students' abstract and innocuous posters on prejudice removed from corridors the night after they were put up, lest seeing them cause an overreaction to the attention given the minority students.

An anti-prejudice curriculum for many levels developed by two Brookline eighth-grade teachers, "Facing History and Ourselves," has gained national prominence as a moving way to confront anti-Semitism and racial prejudice. It has led to a nonprofit foundation that trains teachers to deal with prejudice in classrooms. Students are required in several of the lessons to coordinate the different perspectives of a Holocaust victim, victimizer, leader, resister, and bystander. They build on each other's feelings and gain support to face some shocking truths about negative human potential. The curriculum requires in-depth discussion and putting the emphasis on the reasoning of the resisters and rescuers so that the situational negatives do not become overwhelming.[13]

While the Facing History Foundation has grown to the point of guiding teachers nationally, few now have the training to offer historic facts about prejudice in such an immediate, emotionally moving way, let alone bring students to relate these facts to the way prejudice has affected their own lives. Still, there are less direct ways to induce thoughtfulness. In Cleveland, a court ordered that to reduce prejudice and segregation, students must explore the local history of the subject. Local history piques interest when it is tied to students' own issues, and computer networks allow access to fresh reports in newspapers and magazines. Researching news stories to learn about and explore their interest in gangs led students in one school to themselves introduce the broader topics of prejudice and violence.

In schools where teachers are in danger or explosive feelings exist, it may be necessary to shelter education about prejudice under the rubric of moral or speech-and-assertiveness education. The teacher or discussion leader must constantly insist that the discussion is about respect and must show respect. Still, its goal is to make visible what people do not want to know about themselves and their society. Herbert Kohl argues that teachers must take training in this area, because those who avoid confronting ethnic and social class issues risk losing the respect of students and "turning them into passionate school avoiders."[14] Somehow, school has to again become a place where students can enjoy voicing their evolving opinions without fear, knowing they will be heard and cared about, not diminished, ignored, or punished by ostracism or rude rejoinders.

Teachers might ask: Are we equal? Are rich and poor students given the same opportunities in school? Do middle class students care more about supporting their car's performance than a high-performance work ethic at school? Is tiredness from a boring job compatible with the understanding and effort needed to get top marks, along with the knowledge, flexibility, and creativity needed later for a great job? Will there be great jobs if your weekly four-and-a-half hour homework time is the same as the daily time in Japan and Europe?

MORAL EDUCATION

Teachers who are interested in raising moral issues might be more comfortable at first to choose an area of their own subject in which they feel confident, then research it further to obtain a series of provocative questions to pose to students. The short course for discussion leaders offered by the Great Books Foundation teaches Socratic questioning — raising an issue in provocative ways until students observe the contradictions in their own answers.[15] In a few sessions teachers learn to tease out the moral dilemma at the core of every classic document and piece of literature then find some related subsidiary dilemmas that help elucidate and resolve the core issue.

For example, an American history teacher could note that each British subject in America in 1776 had to decide whether revolution was justified. The fact that the Declaration of Independence presented a moral dilemma to some members of the British parliament as well as to American Tories challenges students at stage two, who believe that each person defends only his own interests. The inadequacy of stage two would be exposed if, near the end of a staged debate between Americans assigned to be loyal to England and groups of patriots from various colonies, a drama student were to pop up in the cloak of Pitt and read them some of his speech to Parliament. Students might list Pitt's principles as the actor emphasized them, then vote for or against their persuasiveness.

The paperback book *Great Courtroom Battles* also provides some pivotal historical dilemmas that students could argue. Some imply questions as to whether and why judges should have final power in redressing minority rights, not only for ethnic groups but also for any small group with an unpopular, but fair, issue.[16] Are majorities usually right? If not, how can one adhere to the values described under stage three? A discussion could logically lead to concern for the existing balance of power among the branches of government as well as the uses of politics to advance civil and minority rights.

For example, should Boston's Judge Garrity in the 1970s have had the power to polarize his city by busing black students to South Boston, as described in J. A. Lukas' *Common Ground*?[17] How should such conflicts be prevented or resolved, if not by courts? The teacher should remain neutral at first to allow students to express themselves, but taking no position even after the students have taken theirs undermines the demonstration of caring that is an essential aspect of moral education. Sometimes, though, the larger issues may be left unresolved so as to challenge students to continue to think. Thinking is also stimulated by studying other cultures as having evolved to express their values. For example, the Kwakiutl Indians of the Northwest accumulated blankets in huge stacks to establish status, and the highest status came with a big party, a potlatch, to give them all away. Does this mean they were like the poor, generous hippies of the Northwest in the 1960s, or is it not so easy to understand another culture? What acts might be altruistic?

Writing centers in high schools raise the level of moral thinking as they encourage teachers to get students to notice interesting aspects of their cultures and themselves. Many centers suggest assigning daily exercises that allow uncorrected flows of feeling. These promote emotional growth as well as growth in writing ability. The easier writing becomes, the more likely it is to refine thinking.[18]

Students can learn analytical techniques through parsing their own works. The words underlined below might be kept on permanent display and used to analyze not only student essays but also an historical story, a book report, or, perhaps, a letter to a friend, set in the past. The teacher begins by writing and underlining the word analysis. Under that word go any ideas in the story referring to three subcategories of context: the social, the economic, and the cultural. Next, students might draw pictures or cartoons that illustrate one of these elements of context from the chosen work. A classmate could then describe someone's picture in such detail that others become able to reproduce it without seeing it. Some results might be humorous, but accurate description can then be underlined as an important tool of thinking. From there, the context that produced the events and feelings can be further explored in terms of the quality of life in the story, the happiness of the people, or their assumptions about life. This leads to a summary, or synthesis, a process that ends in formulating meanings, and then a relevant moral question. Concept formation is the final stage, a generalized answer to the meaning questions, using bits of information to produce some abstract principles that seem to underlie what mattered to the people in the story.[19]

Knowing how to analyze prepares students to examine writings explicitly about moral judgments, including those of Plato, Aristotle, Thoreau, Lincoln, King, and current moving authors. One goal is to recognize assumptions under which people think and act, using a context-sensitive approach; another is to relate standards of morality to their own lives, including future marriage and obligations to children.

In another approach, the teacher might ask what abstract ideas matter to students in the class. Freedom, power, group loyalty, ownership, equality, patriotism, winning a just war, the law, the Constitution, and personal relationships could be suggested. The list could be thoughtfully and privately put into each person's order of importance and then examined for incongruities by way of group discussion. Rokeach's repeated use of such a list with college students and television viewers, most of whom gave a high rating to freedom but put equality far down, proved that the technique of generating cognitive dissonance works to reduce prejudice, even when tested behaviorally months later.[20]

The essential processes in becoming a moral person are looking out for and identifying moral situations, recognizing feelings, applying standards, evaluating options, and following through with behavior. One idea might be to have students inscribe these words on the first page of a notebook. The teacher could require one notebook entry per week describing a personal or public moral situation, with the understanding that all entries would be kept confidential. No grade on the quality of writing or spelling should be given, because teachers would not want these judgments to interfere with the kind of moral growth that includes coming to own one's values and making a commitment to act on them.

KOHLBERG'S EXPERIMENTAL SCHOOLS

A true community can influence even hardened urban teenagers to consider moral issues. Kohlberg started five small "just community schools" within public high schools. Adolescents shared responsibility with their advisors for creating a fair and considerate environment, rather than view their school as the typical "world of invoked authority at the stage one level, instrumental exchange at stage two, and some informal loyalties to friends at stage three" Kohlberg described. He added that the stage four world of organized society cannot be understood by those who, with their families, have no roles of power or means of participation in the mainstream.[21] Students need to experience power in classroom discussions where higher stage views are expressed and in student government with everyone participating and taking responsibility for the climate of the school.[22]

Teachers and students in Kohlberg's experimental schools did become partners in avoiding or adjudicating abuses, after a period of a year or more in which commitment to their special school-within-a-school was established and peer pressure to avoid disturbances began to work. "We train students in listening skills, we provide opportunities for role-taking, and we teach and model advocacy skills," wrote Elsa

Wasserman, a counselor at the first experiment, called Cluster, in Cambridge, Massachusetts. She observed the poor, urban ninth graders benefiting from the Cluster community and felt bad for those outside of it in the larger school, of which she later become principal. "Most of them felt, in one way or another, that they had been treated unfairly. As they saw it, their only recourse was to write on the walls, harass other students and staff, and be a general nuisance to school property and neighbors."[23]

Cluster was not without its problems, however. When this book's authors invited a group of students home for a spaghetti dinner, they arrived with a gift consisting of more than enough food, but all stolen from a supermarket where one of them worked. They thought this was a good joke with which to start the party. The store could afford it, and they found stealing to be moral, in that it was for their own group and motivated by friendship.

In a community meeting that year, the students said: "You teachers are always on our backs. We've made a rule [not to steal from each other]. What more can you want?" The following year, they became more concerned about whether their school was a community, frequently bringing up trust and caring. They resolved to make up from their own pockets any stealing that went on within their group. Although the students in no way adopted niceness, they acknowledged responsibility to maintain a climate of trust they had not known before. However, this did not immediately spread to a resolve not to steal outside of school.

Racial issues emerged during Cluster's early period of mistrust. Kohlberg wrote cautiously, "Our experience in the Cambridge Cluster School, half black and half white, showed a movement from some antagonism to separation with a certain degree of respect to some social integration between racial groups."[24] Lockwood, testing these and other students, found that education that involved active perspective-taking in frequent community meetings raised moral stage by a half-stage in a school year or less, while other groups that experienced a preaching type of character education remained almost the same.[25] The Cluster faculty struggled to the point of exhaustion and described it as a major step forward when the whole group voted for more racial balance among new members out of concern for the current black members, even though some of their white friends were ahead on the waiting list.[26]

Kohlberg learned along with his students. Although he started similar "just community" schools-within-schools, he became steadily more convinced that the schools' atmosphere of caring helped raise moral stage more than the noisy debates over fairness issues established for intellectual challenge. In 1978, he wrote: "Some years of active involvement with the practice of moral education at Cluster School has led me to realize that my notion . . . was mistaken. . . . The educator must be a socializer teaching value content and behavior. . . . This is true, by necessity, in a world in which children engage in stealing, cheating and aggression."[27]

SEPARATE PROGRAMS FOR SCHOOL CHANGE

Apart from programs addressed specifically to prejudice or moral judgment, there are many changes being tried in secondary schools around the country that ought to be brought together under a school-for-caring rubric to show the benefits of synergy. Specific programs that are appropriate for all schools deal with local management, parent volunteering, smaller schools and schools-within-schools, in-service training for teachers, health care, and service clubs. Albert Shanker, president of the American Federation of Teachers, has long proposed that groups of from 6 to 12 teachers design and run their own school or school-within-a-school. Such experiments have been funded as charter schools during the past five years in more than 27 states.

To reduce the influence of city politics on the 541 public schools in Chicago, there are now governing councils in each school made up of six parents, two other citizens, two teachers, and a principal.[28] Thematic improvements, such as literature-based reading and "staff development before student development," are sought. Parents are untrained, except in their own politics, and some dissension with administrators has erupted. The Comer method of choosing parents for governing councils from among those who have already demonstrated cooperative skills while volunteering would presumably reduce such disagreements, as would downsizing.

Parents often criticize schools without realizing they can help. Administrators should try to transform complainers into workers for change. Even apathetic or fearful minority parents can be induced with small stipends to tutor, supervise homework, assist teachers, and offer their own experiences for multiethnic orientation sessions and their support for celebratory and recreational activities. As they experience friendliness and adopt more of the school's values, so, too, might their children.

At the very least, parents need a place to meet with other parents to agree on rules concerning homework, chores, curfews, cars, TV watching, and dating. Most might learn from the best teachers how to urgently and effectively oppose drugs and adolescent misadventures, how to find their child's unique talents and foster them, how to get homework done without destructive confrontations, and how to help the school improve. Training parents to do some of these things led to successful reinforcement of school lessons at home in 16 of 17 situations studied by Walberg in 1982.[29]

How can teachers do all this? They may soon have to declare themselves incessant learners with year-round jobs. Consensus is growing that a faculty's summer ought to be spent in workshops. The bottom up theory of motivating school change might imply a range of workshops chosen from a self-generated list of areas of interest. Typical concerns could be classroom discipline, how to motivate students, cooperative education, values and multiethnic issues, philosophical thinking, moral dilemmas for particular subject areas, curriculum development, community liaisons, and working with volunteers. In the weeks before school starts, the groups pursuing any of these options could share with those pursuing others what they have learned. Recognition of the power they have gained by listening to each other leads to implementations. Only when teachers feel a sense of authority and take control as the trusted core of an enormously important educational enterprise can they inspire the sense of community the students need. In Montgomery County, Maryland, for example, teachers who devised their own multiethnic curriculum in a summer workshop taught other teachers how to insert it into their regular classes, then met regularly all year for the mutual support needed to implement attitudinal changes.[30]

Teachers must eventually join together to bring about whole-school reform. Starting a school-within-a-school and creating smaller classroom groups to increase student participation has been shown in New York to reduce absenteeism and tracking. Deborah Meier has concluded that "unless we start thinking small, none of the recent consensus that has developed around needed school reforms is remotely feasible." She insists that while drugs, violence, and vandalism must be eliminated before a positive atmosphere can begin, "the solutions appropriate to a large, anonymous school — metal detectors, quasi-military pass systems — increase the depersonalization that contributes to anti-social behavior."[31] Her success is now prompting numerous downsizing innovations across the nation.

Health care in schools is another way to foster a caring ethic and involve parents and outside agencies. New Jersey is pioneering this area by incorporating into more than 30 high schools youth service centers featuring health and addiction care, along with referrals to community agencies, bilingual family counseling, and vocational or recreational education. Some also offer child care, parenting skills, and outreach to dropouts.[32] Many such desperately needed programs are also offered individually in high schools elsewhere. English High School in Boston, for example, developed a parenting and nursery program for its students that allowed some 300 young mothers to remain enrolled, most of whom thought they would have to leave school when they became pregnant.

Experimental programs are springing up all over. English High also began a three-year "International College-Preparatory Program" that focused on building communication skills, self-confidence, and cultural support among ambitious Hispanic and other minority students. A secondary school in Dade County, Florida, has accomplished "profound changes in human relations" by assigning the same teachers to each set of students for four years.[33] Some Minneapolis schools allow high school students to suggest and plan human relations topics that appeal to them, then work out their learning in a way that allows both students and teachers to become invested in the topic. As Paulo Freire says: "Learners ought to create their own preferred world."[34]

Some other examples of programs that meet the needs of students in many places are ethnic clubs with outreach programs; service clubs, such as Students Against Driving Drunk (SADD), and Students Against Violence and for Education (SAVE); and clubs for theater, cheerleading, student government, sports, and other hobbies. These give many more students a chance to lead and achieve visibility while also fostering community. They provide a needed place to share common interests during a release from the daily grind of school. However, club members need to become more conscious that not all students can belong, and those who most need companionship may feel that cliques of popular students intimidate them or keep them out of the clubs. School administrators should concentrate on the fact that adolescents who gain acceptance can have vastly improved academic motivation, which means first paying attention to their social and recreational needs. If there is not a club for each teenager, more are needed. After-school jobs, school-to-job links, sports, and volunteering should be arranged and supervised to keep every student connecting these with their learning and their staying out of trouble. Small group discussions eliciting attitudes toward such activities could draw out the opinions of isolates and make the school warmer — a place of growth, rather than of coercion.

YOUTH SERVICE

Discussing the moral issues uncovered while volunteering outside the school helps students recognize that their lives have moral relevance to the community. Engagement in volunteering outside the school to help the needy during the student's critical period for deciding values creates a state of mind in which morality is no longer just an abstraction. Young people who work with the old, the handicapped, and the mentally and physically ill are almost always moved. Under a wise discussion leader, the sense of wonder and pain that comes from taking a deeper look at life in the presence of supportive friends allows expression of the kind of uncertainty about what is needed and what is right that may foster everyone's development.

Volunteer youth service for adolescents took hold in the second half of the 1980s in New York, Detroit, Atlanta, and other cities, as well as in some 200 public and private high schools all over the United States. The California Conservation Corps, begun in 1971, now manages 2,000 youths in a year-round residential program. At least 18 year-round and 50 summertime environmental youth service programs are also in effect at various state and local levels, with a mixed group recruited as part of multiethnic education. Presidents Bush and Clinton have both called for a federal/private partnership to put suburban young people into the cities "where the want is," and, in 1993, Congress, which has for many years debated various forms of youth service, voted some significant money for the largest civilian service since the Civilian Conservation Corps expired 52 years ago. With a budget of $1.5 billion over three years divided among states, universities, and other grant applicants, the number of "AmeriCorps" participants should be 30,000 by the end of 1995.[35]

New York City's Youth Service Program began in 1984 and grew to 1,000 18-year-olds soon afterward, without involving schools. Sponsoring agencies are either public or non-profit groups in need of help. Ten million dollars were appropriated, from which corps members received $80 per week, plus either cash or an educational entitlement at the end of their service year. Half of the year is spent in conservation work and half in service to needy persons.

Recently, charismatic young adults have also bypassed school bureaucracies and persuaded governments and businesses to let them start programs for city youths ready to offer their services. Kansas City youngsters work for $3 per day, while San Francisco pays its volunteers more from bottle-return receipts. Although Kansas City's young workers are called disadvantaged, they write in diaries about their hopes and ideals, and their leaders report that this writing "inspires them to read Emerson and Thoreau." In Boston, young professionals raised $225,000 from business, parties, and direct mail to start a widely admired and imitated program called City Year. They pay volunteers $60 per week plus a $1,000 scholarship for completed labors. "We are not inventing youthful idealism, we're just getting out of its way," says a founder, Michael Brown.[36]

The mayor of Springfield, Massachusetts, has instituted a school-sponsored service requirement for graduation that extends down to young children. They begin by bringing their gifts and creations to some new friends in nursing homes.[37] It is also mandatory for graduation from Atlanta schools that students offer various kinds of help, such as tutoring, repairing vandalized housing projects, and cleaning up parks. They accept that since they are educated at public expense, they should give something back.[38]

What is still needed is more joining of such programs to moral education that involves processing in small groups the experiences the young people are having. This might lead to discussions about the level of benevolence that citizens ought to apply through taxation, as opposed to volunteering. Especially moving are comparisons between others' needs and one's own, tying feelings to judgments about fairness.

Teachers now run many small school-based programs, but they are hard-pressed just to get the work done and generally neglect some of the rewarding educational aspects.

A serious problem for schools trying to integrate themselves into the community through student volunteering is lack of discipline among adolescents. Moral education should come first. Stealing from apparently affluent institutions, businesses, or individuals said to have too much is an issue that requires searching discussions. Urban students' shoplifting undermined the outset of the Parkway Program after the Philadelphia schools, in the 1970s, had obtained merchant cooperation for apprenticeships. Perhaps students who want sponsorship from their school for outside work should discuss cheating and stealing, writing down their ideas until they can affirm an ethic of honesty in terms of the need for a wider sense of community and order. This begins with desire for respect for their group. Essays on why money that could go for schools goes for prisons and what better to do about crime might influence some to abandon dishonest rationalizations.

Private and religious schools explicitly connect service work with higher values. They teach that the self-denial involved in behaving morally will, in the end, serve the student as well as the community. Sociologists J. S. Coleman and Thomas Hoffer agree that the chief reason urban Catholic high schools retain students, even though many of them are poor, potential drop-outs, and from non-Catholic families, is the schools' definite value orientation.[39] Many such schools also express their ideals through community-assistance programs.

A Quaker Youth Service network at the Westtown School in Pennsylvania was initiated in order to develop empathy among its mostly affluent volunteers. Industry and private foundations donated $68,000 in the first four years of the experiment, which was described to them as making productive use of after-school hours. Some 160 unpaid positions are filled by the students each year in local service agencies. Funds are spent solely on transportation to job sites and providing faculty for discussions to help students understand people's needs. Students now say they are surprised by their own caring and willingness to work without pay. At a nursing home, several of them described a feeling of commitment to helping out with problems of the aged that had become vividly real. Teachers report that outstanding writing was turned in by volunteers considering "universal ethical principles that make civilization possible."[40]

Eighty-two percent of a random sample of teenagers surveyed in a 1989 Gallup Poll said they have a need to help others that would make them interested in joining a national youth service corps. Most said they would join a program that paid $3,000 at its end for further education or training and also supported them at $100 a week while working.[41] While the president and Congress have acted on this information, the Peace Corps and Vista still turn away tens of thousands each year. Labor unions, whose members have families to support, have in the past opposed this subsidized work as "ineffective." Whether community service results in real help to poor areas or help with college tuition, it is clear that a massive pool of young workers believe they have the time and energy to rebuild the infrastructure of caring and discipline that society needs, as well as gain in self-knowledge.

CONCLUSIONS FOR EDUCATION

Adolescents most urgently need to see the connections between what they learn and how they live. To do this, they must be in touch with their own deepest aspirations as well as the needs of the wider world.[42] Becoming interested in the world's needs and in schoolwork as a way to contribute may well depend on believing that what they think and feel matters. While many idealistically say they believe societal problems can be solved, most seem unaware that they themselves have a role to play. They want to confront hypocrisy about racism, or so Tom and other teenagers in our study claimed. Nevertheless, without knowledge or experience of how they might act effectively, most will opt for a cynicism, mild or virulent, that undermines their desire to create change.

Apart from personal effectiveness, allegiance to and support from a small group, even one at a pre-moral stage of thinking, is the teenager's main desire. A close second must be to make sense of events and create meanings to live by. Working with and sharing every group's concerns for its own members offers the school its best opportunity to leverage new insights, boosting them with the emotional appeal of respectful relationships with adults. Outside the classroom, in service among people who lack hope, students' suspicions may be confirmed that the real world can never be ideally rewarding. To learn this, describe it, complain about it, and yet keep on working is to become mature.

THE CASE STUDY CHILDREN IN HIGH SCHOOL

Five years after our first meeting, the students in the long-term study, now tenth graders, were full of adolescent protests and desires. Each, nevertheless, psychologically resembled his or her previous self to a surprising degree. They certainly had no sense of being protected by their privileged status or by a moratorium on moral decision making. Rather, they felt under pressure to be assertive while not making serious mistakes in lives already full of adult temptations.

The students were interviewed and tested for prejudice and moral stage again in their last year of high school. At this senior testing, they had become even more comfortable with and sure of their ideas. Three of the 17 who remained from the original group had advanced a full moral stage since grade seven. Six were mostly at stage four, six mostly at stage three, and five mostly at stage two. Two of the stage twos had some admixture of stage three and two some of stage one, while Pat, still seeming emotionless and depressed, was a pure stage two and the only student with no advancement of stage. Only those in the stage four group showed little or no prejudice. The others expressed their discontent with the results of the partial integration of their school, now showing their bias toward their own group, black or white.

The four students in the case studies who remained mostly at premoral stages were Pat and the three Metco students. Pat's family was joyless, and the others had lost their fathers in ways that seemed unfair and also related to the racism of society, which allows black men to live in frustration and rage, die young, or drift into prison. Nevertheless, positive elements in the lives of the three black children provided hope that their progress would continue.

At age 15, Pat described his environment in flat tones: "In high school people hate blacks and Jews more, in general. Maybe you got mugged, you know. Now they get everything they want. They should get the leftovers, because we were here first. I get mad when I hear you can't legally carry a gun. That's in the Constitution."

Pat seemed disinterested in the interview, but he disclosed that "all the bused-in kids think they're 'Joe Cool,' and that's why all us kids here hate them. Especially the black girls; they are the absolute worst." For Pat to try to figure out why the small group of blacks behaved defensively would have been to take interest in their stories or how they think. This he could not do, because he always disliked stories and avoided others' controversies.

Absolute consistency in non-involvement was Pat's method of portraying manhood. His arrested social thought thus appears to be a deliberate oversimplification of life in the service of a lonely and deflated ego, which had found this method to shore itself up. Pat said he believed people do not care about each other, and he, at least, was doing no harm. However, the fact is that his personal philosophy, however cool, remained throughout adolescence as unelaborated and as low in stage as a young child's. It appeared he had not experienced much in the way of friendship. In junior high, he said: "I had Gene, but nobody liked him. Including me." In his senior year, still at stage two, Pat said:

Prejudice is okay if you know they are prejudiced against you. You can never change people, not even yourself. The purpose of life is to do what you want. There's no right or wrong: just do what you feel. People who wreck their lives had their chance; everybody does. I go to church, but I'm not sure why. Just to be safe, I guess.

At age 18, Pat had a girlfriend, but still had few outside interests. Asked for his values, he replied:

People talk unselfishness. Being unselfish doesn't help you to live any longer. There's nothing, no cause, that I would die for. You should live one day at a time, 'cause that's all there is. My values? I want to be a computer technician or else a lab person. You should stay away from minorities. Why ship them to the suburbs? It makes no sense. The more people fuss around trying to help, the more they start up new problems. Anyway, black people will always attack you sooner or later, because they have been put down.

Pat's grade school teachers would be saddened to hear him justify the withdrawal from others that followed his annoying liveliness when younger. The question that must be asked is whether they, or his later educators, during the thousands of hours this very bright boy spent in school, could have "bent the twig" differently. Perhaps more support given to his lonely mother or family counseling might have reached him. In response to Pat's provocations, it might have worked to set up a program at school like the one Jo had for her shyness or those for lonely bullies that Selman writes about to get him to relate to a friend and perhaps to tutor some less gifted peer.

At age 17, Leah had matured from the unhappy, rebellious stage she showed earlier. She was one of the few black students in Metco who did not plan to go to college, and she was looking forward to graduation. Her gender prejudice threatened to harm her future, however. "I just want to get friends, so that I can just sit down quietly and talk about things with them. And get a boyfriend, but not for marriage, because men have nothing better to do than start fights or wars! I feel terrible if I do anything wrong, but boys don't. Lots of people don't."

Leah graduated at stage two but still with some stage one, as shown in: "Obey the law, or you'll be in trouble. But if somebody gets away with something against blacks, I'll do the same to them, and more. I'll just keep following suit until everybody follows me, and then whites will have a crisis on their hands!"

Leah had been known as a disturbed little girl, constantly calling attention to herself. She was given counseling in high school and felt better about herself as she matured. Nevertheless, her simple moral assumptions went uncorrected in her classes, those for the slower students. Her ability to articulate feelings about racism was not rewarded. It was probably viewed as threatening.

Ella took a path opposite to Leah's, finding more self-esteem and safety in keeping most of her thoughts to herself. This did not work very well, because in tenth grade Ella seemed more sullen and less compliant than before. Her acceptance of being a black girl still had an element of passivity and bitterness, as in Ella's response to a story about a man who had to relinquish his house so a road could go through. "Probably he's black. All he can do is let them plow through and destroy everything. That's the way it goes."

In twelfth grade, Ella remained depressed, fearful, and confused. Young black men frightened her. She still liked life in the suburbs but did not believe she could or should be accepted by whites. Her emphasis at age 17 on achieving racial separation through assertion still represented a stage two trade-off, as well as a very sad loneliness:

People shouldn't have to integrate if they don't want to. I don't understand the whole busing thing, since we black people don't need help; we don't want help! Leave us alone, because there's too many toughs among white people. We're only going to be in trouble leaving our own. There's no need to do what white people say, their laws. We can do what we want, if they see it or not. We have the power. Here nobody bothers me, and I bother nobody.

Ella stated that anger and even killing are justified by the need of each person to further his own rights. Perhaps she needed this self-defense to escape from feelings of subservience, and move toward stage three. Ella said, "I am going to go to college. I think I will like it better than high school, because people are more nice, and they help you."

This resolution implies further growth, and her comments imply that in becoming middle class Ella is unlikely to accept a morally numbing sense of class status as thoughtlessly as students more privileged from birth. Perhaps the feelings of loneliness, loss, and rebellion in the four low-stage adolescents presage a greater moral depth in adulthood.

Roy, with his more active temperament, quick intelligence, and solid early attachments to both parents, should have even more chance of profiting from higher education. However, a threat to that outcome existed in his apparent adolescent identification with some less favored friends in the ghetto, creating for himself in imitation of them a double or false self. So far, this self was full of bravado and readiness to mock but not seriously challenge the white-dominated world.

Roy was re-accepted into the suburban school the year after he was suspended. At age 17, he retained and expanded his manipulativeness, perhaps to the level of an incipient character disorder, but he rejected violence. At stage two, with some stage three, he said he would not steal a drug to save his wife's life.

No use getting myself shot. I'd get something on the druggist and blackmail him out of it. Make up a lie that it made my wife worse! But I'd save her somehow. Treat others like you want to be treated means love your wife. But not a stranger. There could be a good reason he's in trouble. If you do something wrong, your conscience could get you. Like flashbacks, it could be bad, seeing yourself found out.

Roy was the first interviewee to come out strongly for Metco, saying it had given him the chance to go to college.

I lost a lost of friends by coming out here. I didn't want to. But my two sisters are in college, and now I can go, too. I read a book a night, 200 pages, speed reading, like my sister taught me, for a scholarship. I've missed being in trouble, except once. I got a shotgun in my face in a store shootout. I didn't tell my mother. She'd make me come in at 12 instead of 2! She gives me seven dollars allowance. I want a mini-bike, but police would probably take it for their own kid. I hate to work, so much — especially floors and dishes! You got to go to college if you don't like that work, 'cause nothing is going to happen to help black people.

Roy was definitely in need of a moral focus. Moral illiteracy in the wider culture, which robs teachers of the courage to speak out on what they know is right and robs students of the sense that they are trusted to respond sincerely, in the end leaves adolescents in a lonely limbo. Whether discussion alone could provide Roy with a moral focus and confidence in his community's future is unknown but unlikely. The fine school in the suburbs still felt unfriendly. Attendance at a black college with a clear sense of mission could help.

Three of the four white girls in the case study group had in common a preoccupation with defining their own femininity, attractiveness, and attitudes toward the opposite sex. While entirely natural, this probably made them less oriented to larger issues where the need for principled morality would arise. Jo was different. At moral stage three and stage four, she retained the concern for others she had developed in grade school, and she was consciously critical of her own and others' attitudes.

People are trying to do something about the injustices to black people. I don't think they should go around with a big chip on their shoulder. In elementary school when the first couple of black kids came, we thought, WOW, they are black, and that was really neat! After awhile, we forgot. When we all got to junior high, there were more black kids. It seemed like they all hung around together. But there still wasn't that much prejudice. Then at the high school, a lot of them are really offensive, and they do have a chip on their shoulder. Still, some of my really good friends are black. There are other black kids that I can't stand. They go around in groups in the hall, bump people, and they won't let you go into the bathroom. That causes a lot more prejudice. A girlfriend of mine was going to her locker and a bunch of about eight black guys started pushing her around and saying obscene things to her. She started crying. Then a big bunch of girls came out of the locker room and theyh left her alone. Something like that really causes a lot of resentment. Now, after every practice the kids stay together. I feel — I think I'm a lot more prejudiced right now than I've even been in my life. The one thing about that incident was that that girl went to the principal. She was really shaken up. But nothing was done about it. He just said, "Don't worry about it." That wasn't fair, so some of us went to him. He said, "What's the matter, are you prejudiced? Are you trying to cause racial trouble here at school?" It wasn't that at all. They did something wrong and they should have to pay for it. If it was white guys that did that to a black girl, they probably would get sent to court or something. We shouldn't have to be afraid of them. But my ideas like that bother me. Maybe the black kids do that because the white kids all hang around together.

Jan, Beth, and Meg were less oriented to others' needs, being preoccupied with personal issues. Beth had a steady boyfriend and talked about marriage "although not necessarily to him." Her earlier interest in low-income housing was now forgotten. Meg's broken family and her early boy-craziness led her to some serious, but emotionally biased and gender-prejudiced, considerations of intimate relationships.

Jan, like Leah, seemed afraid of male violence as well as the increasing pressure within her culture that adolescent girls should be as tough and independent as boys. Jan, midway between stages two and three at age 15, was trying to accept her own emotions as she remarked:

I'm not really that prejudiced, except they get all the jobs, blacks do. All my prejudice is is *fear*. And I'm not afraid of black girls, because they used to be my friends. But I always think of the guys starting a fight. Yet I'm not so afraid of the hard guys who hang around who are white. But I never really think of blacks as kind or gentle. Most of them act really cool and tough and stand up for what they believe in, no matter what it takes. To a teacher, a principal, whatever. I don't want to be caught in an alley alone, you know! Even when I'm talking to black boys, I kind of shake. Although Roy treats me nice, I'm afraid of him. I think I'm afraid of men.

Angry black people make me feel so helpless! What can you do? They'll always just scream "prejudice" if you get angry back, when they started it. I think they should feel honored to be in our school, not feel it's their place. I would never take the law or the rules in my own hands. Because God made life as a test, and you might fail. And there's a time to die!

Jan's mother, like Beth's, made frequent moralistic and unconsciously racist remarks, but Jan's rule-oriented and religious family also enjoyed and celebrated their closeness. Jan seemed to doubt herself but not her parents or her faith, perhaps because she felt forbidden to think deeply and even more feared being overwhelmed with insecurity. She strove toward honesty, wanting, as she said, "to be more perfect."

Beth, at age 15, had also not progressed beyond a stage three awareness of how society should work. She enjoyed the economic and social benefits of her relatively wealthy family, but she still had simple ideas that problems would go away if people could be more fair while retaining their sense of status and privilege. "There's nothing you can do about people who don't care enough to help themselves. Like black kids who don't take advantage of the chance to get educated. They think they're too cool for us, when we try to integrate things. They either fight us or stand around with their noses in the air."

Beth was, in spite of herself, becoming more like her mother, perhaps seduced by the comfortableness of a family and school where there was no discussion of prejudice or suburban obligations to the problems of cities. Metco was supposed to have stimulated such discussions but, instead, may well have served as a token effort that granted relief from them. The white high school students reacted with disdain and rejecting body language to the defensive behavior of individual bused-in black students, who were never brought to understand their own reactions, either. If they had been, they might have understood the opportunity they had to change prejudices by offering laughter, friendliness, and words to challenge the smug notion that they were outsiders who should feel "honored" in their own school.

At age 18, Meg was more than ever locked in conflict with her parents. Nevertheless, she had become mostly stage three, with some stage two. She was firmly opposed to prejudice:

Racism is appalling. I understand what they were trying to do with busing. The idea was that going to school together would make people less prejudiced. But it had the opposite effect, because people had no choice. Black people shouldn't have to act friendly, because they have to get what they want. In our school they do get it! I have black friends, but they changed an awful lot in high school. We got more awareness. But I would only fight for myself. This place is so big and unorganized and nobody is in touch with their teachers. It's kind of lonely, but I have about 50 friends, people I know.

Meg felt loyalty toward her friends and accepted their norm of looking for hypocrisy in adults to protest. Still, she graduated with almost no intuition that there are principles of morality that could conceivably improve upon the judgments she made to correspond with her chosen and necessary attachments. She thought for herself, but her thoughts seem influenced by her previous strong need for a reference group and her continuing determination to prove independence.

The two remaining students, Sal and Tom, were more caring and thoughtful. Sal, in particular, had emerged from his fifth-grade childishness. At stage three and stage four, Sal was without prejudice and strongly against it. He was close to his family and looked forward to college the following year.

Up at the high school kids think and act on their own will. They're not persuaded to think any one way. If they like blacks or whites, they act like it. If they hate the whites, they act like it. In senior high you put your acts to be like your thoughts; no difference there. But people should open their eyes and see what they are missing when they don't have a friendly and neighborly attitude. It's not worth it to be stingy and selfish. That ends up with wars and riots. And what kind of a name you get!

Sal's open personality won him favor with both adults and peers, and retaining the right to think for himself made him seem interesting to them. Fairness was very important to him, as he often said. He was elected to school office, and could have been a role-model for altruism among the more typical students had he been offered an opportunity to be a volunteer tutor or a discussion leader.

In grade and middle school, Tom had seemed bent toward college by his sister's attentions, which extended even to sharing her volume of Plato. However, by age 15, Tom backed away from both his previous idealism and his interest in higher learning. He got a job, and, as he seemed to predict earlier, became a casual, non-leading member of his peer group. About himself at this age, Tom said:

Your thoughts change, you change to not like some kinds of people. In high school you choose your friends carefully. In grade school, you are more unaware, and don't really meet people, and you're not looking for anything bad in people. You don't think of stuff like that in grade school. Then you meet a lot, and that includes some rotten apples. I pick for friends the kids that are not immature, that are more cool, and let everybody do what they want to do. I used to think that everybody should help blacks, like lean over backwards. But now I think they should help themselves. Because here [in high school] they are just turning everybody off, acting so smart. They'll never get anywhere until they come to, and figure out how to join the world and make compromises with other people. They just think they're cool, but cool is not an act. . . . Cool is being careful before you jump in. I don't know what I think, completely. Thoughts change as you grow up, but nobody talks about these things. My cousins don't seem so prejudiced to me now. I kind of agree with them. Like, watch out.

Tom, at age 18, tested at stage four, with some elements of stage five, and was against all prejudice. It is sad that he no longer believed that he could help others. Asked if he still wanted to be a politician, he said:

Now I want to be an electrician. Just have a life. Like, have a house. There's no sense in trying to figure it out for other people, any more than living to please them. What can you do? Politicians, they can't do anything, you know. Government has to be by consensus, so they're bought, in general, in one way or another.

Tom decided to stay in his small town and not attend college. He felt he had had a look at the wider world and did not like what he saw. His solution, like most people's, was simply not to look at it too much. "I really like it here; it's enough." The loss to society of Tom's former idealism, his concern, and his potential for civic leadership is emblematic of what was wrong with even the best public schools.

9

Conclusion

Tom's refrain of "What can you do?" was echoed by his classmates, almost all of whom graduated happily enough but with discouraged feelings about their own ability to contribute to society. Most still harbored some ethnic prejudice and cultivated indifference. Despite the well-intentioned efforts of their school, parents, and community, the prejudiced and premoral assumptions of these students went essentially unchallenged, let alone enlightened, throughout their educations.

Pessimism and discouragement among young people have clearly worsened during the 1980s and 1990s. There is less trust that adults have answers. The decade following a national commission's 1993 *A Nation at Risk* and the corresponding shelf-load of books on school reform[1] has produced little change in most schools, while ever greater numbers of working mothers and lonely single parents depend more on schools to help rear their children. They want reform to focus more on care than on competition, agreeing with Betty Sichel that

The extent to which bonds of caring, relationship and support have been loosened, even at home since divorce became commonplace, mean schools must take over. The habits of the heart of even the leading segment of society are heartless habits that concentrate on personal success, material fulfillment, and newer forms of individualism.[2]

And indeed, America has lost its sense of direction, "tis all in pieces, all coherence gone,"[3] if we can accept that nearly half our children are battered by divorce, poverty, or even homelessness; many affluent ones are buying drugs; poor children in cities are selling drugs, carrying guns, and being shot; the average age of juvenile murderers his under 16; one-fourth of young black men are locked up or have criminal records; and nearly 60 percent of black and Hispanic students leave school in a semi-literate state before the tenth grade. The schools did not cause the material poverty situation, but correcting moral and spiritual poverty has been education's major goal throughout history. The public schools are still our last best hope to effect basic morality, encourage people to volunteer their time and money, and help parents mobilize the large reservoir of latent energy that exists in their fierce love for their children. Perhaps by recognizing the need to make parents a part of the schools, along with the need to educate children morally and with different methods at each stage, change will come.

However, it may not. Society has been coarsened and desensitized by its entertainment media making bad news more familiar and exploiting it, as well as by its "rights revolution" not being accompanied by a revolution in sense of responsibility. Teachers who recognize this must aspire to school and societal leadership, with a consequent enhancement of their status, salaries and satisfaction. They must first guide other teachers and parents of the "fast-track" students not to kill reforms, such as the charter schools movement, with fears and protests about their own security and autonomy. Empowerment is uncomfortable; it is easier to hide in a private classroom and let princihpals make decisions, protesting, perhaps, that those in the vanguard of reform are "his pets." Schools of education should more vigorously promote reforms, perhaps offering free workshops to oppose these human tendencies among their graduates with the same inspiration they give to their current students.

MOTIVATING STUDENTS

Successful teaching at any age begins with the child's concerns. Amazingly, this fact has been forgotten in discussions of reform during the last two decades. To bring about both caring and social mobility, we mandated busing for racial balance, considered parental choice, sought vocational training for the economic advancement of corporations, turned some schools over to businesses, ordered teacher accountability through uniformity of curriculum and more paperwork, accepted publishers' pap-laden multicultural texts, and mandated standardized testing as the bottom line. Of course, there were specific successes, but none of these remedies went to what is really wrong: the unmet emotional and inspirational needs that leave many school children unproductive and, therefore, candidates for the gradual loss of self-esteem that leads to still more unproductiveness. Reform in all but a few places is still not driven by any backward mapping from those needs.

Margaret Goodwin, coordinator of a reach-out program for the Boston schools at Massachusetts Mental Health Center, does understand. "What we're seeing and what a lot of teachers are seeing, particularly in the last few years, is that it's really hard for [students] to learn to read and write if they don't feel that they have a future or they don't feel they have control over anything, or that they're not worthwhile," she says.[4] In other words, children need to feel that they matter in order to want to succeed. They are bright-eyed in the first grade, thrilled with their discoveries, but something happens in the years following as they measure themselves by watching their teachers' tired disappointment and the dreaded tests and messy papers sent home. Why try? Those trapped in cities look around as they enter adolescence and think: "I'm average, don't like school, doing no better in school than those people hanging out in the street did, so that's my life. School's irrelevant. Useless."

According to them, these dropouts' choices are soon limited to two: welfare or crime. Pregnancy and young parenthood offer a brief sensation of love and status. Then mere children ask: "Who's gonna feed my baby?" and, with less hope, "Who's gonna hire me?" Although they seem blameworthy for giving up on education, their lack of support for achievement probably began in preschool years or while behind in first grade, too young to be responsible and too often already emotionally agitated and distracted by the conditions of poverty.

The schools have long since ceased functioning as equalizers. The Coleman Report, prepared for the U.S. Congress in 1966 at the height of the civil rights movement, showed how public schools in poor neighborhoods actually undermine the struggle for equality. Social class, family background, and lack of jobs and money determine student achievement because they shape not only school funding but also attitudes toward the environment of study, including trust in teachers, familiarity with books, language, and discerning reasons for events.[5] Teacher attitudes toward children who cannot conform and do not perform then perpetuate the problem, because the teachers become discouraged. Poor schools that lack leadership do not support teachers emotionally. However, teacher salaries have risen, so funding for them is much less the problem within the schools than low expecta-tions, an overwhelming bureaucracy, crumbling buildings, too many children, and, most of all, the emotional intangibles of lack of vision and leadership.

Material incentives do not work. One of the most concerned state legislators introducing a reform bill announced in 1993: "What education reform is really all about is very simple, to give all our children better skills to compete in the global economy, and to make equality of opportunity less of a myth."[6] However, excellence is unobtainable whenever business and efficiency are education's primary concern. The spiritual vacuum expressed in the often quoted "the business of America is business" demeans the huge number of churchgoers and character-oriented parents in the United States, and ignores the wholly different nature of business and educational ventures. Children are not commodities, and they prove it by refusing to learn when they are so treated.

A dozen years, yards of editorials, and millions of dollars since the latest wave of school reform began, we still lack awareness that its central issue ought to be showing children their own worth and that of others by promoting the primacy of human bonds, all human bonds, over humanity's normal and legitimate commercial, competitive, and daily survival goals. One must bend down to children to know what they care about, which is more about being proud, being friends, and being cared for than about global competition. If we do not listen to their simplicity, sweetness, idealism, and yearnings at each moral stage, their learning will continue to be impeded by their lack of motivation, and progress toward either excellence or equality of opportunity will remain a myth. Neither they nor their parents know the practical steps from simplicity to success, but, from our models, we know that moral growth and academic excellence are possible even in core cities. Comer schools and Central Park East Secondary School have managed to vastly improve test scores at the same time as giving more attention to productive interpersonal relationships. In their view of human nature, sociability, emotion, imagination, and reason interpenetrate one another, and each depends upon the other being nourished.

A preschool for poor children in Carpenteria, California, offers an example of how respect for a culture provided relief from the kind of failure that results from a perception of ethnic prejudice and disrespect. The question planners asked themselves was, "What is right with our client families that could help us prevent damage to children and assure their early success?" Scores on a School Readiness Inventory were amply raised by involving parents and by teaching in Spanish, even though the preschoolers would have to respond to the inventory in English the following year. Families thought their culture was valued, especially its assumption that belonging is for everyone and not something a child earns. They were happy, and the little children then felt celebrated. The preschoolers were taught in several areas: conversation, learning new ideas, concepts, and Spanish vocabulary. A fifth item — creative thinking and problem solving — caused an especially noticeable effect the following year. The children appeared particularly alert, focused, and interested in learning as they went through grade one. Five times as many of them became fluent in English as children in a similar-sized group that had been taught in the old way in a bilingual preschool.[7]

STAGE-APPROPRIATE EDUCATION

Educators in this era of science who need a firm foundation to underpin reform look for it in psychological research. Unfortunately, psychology has often described people in terms of reason, drives, forces, needs, emotions, physiology, and so on, as if each were separate.

Psychology became a major source of sterility in schools at the same time that it supplied information everyone needs. The three types of research — the cognitive-developmental, the clinical, and the social psychological — do provide different and necessary insights into how children think. Three resulting educational models for moral education are current: the moral judgment model provided by Kohlberg, the more clinical and insightful extension of it based on the ethics of care of Blum, Noddings, and Gilligan, and the newly resurgent character education model described by Kilpatrick, Lickona, Ryan, and Wynne. They urge that we learn from the past and use more discipline.[8]

We have attempted to resolve the enormous tension between advocates of these models by pointing out that children do not think like adults and that character education fits the need for security and for good habits among the youngest children. Those who lack discipline may be unable to make good use of increasing their freedom to actively construct their own moral beliefs, a freedom that could be offered through the Kohlberg model in secondary school. However, without the insights of the care model, which stresses creating and maintaining meaningful individual relationships, moral development among the young stagnates, and the most intellectually elegant moral judgments of older people become prideful and sterile.

In this book an attempt has been made to integrate the goal of reducing prejudice with the broader, perhaps easier, goal of fostering childhood moral development. We discussed several reasons for the ways children think about other groups, and presented some causes of their errors that are not necessarily linked to adults' prejudices, or even to their own negativity. An emphasis on gentle, but persistent, discipline and the child's need to be good led us to the ways attractive children charm adults into mentoring them, and, from this, the ways adults are motivated to become exemplary parents or teachers. The process for each side is like a joined spiral — a double helix.

Parents and educators should be able to develop or locally modify a comprehensive, age-related, anti-prejudice curriculum and a range of school changes to create an atmosphere of acceptance that favors both academic and moral growth. Multicultural awareness is less divisive — because human differences take on less importance — when children are taught the basic virtues of generosity that make civilization possible. Three broad routes are suggested. First, influence children's current and future behavior by opposing blame and harsh judgments, modeling caring and cooperation at school, and instituting community service outside. Second, invite parents to help manage and enjoy the resources of the school while they learn how to further promote in children the disciplined habits and sharing that enhance trust. Third, advance children's self-esteem, school achievement, and stage of moral judgment by teaching and institutionalizing self-governing skills and ideas that elicit attitudes of fairness, willingness to work, creative imagination, and warmth toward others, including those who are different. All this must first be discussed, agreed upon, related to appropriate ages and stages, and practiced locally in summer and follow-up workshops for teachers in scaled-down schools. Each teacher should be working with no more than 80 students (according to Sizer's experience), because what matters is students and teachers getting to know each other and teachers gaining the time and opportunities to grow in advance of their pupils.

The specific moral and anti-prejudice education we recommend is different for each of the three levels of schooling, because it should roughly correspond to children's changing structures of thinking. In preschool and elementary school years, learning and acting upon some prescribed simple, but universal, values and insisted-upon work habits has the purpose of etching in the child's character the discipline and habits of cooperation that respond to stage one insecurities and promote learning. Myths, stories, and concrete examples allow recentration to occur around their symbolic meanings and the child's imagination to flourish as structures of thinking change. Becoming interested in the concerns of others leads stage two children to begin to recognize stage three values. Teachers who love children model the attitudes they want to elicit. For adults as well as children, virtue becomes a relational state, made more continuous by responses from each other.

Awareness of everyone's need for support is particularly important in middle school when children act out roles of future independence, pushing adults away. Even before this, when children start to organize their perceptions into personal opinions, around age 9 or age 10, they also begin to be confused about what now seem their overly innocent previous convictions. Peers seeking a false sophistication influence each other into premature adolescence. Reading scores often start to slump, and the head start advantage given to poor children disappears when no further enrichment is offered. Some begin to blame prejudice for what is wrong with their school.

Middle schoolers especially need intellectual attention to their emerging values and inconsistent opinions. The sophistication they crave lies in knowledge, not in their quick pronouncements and pretense of uncaring. Mentors, or small advisory groups, such as those at Shoreham-Wading River Middle School, enable these children to work out in an intimate, supportive setting their hopes and conflicts and their possible rationalizations for too little studying. After age 12, it is much more difficult, although not impossible, for adults to create a community that attracts a rebellious or drifting child, now clinging to peers. Each needs an identity that includes a skill or a small area of knowledge at which he or she will be helped to become truly good. Real-life situations, such as community service, give these students new opportunities to value themselves, share their lives, and clarify their own moral choices.

High school students should be steered toward graduating near stage four. They need carefully crafted requirements to practice thinking, speaking, and writing more analytically and critically and with society in mind, not just themselves. Movement to higher moral stages is more likely and natural when constraining circumstances and personality defenses are breached through writing in diaries, giving speeches, and engaging in intimate discussions that turn upon the rights of others and how their own group can achieve, not just protest. The educational device of a guided discussion after helping other kinds of people works better than exhortations about brotherhood. After all, arguments must seem relevant to experience before their conclusions can be self-chosen.

Unlike in grade school, inculcating or grinding in specific moral values in no way fits the self-image of America's liberated high schoolers. Even to approach them requires strong resolution. When the mechanisms for thinking about and acting upon questions of right and wrong are framed and established early in life and are continuously fueled by sharing hopes and pride of accomplishment with teacher/ mentors in small schools, adolescents are more open. They can be jollied and chided into accepting adult participation in honest discussions of some of their values, such as those implied in the 1960s slogan "For the time of your life, live the life of your time" (you're only young once). Then, teachers who have learned the respect for their high spirits that is inherent in using counseling skills can raise relevant issues with individuals or small groups — the need for fun, love, and belonging — and relating these to the bad effects of prejudice, violence, drugs, premature parenthood, bonding through cynical disillusion, and the lesser self-defeating behavior of not studying. When teenagers do experiment in an unhealthy way, an elastic safety net ought to exist for bouncing most of them back into the common sense that exists beneath their bravado. Often, only one dedicated and caring adult can marshal enough resources to confirm those not psychopathic or mentally ill in the paths and purposes of a meaningful life, including the vital transition from school to job.

TEACHER RENEWAL

Not only listening and counseling skills but also ability to recognize the moral dimensions of various school-related incidents and teachable moments must be cultivated through continuing teacher education. This should include understanding the irrational aspects in the pull of different kinds of cultures for which the child is not responsible and should not be blamed. Loosely estimating both cultural effects and stages of moral judgment and what might be needed to change them is a way to add clarity to lesson plans, but all such judgments of individuals should be held only tentatively and preferably by teachers privileged to know the same child for along time. Private note cards, one kept for each child, are a way to start monitoring individual aspects of children's moral growth and what subtle prods might be effective without being intrusive.

Understanding moral development as proceeding from the underpinnings of a stage of judgment and not just from incidents of behavior should enable teachers to deal more effectively with prejudice. When children and adolescents search for and invent negative internal dispositions in others that supposedly account for behavior that has offended them, teachers must listen to their concerns but question them and note their thought processes for future challenge. They must mediate all disputes at once, bringing the children together to get them talking and to reiterate the danger of the self-fulfilling prophesies that misunderstandings and stereotypes turn into. Disputes are to be respectfully treated as real sources for anchoring hypothetical moral discussions that interest students because they relate to their own lives.

School and home should not double-team the child in judging him, but rather agree on strategies to meet the child's the need to judge himself favorably. The locus of moral development lies not only in the child's behavior and underlying judgments but also in the still more deeply buried area of self-esteem. Self-esteem depends on the youth's constant observation of his or her personal likability, behavior, success in school, strength, motivation, and, not least, emotional relationships with family.

Good teachers have always known that the way to motivate students is to structure learning opportunities in which they must take seriously their deepest concerns, as well as the more superficial questions that would interest them if they knew they would be able to find the answers for themselves. Profound appeal exists in what they need to know to keep them up or down in the future about love, human relations, and fairness issues that invite a passionate response and can be debated with an older, cooler head. More superficial school-type studies have relevance only to the extent that students become able to give up the deep sense of the unimportance of their lives that they harbor because they are young and exaggerate others' uncaring. They need teachers who talk about profound issues and who live by what they teach, becoming optimistic and active as citizens of their schools and communities.

Good teachers also need the support of enlightened principals and school superintendents. In what could serve as a model for others, one superintendent in Wisconsin recently offered "a profound commitment" to values development through managing by consensus, abolishing all signs of status (such as his parking place), and establishing a continuous feedback loop to himself by way of complaint forms that promise immediate attention and personal contact to discuss ideas.[9]

CHANGE AGENTS

A teacher who wants to be an agent of change could begin by developing an initiative to solve a particular problem, such as bored girls in exclusive cliques, boys who harass minorities, turned-off latchkey children, or students who talk back or do not do their homework. She then could find allies among other teachers, and approach the principal or superintendent for an in-service course or a workshop that produces an assessment of needs and possible solutions. A mental-health professional in the school is generally a good resource. Friends, both inside and outside the school, can help expand awareness of such an initiative as a high-profile small study or experiment, one not including the whole school, by putting it on the news agenda, seeking out experts, disseminating minutes of meetings, writing letters, and finding donors for a special program or community party at which the needs assessment and possible changes are shared. It is important to start small, to do no grandstanding and make no promises, to offer praise and support for those doing behind-the-scenes work, and to involve established leaders in new roles while avoiding top-down leadership. Everyone must be invited who wants to be because their objections need to be heard if reform is not to be sabotaged.[10] Working groups can serve as the nucleus for larger reforms, convincing potential saboteurs to take positive roles.

Literature about sabotage and the difficulties involved in bringing about real change is accumulating. School-based management might well evolve from the above initiatives, but if reform stops there without reaching students the usual discouragement will follow. Smallness is the key to reaching students. Economies of scale imply big schools, but they become the pawns of their own bureaucracies. Then rules and reforms are likely to be poorly supported and abandoned at the school level, where teachers are tired of being treated as low-prestige nonprofessionals by politicians.[11]

Ownership, enthusiasm, new insights, and skills are generated only by the bottom-up reform process. Politicized urban systems must be returned to small groups of teachers, parents, and children, a process already started with chartered schools in Philadelphia and New York City and in a dozen states. Teachers prefer to learn from internal rather than external consultants. However, leaders arising from the ranks can also become threatening. Preexisting power bases require respect and persistent dialogue. When dissent arises, it must be kept in mind that creating a caring community is the overall goal, a place where adults feel sufficiently known and supported by other adults that they can personalize education for the young. Dissent is often handled best by surrounding it with care in a small focus group, which then expands.

Similarly, a parent might start a movement by mobilizing the concerns of families who might benefit. For example, when Robert Moses' adolescent daughter was no longer willing to allow him to prepare her for algebra classes in the city of Cambridge, Massachusetts, he appealed to her teacher and was given the opportunity to tutor at school. He then observed how few black students made the pre-college track. He adopted the goal of creating a different culture of learning by appealing to their parents for help. A consensus statement sought from these parents revealed how much more favorably they regarded their children's abilities than did teachers' written evaluations. Apprised of that, many parents volunteered as tutors, some learning algebra themselves on Saturday mornings. Now, algebra is required of everyone in the system, and several black students make the highest track in the high school each year.[12]

The chance for an equal opportunity in life that begins — and too often ends — in childhood demands that school personnel and parents become moral leaders, not political followers. Schools must get ahead of their communities on the issue of character-building during the early years. We now know much about the psychological elements necessary for successful educational reform. What is required is the will to carry out the programs and reforms and the personal growth they imply.

Since the public recognizes that it is cheaper to provide money for education than for prisons and possible reform later, a number of states and charitable foundations have matching funds for innovative local programs. Chartering new schools and schools-within-schools is a real option. The federal government and several other jurisdictions now offer large sums to expand both charter opportunities and youth service opportunities.

Businesses are also being generous to schools, but they are always overly oriented to organization and final results. Business leaders must understand that children cannot be commercialized, such as by advertisements offered in school. The needs of children are not those of adults, and they need their own place to express their own interests. They need spiritual interests, not material ones. Getting them to care about a long-term need to learn and be grounded in and committed to the community and the people they know is different from and prior to their being able to achieve the long-term academic successes that benefit business in global competition.

Money will be needed for charter schools and for initial costly downsizing. More federal money needs to be allocated to states, and state and local funding made more equal, if we do not want social class at birth to limit or perpetuate a child's status. In 1978, the federal government provided 9.8 percent of educational costs; by 1987, it had declined by one-third to 6.4 percent. The kinds of reforms advocated here are not especially costly. Some early success with school reform would almost certainly have the effect of drawing more investment.

A society that fails to pass on its core values will die. We can be different. Unlike other nations now warring or splitting because they tried to function in a multiethnic arena without attending to issues of equality and mutual understanding, we have considered ourselves committed to a creed of equal opportunity "with liberty and justice for all." How deeply do we dare disillusion a ten-year-old who, after being required to repeat that phrase daily, remarked: "Americans are the best, because we help everybody. There's a statue that says on the bottom that all the homeless can come to New York, the Statue of Liberty. We want the world to be free, and so everybody can be happy and get enough money here!"

There is no way to teach caring without caring. Real efforts to distribute justice in jobs, housing, health, and child care depend upon the moral education and willingness to volunteer of all of us. It is late now. Schooling alone, or any single solution, is bound to fail as race prejudice and worn places in the societal fabric threaten proud cities and, thus, the nation, with coming apart. Home, school, and government must at once and in many simultaneous programs manifest a heightened sense of respect for each group of people and a willingness to share and to work harder to meet the developmental needs of every individual child.

Notes

PREFACE

1. "Desegregation Requires More than Buses and Maps," *The Harvard Education Letter* 10 (1994): 3.

2. J. Braddock, R. Crain, and J. McPartland, "A Long-Term View of School Desegregation," *Phi Delta Kappan* 66 (1984): 4, 259–64.

INTRODUCTION

1. J. Piaget, *The Moral Judgment of the Child* (Glencoe, Ill.: Free Press, 1932, 1948), p. 122.

2. L. Kohlberg, *Essays on Moral Development*, Vol. 1: *Moral Stages and the Idea of Justice* (San Francisco: Harper & Row, 1981), pp. 123, 409–12; L. Kohlberg, C. Levine, and A. Hewer, *Moral Stages: A Current Formulation and a Response to Critics* (New York: Karger, 1983). For critical reviews of Kohlberg's stages in education: S. Modgil and C. Modgil, *Lawrence Kohlberg, Consensus and Controversy* (Philadelphia: Falmer Press, 1986); R. S. Peters, *Moral Development and Moral Education* (London: Allen and Unwin, 1981); J. C. Gibbs, "Kohlberg's Stages of Moral Development: A Constructive Critique," *Harvard Educational Review* 47 (1977): 1; J. C. Gibbs and K. F. Widamon, *Social Intelligence: Measuring the Development of Socio-Moral Reflection* (Englewood Cliffs, N.J.: Prentice-Hall, 1982); C. Bereiter, "Educational Implications of Kohlberg's Cognitive-Developmental View," *Interchange* 1 (1970): 25–32; E. V. Sullivan, *Kohlberg's Structuralism: A Critical Appraisal* (Toronto: Ontario Institute for Studies in Education, 1977); C. Dykstra, "What Are People Like? An Alternative to Kohlberg's View," in *Moral Development Foundations: Christian Alternatives to Piaget/Kohlberg*, ed. D. M. Joy (Nashville, Tenn.: Abingdon Press, 1983), pp. 153–62; K. Gow, *Yes, Virginia, There Is a Right and Wrong!* (Toronto: John Wiley, 1980). For replies to these critics, see: L. Kohlberg, *Essays on Moral Development*, Vol. 2: *The Psychology of Moral Development* (San Francisco: Harper & Row, 1985), pp. 320–85; Kohlberg, *Essays*, Vol. 1, pp. 183–89; A. Blasi, "Bridging Moral Cognition and Moral Action: A Critical Review of the Literature," *Psychological Bulletin* 88 (1980): 1–45; A. Blasi, "Moral Cognition and Moral Action: A Theoretical Perspective," *Developmental Review* 3 (1983): 178–210.

3. C. Gilligan, *In a Different Voice: Psychological Theory and Women's Development* (Cambridge, Mass.: Harvard University Press, 1982). See also J. Attanucci, "In Whose Terms: A New Perspective on Self, Role and Relationship," in

Mapping the Moral Domain: A Contribution of Women's Thinking to Psychological Theory and Education, ed. C. Gilligan, J. V. Ward, J. M. Taylor, and B. Bardage (Cambridge, Mass.: Harvard University Press, 1988); M. Belenkey, B. Clinchy, N. Goldberger, and J. Tarule, *Women's Ways of Knowing: The Development of Self, Voice and Mind* (New York: Basic Books, 1986).

CHAPTER 1

1. B. Lasker, *Race Attitudes in Children* (New York: Henry Holt, 1929).

2. T. Adorno, E. Frenkel-Brunswik, E. Levinson, and R. Sanford, *The Authoritarian Personality* (New York: Harper, 1950), pp. 128–42, 222–80. See also J. Kirscht and R. Dillehay, *Dimensions of Authoritarianism: A Review of Research and Theory* (Lexington: University of Kentucky Press, 1967).

3. J. Kagan and H. Moss, *Birth to Maturity* (New York: Wiley, 1961).

4. B. Kutner, "Patterns of Mental Functioning Associated with Prejudice in Children," *Psychological Monographs* 72 (1958): 460.

5. M. E. Goodman, *Race Awareness in Young Children* (Cambridge, Mass.: Addison-Wesley, 1952), pp. 142, 163.

6. M. Radke, H. Trager, and H. Davis, "Social Perceptions in Attitudes of Children," *Genetic Psychology Monographs* 40 (1949): 440.

7. G. Allport, *The Nature of Prejudice* (Garden City, N.Y.: Doubleday Anchor Books, 1958), p. 7.

8. Ibid., p. 309.

9. Ibid., pp. 317–19.

10. K. Clark, *Prejudice and Your Child*, 2d ed. (Boston, Mass.: Beacon Press, 1955, 1963), p. 24.

11. L. Kohlberg, "A Cognitive-Developmental Analysis of Children's Sex-Role Attitudes," in *The Development of Sex Differences*, ed. E. Maccoby (Stanford, Calif.: Stanford University Press, 1966). See also M. Alejandro-Wright, "The Child's Development of the Concept of Race," Ed.D. dissertation, Harvard University Graduate School of Education, 1980; J. Porter, *Black Child, White Child: The Development of Racial Attitudes* (Cambridge, Mass.: Harvard University Press, 1971), p. 37.

12. J. Piaget and B. Inhelder, *Mental Imagery in the Child: A Study of Imaginal Representation*, trans. P. A. Chilton (London: Routledge and Kegan Paul, 1971), pp. 270–82.

13. Allport, *Nature of Prejudice*, pp. 173–75.

14. W. Lippman, *Public Opinion* (New York: Harcourt Brace, 1922).

15. H. Tajfel, "The Roots of Prejudice: Cognitive Aspects," in *Psychology and Race*, ed. P. Watson (Chicago: Aldine, 1973). See also H. Tajfel, "Cognitive Aspects of Prejudice," *Journal of Social Issues* 25 (1969): 79–97.

16. R. Gould, *Child Studies Through Fantasy: Cognitive-Affective Patterns in Development* (New York: Quadrangle Books, 1972), p. 32.

17. R. L. Leahy, "The Development of the Concept of Social Class," in *The Child's Construction of Social Inequality*, ed. R. L. Leahy (New York: Academic Press, 1983), p. 104.

18. Goodman, *Race Awareness*, p. 263.

19. J. Piaget, *The Language and Thought of the Child* (New York: Harcourt Brace, 1926), p. 187.

20. P. A. Katz, "Attitude Change in Children: Can the Twig Be Straightened?" in *Towards the Elimination of Racism*, ed. P. A. Katz (New York: Pergamon, 1976), p. 229.

21. See R. D. Ashmore and F. K. DelBoca, "Psychological Approaches to Understanding Intergroup Conflict," in *Towards the Elimination of Racism*, ed. P. A. Katz (New York: Pergamon, 1976), pp. 88–89.

22. J. Piaget, *The Child's Conception of Physical Causality*, trans. M. Gabain (Patterson, N.J.: Littlefield, Adams, 1960), pp. 301–3.

23. D. W. Winnicott, *Deprivation and Delinquency*, ed. C. Winnicott, R. Shepherd, and M. Davis (New York: Tavistock Publications, 1984).

24. J. Flavell, "The Development of Inferences about Others," in *Understanding Other Persons*, ed. T. Mischel (New York: Basil Blackwell, 1974); R. Selman, "Taking Another's Perspective: Role Taking in Early Childhood," *Child Development* 42 (1971): 21–34.

25. L. Semaj, "The Development of Racial Evaluation and Preference: A Cognitive Approach," *Journal of Black Psychology* 6 (1980): 59–79.

26. R. Selman, *The Growth of Interpersonal Understanding: Developmental and Clinical Analyses* (New York: Academic Press, 1980).

27. W. Damon, *The Moral Child: Nurturing Children's Natural Moral Growth* (New York: Free Press, 1988), pp. 24–25.

28. J. Piaget, *To Understand Is to Invent: The Future of Education* (New York: Grossman, 1973). Written for UNESCO in 1948.

29. See E. Erikson, "The Concept of Identity and Race Relations: Notes and Queries," *Daedalus* 95 (1966): 145–71; E. Erikson, *Childhood and Society* (New York: Norton, 1950, 1963).

30. See J. Bruner, *Acts of Meaning* (Cambridge, Mass.: Harvard University Press, 1990).

31. See C. W. Branch and N. Newcombe, "Racial Attitude Development Among Young Black Children as a Function of Parental Attitudes: A Longitudinal and Cross-Sectional Study," *Child Development* 57 (1986): 712–21.

32. W. G. Stephan and D. Rosenfeld, "Black Self-Rejection: Another Look," *Journal of Educational Psychology* 71 (1979): 708–16. See also, E. Erikson, "Identity and the Life Cycle," *Psychological Issues* 1 (1959): 38.

33. H. Cohen and G. Weil, *The Tasks of Emotional Development: A Projective Test for Children and Adolescents* (Lexington, Mass.: D. C. Heath, 1971).

34. L. Semaj, "The Development of Racial Evaluation and Preference: A Cognitive Approach," *Journal of Black Psychology* 6 (1980): 59–79.

35. Damon, *Moral Child*, pp. 110–11.

36. See L. Kohlberg and R. Meyer, "Development as the Aim of Education," *Harvard Educational Review* 42 (1972): 449–96.

37. See H. Tessman, *Children of Parting Parents* (New York: Jason Aronson, 1978), pp. 359–61.

CHAPTER 2

1. J. Kovel, *White Racism: A Psychohistory* (New York: Random House, 1970), p. 49.

2. H. S. Sullivan, *The Interpersonal Theory of Psychiatry* (New York: Norton, 1953), p. 216; E. Erikson, *Childhood and Society* (New York: Norton, 1950, 1963), p. 241.

3. T. Adorno, E. Frenkel-Brunswik, E. Levinson, and R. Sanford, *The Authoritarian Personality* (New York: Harper, 1950), pp. 222–30.

4. D. B. Harris, W. H. Gough, and W. E. Martin, "Children's Ethnic Attitudes: II. Relationship to Parental Beliefs Concerning Child Training," *Child Development* 21 (1950): 169–81.

5. E. Frenkel-Brunswik, "Children's Attitudes," *Journal of Orthopsychiatry* 21 (1951): 543–58; E. Frenkel-Brunswik and J. Havel, "Prejudice in the Interviews of Children: I: Attitudes Toward Minority Groups," *Journal of Genetic Psychology* 82 (1953): 91–136. See also D. Byrne, "Parental Antecedents of Authoritarianism," *Journal of Personality and Social Psychology* 1 (1965): 369–73; D. L. Mosher and A. Scodel, "Relationships between Ethnocentrism in Children and Authoritarian Rearing Practices of Their Mothers," *Child Development* 31 (1960): 369–76.

6. S. Coopersmith, *The Antecedents of Self-Esteem* (San Francisco: Freeman, 1967).

7. D. Milner, *Children and Race* (Beverly Hills, Calif.: Sage, 1983), p. 62.

8. F. E. Aboud, *Children and Prejudice* (New York: Basil Blackwell, 1988), p. 89; A. G. Davey, *Learning To Be Prejudiced: Growing Up in Multiethnic Britain* (London: Edward Arnold, 1983); C. W. Branch and N. Newcombe, "Racial Attitudes of Black Preschoolers as Related to Parental Civil Rights Activism," *Merrill-Palmer Quarterly* 26 (1980): 425–28 (*inter alia*).

9. See N. Eisenberg, *The Caring Child* (Cambridge, Mass.: Harvard University Press, 1992); R. Coles, *The Moral Life of Children* (Boston: Atlantic Monthly Press, 1986).

10. See D. Franklin, "Charm School for Bullies," *Hypocrites* 3 (1989): 75–77; J. Gibbs, "Social Processes in Delinquency: The Need to Facilitate Empathy as Well as Sociomoral Reasoning," in *Moral Development through Social Interaction*, ed. W. Kurtines and J. Gewirtz (New York: Wiley, 1987).

11. R. Gould, *Child Studies through Fantasy: Cognitive-Affective Patterns in Development* (New York: Quadrangle Books, 1972), pp. 29–55.

12. J. Sandler, H. Kennedy, and R. Tyson, *The Technique of Child Psychoanalysis: Discussions with Anna Freud* (Cambridge, Mass.: Harvard University Press, 1980), p. 256; A. Freud, *The Ego and the Mechanisms of Defense* (New York: International Universities Press, 1966); J. Sandler and A. Freud, *The Analysis of Defense: The Ego and the Mechanisms of Defense Revisited* (New York: International Universities Press, 1985).

13. J. Porter, *Black Child, White Child: The Development of Racial Attitudes* (Cambridge, Mass.: Harvard University Press, 1971), p. 150; P. A. Katz, *Towards the Elimination of Racism* (New York: Pergamon, 1976), p. 84.

14. T. S. Pettigrew, "Personality and Socio-Cultural Factors in Intergroup Attitudes: A Cross-National Comparison," *Journal of Conflict Resolution* 2 (1958): 29–42; Milner, *Children and Race*, pp. 34, 117.

15. See W. M. Kurtines and J. Gewirtz, *Moral Development through Social Interaction* (New York: Wiley, 1987); A. Bandura, *Foundations of Thought and Action, A Social Cognitive Theory* (Englewood Cliffs, N.J.: Prentice-Hall, 1986); J. Aronfreed, *Conduct and Conscience: The Socialization of Internalized Control over Behavior* (New York: Academic Press, 1968); A. Bandura and F. McDonald, "The Influence of Social Reinforcement and the Behavior of Models in Shaping Children's Moral Judgments," *Journal of Abnormal and Social Psychology* 67 (1963): 274–81.

16. M. Rosenberg and R. Simmons, *Black and White Self-Esteem, The Urban School Child* (Washington, D.C.: American Sociological Association, 1971); W. G. Stephan and D. Rosenfeld, "Black Self Rejection: Another Look," *Journal of Educational Psychology* 71 (1979): 708–16.

17. J. E. Williams and J. K. Morland, *Race, Color and the Young Child* (Chapel Hill: University of North Carolina Press, 1976).

18. H. Tajfel, "Intergroup Behavior I: Individualistic Perspectives," in *Introducing Social Psychology*, ed. H. Tajfel and C. Fraser (Hammondsworth: Penguin Books, 1978).

19.   H. Tajfel and J. Turner, "An Integrative Theory of Intergroup Conflict," in *The Social Psychology of Intergroup Relations*, ed. W. G. Austin and S. Worchel (Monterey, Calif.: Brooks Cole, 1979).

20.   R. Ashmore and F. DelBoca, "Psychological Approaches to Understanding Intergroup Conflicts," in *Towards the Elimination of Racism*, ed. P. A. Katz (New York: Pergamon, 1976), pp. 84–85.

21.   W. S. Hall and P. E. Jose, "Cultural Effects on the Development of Equality and Inequality," in *The Child's Construction of Social Inequality*, ed. R. L. Leahy (New York: Academic Press, 1983), pp. 264–67. See also R. L. Leahy, "The Development of the Concept of Social Class," in *The Child's Construction of Social Inequality*, ed. R. L. Leahy (New York: Academic Press, 1983), p. 89.

22.   H. Trager and M. Radke-Yarrow, *They Learn What They Live* (New York: Harper, 1952), pp. 185–231; M. Radke-Yarrow, H. Trager, and J. Miller, "The Role of Parents in the Development of Young Children's Ethnic Attitudes," *Child Development* 23 (1952): 13–53; C. Bird, E. Monachesi, and H. Burdick, "Studies of Group Tensions: III. The Effect of Parental Discouragement of Play Activities upon the Attitudes of White Children toward Negroes," *Child Development* 23 (1952): 295–306.

23.   M. Patchen, *Black-White Contact in Schools: Its Social and Academic Effects* (West Lafayette, Ind.: Purdue University Press, 1982), p. 103.

24.   R. Ashmore and F. DelBoca, "Psychological Approaches," in *Towards the Elimination of Racism*, ed. P. A. Katz (New York: Pergamon, 1976), p. 96.

25.   C. Bird, E. Monachesi, and H. Burdick, "Infiltration and the Attitudes of White and Negro Parents and Children," *Journal of Abnormal and Social Psychology* 47 (1952): 306.

26.   C. Bowerman and J. Kinch, "Changes in Family and Peer Orientation between the Fourth and Tenth Grades," *Social Forces* 37 (1959): 206–11.

27.   J. Condry and M. Simon, "An Experimental Study of Adult versus Peer Orientation," unpublished paper, Cornell University, 1968.

28.   J. Youniss, *Parents and Peers in Social Development: A Sullivan-Piaget Perspective* (Chicago: University of Chicago Press, 1980).

29.   J. Piaget, *The Moral Judgment of the Child* (Glencoe, Ill.: Free Press, 1932, 1948), pp. 275–76. See also J. Piaget, *Judgment and Reasoning in the Child* (New York: Harcourt Brace, 1928), pp. 172–76.

30.   J. Condry, M. Simon, and U. Bronfenbrenner, "Characteristics of Peer- and Adult-Oriented Children," unpublished paper, Cornell University, 1968. See also U. Bronfenbrenner, *Two Worlds of Childhood: U.S. and U.S.S.R.* (New York: Basic Books, 1970).

31.   F. E. Aboud, *Children and Prejudice*, pp. 22–25.

32.   Y. Amir, "The Role of Intergroup Contact in Change of Prejudice and Ethnic Relations," in *Towards the Elimination of Racism*, ed. P. A. Katz (New York: Pergamon, 1976), pp. 245–308.

33.   C. Bullock, *School Desegregation, Interracial Contact and Prejudice* (Washington, D.C.: National Institute of Education, 1976).

34.   W. Hawley, R. Crain, C. Rossell, M. Smylie, R. Fernandez, J. Schofield, R. Tompkins, W. Trent, and M. Zlotnik, *Strategies for Effective School Desegregation: Lessons from Research* (Lexington, Mass.: Lexington Books, 1983); M. Sherif, *In Common Predicament: Social Psychology of Intergroup Conflict and Cooperation* (Boston: Houghton Mifflin, 1966).

35.   M. Billig and H. Tajfel, "Social Categorization and Similarity in Intergroup Behavior," *European Journal of Social Psychology* 3 (1973): 27–52; H. Tajfel and M. Billig, "Familiarity and Categorization in Intergroup Behavior," *Journal of Experimental Social Psychology* 10 (1974): 159–70.

36   C. Glock, R. Wuthnow, J. Piliavin, and M. Spencer, *Adolescent Prejudice* (New York: Harper & Row, 1975), pp. 135–40.

37.   D. J. Armor, "The Evidence on Busing," *The Public Interest* 28 (1972): 90–126; D. J. Armor, "School and Family Effects of Black and White Achievement: A Reexamination of the USOE Data," in *On Equality of Educational Opportunity*, ed. F. Mosteller and D. P. Moynihan (New York: Random House, 1972), pp. 168–229.

38.   Hawley et al., *Strategies*, pp. 110–17.

39.   Glock et al., *Adolescent Prejudice*, p. 42.

40.   Ibid., pp. 151–60.

41.   See P. A. Katz, *Towards the Elimination of Racism*, ed. P. A. Katz (New York: Pergamon, 1976).

42.   P. A. Katz and S. R. Zalk, "Modification of Children's Racial Attitudes," *Developmental Psychology* 14 (1978): 447–61.

43.   W. G. Stephan, "Intergroup Relations," in *Handbook of Social Psychology*, ed. G. Lindzey and E. Aronson (New York: Random House, 1985), p. 600. See also E. Staub, "Steps toward a Comprehensive Theory of Moral Conduct: Goal Orientation, Social Behavior, Kindness, and Cruelty," in *Morality, Moral Behavior, and Moral Development*, ed. W. M. Kurtines and J. L. Gewirtz (New York: Wiley, 1984).

44.   For an understanding of Latin cultures in the United States, see S. M. McGoldrick, J. K. Pearce, and J. Giordano (Eds.), *Ethnicity and Family Therapy* (New York: Guilford Press, 1982), pp. 340–61.

45.   R. E. Carter, *Dimensions of Moral Education* (Toronto: University of Toronto Press, 1984), p. 116. See also H. Howe II, "Giving Equity a Chance in the Excellence Game," in *The Great School Debate: Which Way for American Education?* ed. B. Gross and R. Gross (New York: Simon and Schuster, 1985), pp. 196, 245.

46.   R. Ashmore and F. DelBoca, "Psychological Approaches to Understanding Prejudice," in *Towards the Elimination of Racism*, ed. P. A. Katz (New York: Pergamon, 1976), pp. 105–7.

47.   See D. A. Phillips and E. Zigler, "Children's Self-Image Disparity: Effects of Age, Socioeconomic Status, Ethnicity and Gender," *Journal of Personality and Social Psychology* 39 (1980): 689–700.

48.   G. Gardner, "Personality Development and Childhood Behavioral Disabilities," in *Psychiatry and Medicine*, ed. N. Brill (Los Angeles: University of California Press, 1962).

49.   T. Kochman, *Black and White Styles in Conflict* (Chicago: University of Chicago Press, 1981).

50.   See C. E. Sleeter and C. A. Grant, *Making Choices for Multicultural Education: Five Approaches to Race, Class and Gender* (New York: Macmillan, 1993), pp. 216–17.

51.   S. L. Lightfoot, *The Good High School, Portraits of Character and Culture* (New York Basic Books, 1983), pp. 316, 349.

52.   See A. Steinberg (Ed.), *Adolescents and Schools: Improving the Fit* (Cambridge, Mass.: The Harvard Education Letter Reprint Series, 1993), p. 128.

CHAPTER 3

1.   F. E. Aboud, *Children and Prejudice* (New York: Basil Blackwell, 1988), pp. 22–29.

2.   See L. Kohlberg, *The Meaning and Measurement of Moral Development*, Vol. XIII (1979) Heinz Werner Lecture Series (Worcester, Mass.: Clark University Press, 1981); J. C. Gibbs and K. F. Widamon, *Social Intelligence: Measuring the Development of Socio-Moral Reflection* (Englewood Cliffs, N.J.: Prentice-Hall, 1982); B. Kutner, "Patterns of Mental Functioning Associated with Prejudice in Children,"

Psychological Monographs 72 (1958): 460. Authors' Note: Kutner found the mean I.Q. of his unprejudiced group was 115.5 and the prejudiced group's was 110.8, a difference that is not significant. Most of the moral development research has found the significance of I.Q. to be even less than in my research, the usual effect being chiefly at the extremes. See F. H. Davidson, "Respect for Persons and Ethnic Prejudice in Childhood: A Cognitive-Developmental Approach," in *Pluralism in a Democratic Society*, ed. M. M. Tumin and W. Plotch (New York: Praeger, 1977); F. H. Davidson, "Ability to Respect Persons Compared to Ethnic Prejudice in Childhood," *Journal of Personality and Social Psychology* 34 (1976): 1256–67.

3. R. Ashmore and F. DelBoca, "Psychological Approaches to Understanding Racism," in *Towards the Elimination of Racism*, ed. P. A. Katz (New York: Pergamon, 1976), pp. 73–124. See also D. Fox and V. Jordan, "Racial Preference and Identification of Black, American, Chinese and White Children," *Genetic Psychology Monographs* 88 (1973): 229–86.

4. K. W. Fischer and R. L. Canfield, "The Ambiguity of Stage Structure in Behavior: Person and Environment in the Development of Psychological Structure," in *Stage and Structure: Reopening the Debate*, ed. I. Levin (Norwood, N.J.: Ablex, 1986); D. Cohen, *Piaget: Critique and Reassessment* (New York: St. Martin's Press, 1983).

5. E. Peel, *The Psychological Basis of Education* (London: Oliver and Boyd, 1967), p. 207.

6. See T. Adorno, E. Frenkel-Brunswik, E. Levinson, and R. Sanford, *The Authoritarian Personality* (New York: Harper, 1950), pp. 222–80.

7. E. Useem, "White Suburban Secondary Students in Schools with Token Desegregation: Correlates of Racial Attitudes," unpublished Ed.D. dissertation, Harvard University, 1971. See also M. Hallinan and R. Williams, "Interracial Friendship Choices in Secondary Schools," *American Sociological Review* 54 (1989): 67–78.

8. K. W. Fischer, D. Bullock, E. Rotenberg, and P. Raya, "The Dynamics of Competence: How Context Contributes Directly to Skill," in *Development in Context: Acting and Thinking in Specific Environments*, ed. R. H. Wozniak and K. W. Fischer (Hillsdale, N.J.: Lawrence Erlbaum, 1993), p. 83.

9. See L. Green, "Motivational Antecedents to Maturity of Moral Judgment," unpublished Ph.D. dissertation, University of Chicago, 1974.

10. See N. Haan, *Coping and Defending* (New York: Academic Press, 1977), pp. 103–4.

11. G. Lindzey and D. Byrne, "Measurement of Social Choice and Interpersonal Attractiveness," in *The Handbook of Social Psychology* Vol. 2: *Research Methods*, 2d ed., ed. G. Lindzey and E. Aronson (Reading, Mass.: Addison-Wesley, 1968), pp. 452–525.

12. See D. W. Winnicott, *Deprivation and Delinquency*, ed. C. Winnicott, R. Shepherd, and M. Davis (New York: Tavistock Publications, 1984), pp. 84–156.

CHAPTER 4

1. Kohlberg and Gilligan directed the doctoral dissertation for which these Stages of Respect were developed. F. H. Davidson, "Respect for Human Dignity and Ethnic Judgments in Childhood," unpublished Ed.D. dissertation, Harvard University, 1974.

2. K. W. Fischer (Ed.), *Levels and Transitions in Children's Development* (San Francisco: Jossey-Bass, 1983).

3. L. Kohlberg, *Essays on Moral Development*, Vol. 1: *Moral Stages and the Idea of Justice* (San Francisco: Harper & Row, 1981), pp. 145–46.

4. Kohlberg, *Essays*, Vol. 1, pp. 147–48, 409–10.

5. R. L. Selman, "The Relation of Role-Taking to the Development of Moral Judgment in Children," *Child Development* 42 (1971): 79–91.

6. See R. S. Peters, "Moral Development, a Plea for Pluralism," in *Cognitive Development and Epistemology*, ed. T. Mischel (New York: Academic Press, 1971); R. K. Sparks, Jr., "Character Development at Fort Washington Elementary School," in *Moral, Character and Civic Education in the Elementary School*, ed. J. S. Benninga (New York: Teachers College Press, 1991), p. 181.

7. See S. Aranowitz and H. Giroux, *Education under Siege* (Boston: Bergin and Garvey, 1985), pp. 19–20.

8. T. Lickona, *Educating for Character: How Our Schools Can Teach Respect and Responsibility* (New York: Bantam, 1991), pp. 78–79.

9. See D. Bar-Tal, A. Raviv, and T. Leiser, "The Development of Altruistic Behavior: Empirical Evidence," *Developmental Psychology* 16 (1980): 516–24; R. E. Carter, *Dimensions of Moral Education* (Toronto: University of Toronto Press, 1984), pp. 94–96; B. A. Sichel, *Moral Education: Character, Community and Ideals* (Philadelphia: Temple University Press, 1988), pp. 222–23.

CHAPTER 5

1. L. Kohlberg, *Essays on Moral Development*, Vol. I: *Moral Stages and the Idea of Justice* (San Francisco: Harper & Row, 1981), pp. 148–50, 410.

2. E. Durkheim, *Sociology and Philosophy* (Glencoe, Ill.: Free Press, 1953), p. 391; see also E. Durkheim, *Moral Education: A Study in the Theory and Application of the Sociology of Education* (Glencoe, Ill.: Free Press, 1925, 1961).

3. Kohlberg, *Essays*, Vol. I, pp. 150–52, 410–11.

4. Ibid., pp. 152–68.

5. R. S. Hartman, *The Structure of Value* (Carbondale, Ill.: Southern Illinois University Press, 1969), pp. 112–14; M. Buber, *Between Man and Man* (New York: Macmillan, 1965), pp. 30–33.

6. W. A. Weiskopf, "The Dialectics of Equality," *Annals of the American Academy of Political and Social Science* 409 (1973): 163–73.

7. Kohlberg, *Essays*, Vol. I, pp. 192–201; see also, J. Rawls, *A Theory of Justice* (Cambridge, Mass.: Harvard University Press, 1971).

8. R. S. Peters, *Moral Development and Moral Education* (Boston: George Allen and Unwin, 1981); E. V. Sullivan, *Kohlberg's Structuralism: A Critical Appraisal* (Toronto: Ontario Institute for Studies in Education, 1977), p. 35.

9. C. Gilligan, *In a Different Voice: Psychological Theory and Women's Development* (Cambridge, Mass.: Harvard University Press, 1982), p. 18.

10. R. H. Wozniak and K. W. Fischer, *Development in Context: Acting and Thinking in Specific Environments* (Hillsdale, N.J.: L. Erlbaum, 1983); S. Hoppe-Graff, "The Study of Transitions in Development, Potentialities of the Longitudinal Approach," in *Transition Mechanisms in Child Development*, ed. A. DeRibaupierre (Cambridge: Cambridge University Press, 1989), pp. 1–30; P. L. Harris, *Children and Emotion: The Development of Psychological Understanding* (New York: Basil Blackwell, 1989), p. 96; K. W. Fischer and S. L. Pipp, "Processes of Cognitive Development: Optimal Level and Skill Acquisition," in *Mechanisms of Cognitive Development*, ed. R. J. Sternberg (San Francisco: Freeman, 1984).

11. J. P. Comer, *Maggie's American Dream: The Life and Times of a Black Family* (New York: Penguin Books, 1988).

12. J. P. Comer, *School Power: Implications for an Intervention Project* (New York: Free Press, 1980).

13. J. P. Comer, *A Conversation between James Comer and Ronald Edmunds:*

Fundamentals of Effective School Improvement (Dubuque, Iowa: Kendall Publishing, 1989). See also R. Benjamin, *Making Schools Work: A Reporter's Journey through Some of Americas Most Remarkable Classrooms* (New York: Continuum Publishing, 1981).

14.   J. P. Comer, "Educating Poor Minority Children," *Scientific American* 259 (1992): 42–48.

CHAPTER 6

1.   J. P. Comer, *School Power: Implications for an Intervention Project* (New York: Free Press, 1980), pp. 167–82, 228.

2.   H. Gardner, *To Open Minds: Chinese Clues to the Dilemma of Contemporary Education* (New York: Basic Books, 1989). See also H. W. Stevenson and J. W. Stigler, *The Learning Gap: Why Our Schools Are Failing and What We Can Learn from Japanese and Chinese Education* (New York: Simon and Schuster, 1992).

3.   M. R. Yarrow, P. Scott, and C. Z. Waxler, "Learning Concern for Others," *Developmental Psychology* 8 (1973): 240–60; M. R. Yarrow and C. Z. Waxler, "Dimensions and Correlates of Prosocial Behavior in Young Children," *Child Development* 47 (1976): 118–25; N. Feshbach, "Studies of the Empathic Behavior of Children," in *Progress in Experimental Personality Research*, Vol. 8, ed. B. Maher (New York: Academic Press, 1977); N. Eisenberg and P. Miller, "The Relation of Empathy to Prosocial and Related Behaviors," *Psychological Bulletin* 101 (1987): 91–119; D. Krebs, "Empathy and Altruism," *Journal of Personality and Social Psychology* 32 (1975): 1134–46; J. Kagan, *The Nature of the Child* (New York: Basic Books, 1984), pp. 31–37; M. Hoffman, "Developmental Synthesis of Affect and Cognition and Its Implications for Altruistic Motivation," *Developmental Psychology* 11 (1975): 607–22; M. Hoffman, "Empathy, Role-Taking, Guilt, and Development of Altruistic Motives," in *Moral Development and Behavior*, ed. T. Lickona (New York: Holt, Rinehart and Winston, 1976), pp. 124–43.

4.   See J. E. Grusec and L. Kuczynski, "Teaching Children to Punish Themselves, and Effects on Subsequent Compliance," *Child Development* 48 (1972): 1296–1300; W. M. Casey and R. V. Burton, "Training Children to be Consistently Honest through Verbal Self-Instructions," *Child Development* 53 (1982): 911–19; W. Mischel and H. Mischel, "The Development of Children's Knowledge of Self Control Strategies," *Child Development* 54 (1983): 603–9.

5.   N. Noddings, *Caring: A Feminine Approach to Ethics and Moral Education* (Los Angeles: University of California Press, 1984). See also N. Noddings, *The Challenge to Care in Schools: An Alternative Approach to Education* (New York: Teachers College Press, 1992).

6.   L. A. Blum, *Friendship, Altruism and Morality* (Boston: Routledge and Kegan Paul, 1980).

7.   Kagan, *Nature of the Child*, pp. 124–28.

8.   D. Bar-Tal, "Sequential Development of Helping Behavior: A Cognitive-Learning Approach," *Developmental Review* 2 (1982): 101–24.

9.   H. M. Isen, "Success, Failure, Attention and Reaction to Others: The Warm Glow of Success," *Journal of Personality and Social Psychology* 15 (1970): 294–301. See also D. L. Krebs and B. Stirrup, "Role-Taking Ability and Altruistic Behavior in Elementary School Children," *Journal of Moral Education* 11 (1982): 94–100.

10.   E. E. Werner and R. S. Smith, *Vulnerable but Invincible* (New York: McGraw Hill, 1982). See also Kagan, *Nature of the Child*, pp. 109–10.

11.   See P. Mussen and N. Eisenberg-Berg, *Roots of Caring, Sharing and Helping* (San Francisco: W. H. Freeman, 1977), p. 137; E. Staub, "Use of Role Playing and Induction in Training for Prosocial Behavior," *Child Development* 42 (1971): 805–81;

R. Ionotti, "The Effects of Role Taking Experiences on Altruism, Empathy, and Aggression," paper presented to the Society for Research in Child Development, Denver, April 1975.

12.   W. Damon, *The Moral Child: Nurturing Children's Natural Moral Growth* (New York: Free Press, 1988), p. 119. See also J. Larrieu and P. Mussen, "Some Personality and Motivational Correlates of Children's Behavior," *Journal of Genetic Psychology* 147 (1986): 529–42; N. Eisenberg, *Altruistic Emotion, Cognition and Behavior* (Hillsdale, N.J.: Lawrence Erlbaum, 1986); B. Underwood and B. Moore, "Perspective Taking and Altruism," *Psychological Bulletin* 91 (1982): 143–73; E. Staub, "Steps toward a Comprehensive Theory of Moral Conduct: Goal Orientation, Social Behavior, Kindness, and Cruelty," in *Morality, Moral Behavior and Moral Development*, ed. W. M. Kurtines and J. L. Gewirtz (New York: Wiley, 1984).

13.   V. G. Paley, *You Can't Say You Can't Play* (Cambridge, Mass.: Harvard University Press, 1992).

14.   R. L. Leahy and T. M. Hunt, "An Approach to the Development of Conceptions of Intelligence," in *The Child's Construction of Social Inequality*, ed. R. L. Leahy (New York: Academic Press, 1983), p. 149; M. L. Hoffman, "Developmental Synthesis of Affect and Cognition and Its Implications for Altruistic Motivation," *Developmental Psychology* 11 (1978): 617.

15.   D. Baumrind, "Rearing Competent Children," in *Child Development Today and Tomorrow*, ed. W. Damon (San Francisco: Jossey-Bass, 1989). See also D. Baumrind, "Current Patterns of Parental Authority," *Developmental Psychology Monographs* 4 (1971): 1.

16.   B. Whiting and J. Whiting, *Children of Six Cultures: A Psychocultural Analysis* (Cambridge, Mass.: Harvard University Press, 1975), p. 145.

17.   R. Matthews, "Hawlemont Regional Elementary School," *The Boston Sunday Globe*, July 7, 1991, pp. 57–58.

18.   A. Kohn, "P Is for Prosocial Teaching," *The Boston Globe Magazine*, November 6, 1988, pp. 25, 61–71.

19.   V. Battistich and D. Solomon, "Research on the Child Development Project: Current Status and Future Directions," *Moral Education Forum* 14 (1989): 7–10; E. Schaps, D. Solomon, and A. Watson, "A Program that Combines Character Development and Academic Achievement," *Educational Leadership* 43 (1986): 32–35; R. Beswick, *Character Education* (Eugene, Ore.: Oregon School Study Council, 1992), pp. 20–22; E. B. Fiske, *Smart Schools, Smart Kids: Why Do Some Schools Work?* (New York: Simon and Schuster, 1991), pp. 203–20.

20.   Mussen and Eisenberg-Berg, *Roots*, pp. 125–26; L. Kohlberg and D. Candee, "The Relationship of Moral Judgment to Moral Action," in *Morality, Moral Behavior and Moral Development*, ed. W. M. Kurtines and J. L. Gewirtz (New York: Wiley, 1984).

21.   K. H. Rubin and F. W. Schneider, "The Relationship between Moral Judgment, Egocentrism and Altruistic Behavior," *Child Development* 44 (1973): 661–65.

22.   J. S. Benninga (Ed.), *Moral, Character, and Civic Education in the Elementary School* (New York: Teachers College Press, 1991), pp. 131–96; W. Kilpatrick, *Why Johnny Can't Tell Right from Wrong: Moral Illiteracy and the Case for Character Education* (New York: Simon and Schuster, 1992).

23.   M. Collins and C. Tamarkin, *Marva Collins' Way* (New York: St. Martin's Press, 1982).

24.   M. Weinberg, *The Search for Quality Integrated Education: Policy and Research on Minority Students in School and College* (Westport, Conn.: Greenwood Press, 1983).

25. H. M. Levin, *Accelerated Schools for At-Risk Students* (New Brunswick, N.J.: Center for Policy Research in Education, 1988).

26. A. Steinberg (Ed.), "Reading Problems: Is Quick Recovery Possible?" in *The Best of the Harvard Education Letter* (Cambridge, Mass.: Harvard Graduate School of Education, 1993), pp. 10–12.

27. E. Turiel, *The Development of Social Knowledge: Morality and Convention* (New York: Cambridge University Press, 1983); M. Windmiller, N. Lambert, and E. Turiel (Eds.), *Moral Development and Socialization* (Boston: Allyn and Bacon, 1980).

28. M. Blatt and L. Kohlberg, "The Effects of Classroom Moral Discussion upon Children's Moral Judgment," *Journal of Moral Education* 4 (1975): 129–61.

29. W. S. Hall and P. E. Jose, "Cultural Effects on the Development of Equality and Inequality," in *The Child's Construction of Social Inequality*, ed. R. L. Leahy (New York: Academic Press, 1983), p. 263; N. P. Emler and J. P. Rushton, "Cognitive-Developmental Factors in Children's Generosity," *British Journal of Social and clinical Psychology* 13 (1974): 277–81.

30. See J. Robinson, "Mr. Robinson Regrets," quoting World Bank figures, *The Bosto Globe* October 30, 1991, p. 59.

31. C. Glock, R. Wuthnow, J. Piliavin, and M. Spencer, *Adolescent Prejudice* (New York: Harper & Row, 1975), pp. 171–80.

32. M. Yarrow, P. Scott, and C. Waxler, "Learning Concern for Others," *Developmental Psychology* 8 (1973): 240–60.

33. E. Staub, "The Use of Role Playing and Induction in Training for Prosocial Behavior," *Child Development* 42 (1971): 805–16.

34. See J. A. Banks, *Teaching Strategies for the Social Studies: Inquiry, Valuing and Decision-Making* (White Plains, N.Y.: Longman, 1990). See also V. J. Harris (Ed.), *Teaching Multicultural Literature in Grades K–8* (Norwood, Mass.: Christopher Gordon Publishers, 1992); L. Blair, "Developing Student Voices with Multicultural Literature," *English Journal* 12 (1980): 24–28; A. Goldstein, *The Prepare Curriculum: Teaching Prosocial Competencies* (Champaign, Ill.: Research Press, 1988); W. J. Kreidler, *Creative Conflict Resolution: More than 200 Activities for Keeping Peace in the Classroom* (Glenview, Ill.: Scott-Foresman, 1984).

35. Carnegie Council on Adolescent Development, *Turning Points: Preparing American Youth for the 21st Century. Report of the Task Force on Education of Young Adolescents* (Washington, D.C.: Carnegie Council, 1989), p. 26.

36. C. A. Grant and C. E. Sleeter, "Equality and Excellence: A Critique," in *Excellence in Education*, ed. P. Altbach, G. Kelly, and L. Weis (Buffalo, N.Y.: Prometheus, 1985).

37. J. I. Goodlad, *A Place Called School: Prospects for the Future* (New York: McGraw-Hill, 1983).

38. Shoreham-Wading River Middle School, *Advisory Handbook* (Shoreham, N.Y.: Shoreham-Wading River Middle School, 1989), pp. 2–9.

CHAPTER 7

1. K. W. Fischer and S. L. Pipp," Processes of Cognitive Development: Optimal Level and Skill Acquisition," in *Mechanisms of Cognitive Development*, ed. R. J. Sternberg (San Francisco: Freeman, 1984).

2. Carnegie Council on Adolescent Development, *Turning Points: Preparing American Youth for the 21st Century. Report of the Task Force on Education of Young Adolescents* (Washington, D.C.: Carnegie Council, 1989), p. 26.

3. B. Michael (Ed.), *Volunteers in Public Schools* (Washington, D.C.: National Academy Press, 1990). See also Department of Education, *One on One, A Guide for*

Establishing Mentor Programs (Washington, D.C.: Government Printing Office, 1990).

4. "Where Prejudice Takes Root," *Human Behavior* 6 (1977): 37–38.5. See R. R. Carkhuff, *The Art of Helping: An Introduction to Life Skills* (Amherst, Mass.: Human Resource Development Press, 1977); C. Rogers, *On Becoming a Person: A Therapist's View of Psychotherapy* (Boston: Houghton Mifflin, 1961).

6. S. MacDonald and R. Gallimore, *Battle in the Classroom: Innovations in Classroom Techniques* (Scranton, Pa.: Intext, 1971). See also J. S. Phinney and M. J. Rotheram, *Children's Ethnic Socialization: Pluralism and Development* (Newbury Park, Calif.: Sage Publications, 1987), p. 279.

7. S. Harter, "Effectance Motivation Reconsidered: Toward a Developmental Model," *Human Development* 21 (1976): 34–64.

8. E. B. Fiske, "Lessons," *New York Times*, November 30, 1988, p. B14. See also L. A. Daloz, *Effective Teaching and Mentoring* (San Francisco: Jossey-Bass, 1986); I. J. Crushschon, *Peer Tutoring: A Strategy for Building on Cultural Strengths* (Chicago: Center for New Schools, 1977).

9. R. Slavin and N. Madden, "School Practices that Improve Race Relations," *American Education Research Journal* 16 (1979): 169–80.

10. See *Teaching Tolerance* (Montgomery, Ala.: Southern Poverty Law Center, 1993–94).

11. H. E. Kagan, *Changing the Attitudes of Christians toward Jews: A Psychological Approach through Religion* (New York: Columbia University Press, 1952); P. A. Katz, "Attitude Change in Children: Can the Twig be Straightened?" in *Towards the Elimination of Racism*, ed. P. A. Katz (New York: Pergamon, 1976), p. 223.

12. T. Lickona, *Educating for Character: How Our Schools Can Teach Respect and Responsibility* (New York: Bantam, 1991).

13. C. E. Sleeter and C. A. Grant, *Making Choices for Multicultural Education: Five Approaches to Race, Class, and Gender* (New York: Macmillan, 1994), pp. 209–41. See also R. Enright, W. Enright, I. Manheim, and E. Harris, "Distributive Justice Development and Social Class," *Developmental Psychology* 16 (1980): 555–63; W. S. Hall and P. E. Jose, "Cultural Effects on the Development of Equality and Inequality," in *The Child's Construction of Social Inequality*, ed. R. L. Leahy (New York: Academic Press, 1983), pp. 253–85.

14. P. Eckert, *Jocks and Burnouts: Social Categories and Identity in the High School* (New York: Teachers College Press, 1989).

15. See J. U. Michaelis, *Social Studies for Children: A Guide to Basic Instruction* (Englewood Cliffs, N.J.: Prentice-Hall, 1980).

16. C. Gilligan, N. P. Lyons, and T. J. Hammer, *Making Connections: The Relational Worlds of Adolescent Girls at Emma Willard School* (Troy, N.Y.: Emma Willard School, 1989); D. J. Moir, "Egocentrism and the Emergence of Conventional Morality in Adolescent Girls," *Child Development* 45 (1974): 299–309.

17. W. Zinsser, *Writing to Learn: How to Write — and Think — Clearly about Any Subject at All* (New York: Harper & Row, 1988); A. Harrington and M. Curtis, "Basic Writing: Moving the Voices on the Margin to the Center," *Harvard Educational Review* 60 (1990): 489–96.

18. R. A. Schmuck and P. Schmuck, *Group Processes in the Classroom* (Dubuque, Iowa: W. C. Brown, 1983). See also M. Cole (Ed.), *Education for Equality: Some Guidelines for Good Practice* (London: Routledge, 1987).

19. J. Oakes, *Keeping Track: How American Schools Structure Inequality* (New Haven: Yale University Press, 1985).

20. R. Valdivieso, quoted in *The Boston Globe*, June 12, 1990, p. 16.

21. Slavin and Madden, "School Practices," p. 174. See also D. Johnson and R.

Johnson, "Effects of Cooperative and Individualistic Learning Experiences on Interaction," *Journal of Educational Psychology* 73 (1981): 444–49.

22. T. Lickona, "Character," in *Moral, Character, and Civic Education in the Elementary School*, ed. J. S. Benninga (New York: Teachers College Press, 1991).

23. E. Aronson, N. Blaney, C. Stephan, J. Sikes, and M. Snapp, *The Jigsaw Classroom* (Beverly Hills, Calif.: Sage Publications, 1978).

24. R. Howard, "Development in Elementary School," in *Moral, Character, and Civic Education in the Elementary School*, ed. J. S. Benninga (New York: Teachers College Press, 1991), p. 109.

25. Community Board, *Conflict Resolution: A Secondary School Curriculum* (San Francisco: Community Board, 1987).

26. R. J. Selman and L. H. Shultz, *Making a Friend in Youth: Developmental Theory and Pair Therapy* (Chicago: University of Chicago Press, 1990). See also R. J. Selman, *The Growth of Interpersonal Understanding: Developmental and Clinical Analysis* (New York: Academic Press, 1980); J. Youniss, *Parents and Peers in Social Development* (Chicago: University of Chicago Press, 1980); S. R. Asher and J. D. Coie (Eds.), *Peer Rejection in Childhood* (New York: Cambridge University Press, 1990).

27. Slavin and Madden, "School Practices," p. 110.

28. K. Cushman, "Managing the Change Process," *Horace* (newsletter of the Coalition of Essential Schools, Brown University School of Education) 9 (1993): 3. See also T. R. Sizer, *Horace's Compromise: The Dilemma of the American High School* (Boston: Houghton Mifflin, 1984); T. R. Sizer, *Horace's School: Redesigning the American High School* (Boston: Houghton Mifflin, 1992).

29. E. B. Fiske, *Smart Schools, Smart Kids* (New York: Simon and Schuster, 1991), p. 184.

30. S. Fliegel and J. MacGuire, *Miracle in East Harlem: The Fight for Choice in Public Education* (New York: Random House, 1993), pp. 159–61.

CHAPTER 8

1. R. N. Bellah, R. Madsen, W. M. Sullivan, A. Swidler, and S. M. Tipton, *Habits of the Heart: Individualism and Commitment in American Life* (Los Angeles: University of California Press, 1985).

2. J. W. Getzels, "The School and the Acquisition of Values," in *From Youth to Constructive Adult Life: The Role of the Public School*, ed. R. W. Taylor (Berkeley, Calif.: McCutchan Publishing, 1978), p. 59.

3. C. Glock, R. Wuthnow, J. Piliavin, and M. Spencer, *Adolescent Prejudice* (New York: Harper & Row, 1975), pp. 99, 174. See also "Study Details Racism among Nation's Youth," *The Boston Globe*, April 30, 1993, p. 13.

4. S. Eaton, "Forty Years after *Brown*, Cities and Suburbs Face a Rising Tide of Racial Isolation," *The Harvard Educational Letter* 10 (1994): 1–5.

5. W. Hawley, R. Crain, C. Rossell, M. Smylie, R. Fernandez, J. Schofield, R. Tompkins, W. Trent, and M. Zlotnik, *Strategies for Effective Desegregation: Lessons from Research* (Lexington, Mass.: D. C. Heath, 1983), pp. 110–15; J. W. Schofield, *Black and White in School: Trust, Tension, or Tolerance* (New York: Praeger, 1982).

6. Hawley et al., *Strategies*, p. 121. See also R. C. Rist, *The Invisible Children: School Integration in American Society* (Cambridge, Mass.: Harvard University Press, 1978); N. St. John, *School Desegregation, Outcomes for Children* (New York: Wiley Interscience, 1975), pp. 111–17; J. L. Dryfoos, *Adolescents at Risk: Prevalence and Prevention* (New York: Oxford University Press, 1990); J. Kretovics and E. J. Nussel, *Transforming Urban Education* (Boston: Allyn and Bacon, 1994); R. L. Crain, R. E. Mahard, and R. E. Narot, *Making Desegregation Work: How Schools Create Social Climates* (Cambridge, Mass.: Ballinger, 1982).

7.   J. I. Goodlad, *A Place Called School: Prospects for the Future* (New York: McGraw-Hill, 1983), pp. 163, 289.

8.   C. Beck, *Better Schools: A Values Perspective* (New York: Falmer Press, 1990), p. 19. See also C. Power, "Democracy in the Larger High School: The Case of Brookline," in *Moral Education, Interactional Perspectives*, ed. L. Berkowitz and F. Oser (Hillsdale, N.J.: Lawrence Erlbaum, 1983).

9.   D. J. Armor, "The Evidence on Busing," *The Public Interest* 28 (1972): 90–126.

10. T. S. Pettigrew, "Social Evaluation Theory: Convergences and Applications," in *Nebraska Symposium on Motivation*, Vol. 15, ed. D. Levine (Lincoln: University of Nebraska Press, 1967), pp. 241–318.

11. S. W. Cook, "Cooperative Interaction in Multiethnic Groups," in *Groups in Contact: The Psychology of Desegregation*, ed. N. Miller and M. Brewer (New York: Academic Press, 1984). See also S. W. Cook, "Interpersonal and Attitudinal Outcome in Cooperating Racial Groups," *Journal of Research and Development in Education* 12 (1978): 97–113; M. Hewstone and R. Brown, *Contact and Conflict in Intergroup Encounters* (New York: Blackwell, 1956).

12. H. Tajfel (Ed.), *Differentiation between Social Groups* (New York: Academic Press, 1978); P. A. Katz, "Stimulus Predifferentiation and Modification of Children's Racial Attitudes," *Child Development* 44 (1973): 232–37. See also P. A. Katz and S. R. Zalk, "Modification of Children's Racial Attitudes," *Developmental Psychology* 14 (1979): 447–61.

13. A. L. Stoskopf and M. Strom, *Choosing to Participate: A Critical Examination of Citizenship in American History* (Brookline, Mass.: Facing History and Ourselves National Foundation, 1990).

14. H. Kohl, *I Won't Learn from You* (Bellevue, Wash.: Thistle Press, 1992). See also S. Amster, "Making the Invisible Visible: Anti-Racist Education Goes Beyond 'Let's Appreciate Diversity'," *The Harvard Education Letter* 10 (1994): 6.

15. *Junior Great Books Discussion Handbook* (Chicago: Great Books Foundation, 1990). See also P. Gagnon, "Why Study History?" *The Atlantic* 262 (1988): 43–80.

16. R. Rubenstein (Ed.), *Great Courtroom Battles* (Chicago: Playboy Press, 1973).

17. J. A. Lukas, *Common Ground: A Turbulent Decade in the Lives of Three American Families* (New York: Alfred A. Knopf, 1985).

18. R. C. Riordan, "High School Writing Centers: Students Find Their Voices," *The Harvard Education Letter* 6 (1990): 6–7.

19. Adapted from L. Splitter, "Educational Reform through Philosophy for Children," *Thinking, the Journal of Philosophy for Children* 7 (1988): 32–39. See also D. W. Johnson and R. L. Johnson, "Critical Thinking through Structural Controversy," *Educational Leadership* 45 (1988): 58–64.

20. M. Rokeach, *The Nature of Human Values* (New York: Free Press, 1973). See also M. Rokeach, "Long-Range Experimental Modification of Values, Attitudes and Behavior," *American Psychologist* 26 (1971): 453–59.

21. L. Kohlberg, "An Evaluation of the Effects of High School Democratic Governance on Students' Moral Judgment and Action," revised proposal to the Grant Foundation (Cambridge, Mass.: Harvard Graduate School of Education, 1985).

22. See S. L. Lightfoot, *The Good High School: Portraits of Character and Culture* (New York: Basic Books, 1983).

23. E. R. Wasserman, "Implementing Kohlberg's 'Just Community Concept' in an Alternative High School," *Social Education* 4 (1976): 203–7. See also R. Galbraith and T. Jones, *Moral Reasoning: A Teaching Handbook for Adapting Kohlberg to the Classroom* (Minneapolis: Greenhouse Press, 1976).

24. L. Kohlberg, "Moral Education in the Cambridge Cluster School," in *Moral Education: Theory and Application*, ed. M. Berkowitz and F. Oser (Hillsdale, N.J.: Lawrence Erlbaum, 1985), p. 44.

25. A. Lockwood, "The Effects of Values Clarification and Moral Development Curricula on School-Age Subjects: A Critical Review of Recent Research," *Review of Educational Research* 48 (1979): 325–64. See also A. Higgins, "Research and Measurement Issues in Moral Education Interventions," in *Moral Education: A First Generation of Research and Development*, ed. R. L. Mosher (New York: Praeger, 1980), p. 92; L. Kuhmerker, M. Mentkowski, and V. Erikson, *Evaluating Moral Development and Evaluating Educational Programs that Have a Moral Dimension* (Schenectady, N.Y.: Character Research Press, 1980).

26. C. Power, A. Higgins, and L. Kohlberg, *Lawrence Kohlberg's Approach to Moral Education* (New York: Columbia University Press, 1989).

27. L. Kohlberg, "Moral Education Reappraised," *The Humanist*, 6 (1978): 14–15. See also W. K. Kilpatrick, *Why Johnny Can't Tell Right from Wrong: Moral Illiteracy and the Case for Character Education* (New York: Simon and Schuster, 1992).

28. E. B. Fiske, *Smart Schools, Smart Kids* (New York: Simon and Schuster, 1991), pp. 59–61.

29. H. J. Walberg (Ed.), *Educational Environments and Effects: Evaluation, Policy and Productivity* (Berkeley, Calif.: McCutchan Publishing, 1979).

30. Hawley et al., *Strategies*, p. 115. See also M. Chesler, B. I. Bryant, and J. E. Crowfoot, *Making Desegregation Work: A Professional's Guide to Effecting Change* (Beverly Hills, Calif.: Sage Publications, 1981); W. G. Stephan and J. R. Feagin (Eds.), *School Desegregation, Past, Present and Future* (New York: Plenum, 1980).

31. D. Meier, "In Education Small Is Sensible." *New York Times*, September 8, 1989, I25.

32. Carnegie Council on Adolescent Development, *Turning Points: Preparing American Youth for the 21st Century. Report of the Task Force on Education of Young Adolescents* (Washington, D.C.: Carnegie Council, 1989), p. 15.

33. Fiske, *Smart Schools*, pp. 29–30, 35–59.

34. P. Freire, *Education for Critical Consciousness* (New York: Continuum, 1983).

35. D. E. Eberly, *National Youth Service: A Democratic Institution for the 21st Century* (Washington, D.C.: National Service Secretariat, 1991).

36. S. A. Goldsmith, *City Year: On the Streets and in the Neighborhoods with Twelve Young Community Service Volunteers* (New York: New Press), 1993.

37. "Springfield Serves," *The Boston Globe*, April 2, 1993, p. 36.

38. Eberly, *National Youth Service*, p. 24.

39. J. S. Coleman and T. Hoffer, *High School Achievement: Public, Catholic, and Private Schools Compared* (New York: Basic Books, 1982); J. S. Coleman and T. Hoffer, *Public and Private High Schools: The Impact of Communities* (New York: Basic Books, 1987).

40. J. Towne, quoted in *The Westtonian* (Westtown Friends' School, Westtown, Pa.) Winter 1989: ix.

41. Gallup Poll, June–July 198,9 reported in *National Service Newsletter* 55 (October 1989).

42. R. Sennett, *The Uses of Disorder: Personal Identity and City Life* (New York: Knopf, 1970), pp. 6–20.

CHAPTER 9

1. National Commission on Excellence in Education, *A Nation at Risk: The Imperative for Educational Reform* (Washington, D.C.: Government Printing Office, 1983); M. Adler, *The Paideia Proposal* (New York: Macmillan, 1982); E. L. Boyer, *High School: A Report on Secondary Education in America* (New York: Harper & Row, 1983); J. I. Goodlad, *A Place Called School: Prospects for the Future* (New York: McGraw-Hill, 1983); Education Commission of the States, Task Force on Education for Economic Growth, *Action for Excellence* (Denver, Colo.: Education Commission of the States, 1983); Twentieth Century Fund Task Force on Federal Elementary and Secondary Education Policy, *Making the Grade* (New York: Twentieth Century Fund, 1983).

2. B. A. Sichel, *Moral Education: Character, Community and Ideals* (Philadelphia: Temple University Press, 1988), pp. 222–23.

3. W. B. Yeats, *The Poems of W. B. Yeats*, ed. J. R. Finneran (New York: Macmillan, 1989).

4. M. Goodwin, quoted in *The Boston Globe*, December 20, 1989.

5. J. S. Coleman, E. Q. Campbell, C. J. Hobson, J. McPartland, A. M. Mood, F. D. Weinfeld, and R. L. York, *Equality of Educational Opportunity* (Washington, D.C.: Government Printing Office, 1966). See also U.S. Commission on Civil Rights, *Reanalysis of Coleman's Equality of Educational Opportunity* (Washington, D.C.: Government Printing Office, 1970).

6. M. Roosevelt, quoted in *The Boston Globe*, May 17, 1993.

7. J. Kretovics and E. J. Nussel, *Transforming Urban Education* (New York: Allyn and Bacon, 1994), pp. 339–41; J. Cummins, "Empowering Minority Students: A Framework for Intervention," in *Facing Racism in Education*, ed. N. M. Hidalgo, C. L. McDowell, and E. V. Siddle (Cambridge, Mass.: Harvard Educational Review, Reprint Series 21, 1990), pp. 62–64.

8. E. A. Wynne (Ed.), *Character Policy* (Washington, D.C.: University Press of America, 1982); K. Ryan and T. Lickona (Eds.), *Character Development in Schools and Beyond* (Washington, D.C.: Council for Research in Values and Philosophy, 1992); W. K. Kilpatrick, *Why Johnny Can't Tell Right from Wrong: Moral Illiteracy and the Case for Character Education* (New York: Simon and Schuster, 1992).

9. Massachusetts Teachers' Association, "Needed: Bold Plans to Help Schools," *Massachusetts Education Today* 7 (1991): 3–4.

10. See P. Lyeseight-Jones, "A Management of Change Perspective: Turning the Whole School Around," in *Education for Equality, Some Guidelines for Good Practice*, ed. M. Cole (London: Routledge, 1989), pp. 38–52.

11. See Kretovics and Nussel, *Transforming Urban Education*; K. Cushman, "Managing the Change Process," *Horace* (newsletter of the Coalition of Essential Schools, Brown University School of Education) 9 (1993); *Utne Reader*, September–October 1990, pp. 76–77.

12. R. P. Moses, M. Kamii, S. M. Swap, and J. Howard, "The Algebra Project: Organizing in the Spirit of Ella," *Harvard Educational Review* 5 (1989): 423–43.

Bibliography

Aboud, F. E. *Children and Prejudice*. New York: Basil Blackwell, 1988.

Adorno, T., E. Frenkel-Brunswik, E. Levinson, and R. Sanford. *The Authoritarian Personality*. New York: Harper, 1950.

Alejandro-Wright, M. "The Child's Development of the Concept of Race." Ed.D. dissertation, Harvard Graduate School of Education, 1980.

Adler, M. J. *The Paideia Proposal*. New York: Macmillan, 1982.

Allport, G. *The Nature of Prejudice*. Garden City, N.Y.: Doubleday Anchor Books, 1958.

Amir, Y. "The Role of Intergroup Contact in Change of Prejudice and Ethnic Relations." In *Towards the Elimination of Racism*, edited by P. A. Katz. New York: Pergamon Press, 1976.

Amster, S. "Making the Invisible Visible: Anti-Racist Education Goes Beyond 'Let's Appreciate Diversity'." *Harvard Education Letter* 10 (1994): 5–6.

Aranowitz, S., and H. Giroux. *Education Under Siege*. Boston: Bergin and Garvey, 1985.

Armor, D. J. "School and Family Effects of Black and White Achievement: A Reexamination of the USOE Data." In *On Equality of Educational Opportunity*, edited by F. Mosteller and D. P. Moynihan, pp. 168–229. New York: Random House, 1972.

____. "The Evidence on Busing." *The Public Interest* 28 (1972): 90–126.

Aronfreed, J. *Conduct and Conscience: The Socialization of Internalized Control over Behavior*. New York: Academic Press, 1968.

Aronson, E., N. Blaney, C. Stephan, J. Sikes, and M. Snapp. *The Jigsaw Classroom*. Beverly Hills, Calif.: Sage Publications, 1978.

Asher, S. R., and J. D. Cole, eds. *Peer Rejection in Childhood*. New York: Cambridge University Press, 1990.

Ashmore, R., and F. DelBoca. "Psychological Approaches to Understanding Intergroup Conflicts." In *Towards the Elimination of Racism*, edited by P. Katz. New York: Pergamon, 1976.

Attanucci, J. "In Whose Terms: A New Perspective on Self, Role and Relationship. In *Mapping the Moral Domain: A Contribution of Women's Thinking to Psychological Theory and Education*, edited by C. Gilligan, V. J. Ward, J. M. Taylor, and B. Bardage. Cambridge, Mass.: Harvard University Press, 1988.

Baird, L. L. "Big School, Small School: A Critical Examination of the Hypothesis." *Journal of Educational Psychology* 60 (1969): 253–60.

Ball-Rokeach, S. J., M. Rokeach, and J. W. Grube. *The Great American Values Test: Influencing Behavior and Belief through Television*. New York: Free Press, 1984.

Bandura, A. *Social Foundations of Thought and Action, A Social Cognitive Theory*. Englewood Cliffs, N.J.: Prentice-Hall, 1986.

Bandura, A., and F. McDonald. "The Influence of Social Reinforcement and the Behavior of Models in Shaping Children's Moral Judgments." *Journal of Abnormal and Social Psychology* 67 (1963): 274–81.

Banks, J. A. *Teaching Strategies for the Social Studies: Inquiry, Valuing and Decision-Making*. White Plains, N.Y.: Longman, 1990.

Banks, J. A., and C. A. McGee Banks. *Multicultural Education: Issues and Perspectives*. Boston: Allyn and Bacon, 1989.

Barker, R., and P. Gump. *Big School-Small School*. Palo Alto, Calif.: Stanford University Press, 1964.

Bar-Tal, D. "Sequential Development of Helping Behavior: A Cognitive-Learning Approach." *Developmental Review* 2 (1982).

Bar-Tal, D., A. Raviv, and T. Leiser. "The Development of Altruistic Behavior: Empirical Evidence." *Developmental Psychology* 16 (1980).

Bateman, W. L. *Open to Question: The Art of Teaching and Learning by Inquiry*. San Francisco: Jossey-Bass, 1990.

Battistich, V., and D. Solomon. "Research on the Child Development Project: Current Status and Future Directions." *Moral Education Forum* 14 (1989).

Baumrind, D. "Rearing Competent Children." In *Child Development Today and Tomorrow*, edited by W. Damon. San Francisco: Jossey-Bass, 1989.

———."Current Patterns of Parental Authority." *Developmental Psychology Monographs* 1 (1971): 1–103.

Beck, C. *Better Schools: A Values Perspective*. New York: Falmer Press, 1990.

Beck, C., and E. Sullivan, eds. *Moral Education*. Toronto: University of Toronto Press, 1970.

Belenkey, M., B. Clinchy, N. Goldberger, and J. Tarule. *Women's Ways of Knowing: The Development of Self, Voice and Mind*. New York: Basic Books, 1986.

Bellah, R. N., R. Madsen, W. M. Sullivan, A. Swidler, and S. M. Tipton. *Habits of the Heart: Individualism and Commitment in American Life*. New York: Harper & Row, 1985.

Benjamin, R. *Making Schools Work*. New York: Continuum, 1981.

Benninga, J. S., ed. *Moral, Character and Civic Education in the Elementary School*. New York: Teachers College Press, 1991.

Bereiter, C. "Educational Implications of Kohlberg's Developmental View." *Interchange* 1 (1970): 25–32.

Berkowitz, M. W., and F. Oser, eds. *Moral Education: Theory and Application*. Hillsdale, N.J.: Lawrence Erlbaum, 1985.

Beswick, R. *Character Education*. Eugene, Ore.: Oregon School Study Council, 1992.

Billig, M., and H. Tajfel. "Social Categorization and Similarity in Intergroup Behavior." *European Journal of Social Psychology* 3 (1973): 27–52.

Bird, C., E. Monachesi, and H. Burdick. "Infiltration and the Attitudes of White and Negro Parents and Children." *Journal of Abnormal and Social Psychology* 47 (1952): 688–99.

———. "Studies of Group Tensions: III. The Effect of Parental Discouragement of Play Activities upon the Attitudes of White Children Toward Negroes." *Child Development* 23 (1952): 295–306.

Blair, L. "Developing Student Voices with Multicultural Literature." *English Journal* 12 (1980): 24–28.

Blasi, A. "Bridging Moral Cognition and Moral Action: A Critical View of the Literature." *Psychological Bulletin* 88 (1980): 1–45.

____. "Moral Cognition and Moral Action: A Theoretical Perspective." *Developmental Review*, (1983): 178–210.

Blatt, M. and L. Kohlberg, "The Effects of Classroom Moral Discussion upon Children's Moral Judgment." *Journal of Moral Education* 4 (1975): 29–161.

Blum, L. *Friendship, Altruism and Morality.* Boston: Routledge and Kegan Paul, 1980.

Bowerman, C., and J. Kinch. "Changes in Family and Peer Orientation between the Fourth and Tenth Grades." *Social Forces* 37 (1959): 206–11.

Boyer, E. L. *High School: A Report on Secondary Education in America.* New York: Harper & Row, 1983.

Braddock, J., R. Crain, and J. McPartland. "A Long-Term View of School Desegregation." *Phi Delta Kappan* 66 (1984): 259–64.

Branch, C. W., and N. Newcombe. "Racial Attitude Development among Young Black Children as a Function of Parental Attitudes: A Longitudinal Cross-sectional Study." *Child Development* 57 (1963): 712–21.

____. "Racial Attitudes of Black Preschoolers as Related to Parental Civil Rights Activism." *Merrill-Palmer Quarterly* 26 (1980): 425–28.

Bronfenbrenner, U. *Two Worlds of Childhood: U.S. and U.S.S.R.* New York: Basic Books, 1970.

Brown, A., ed. *Prejudice in Children.* Springfield, Ill.: Charles Thomas, 1972.

Bruner, J. *Acts of Meaning.* Cambridge, Mass.: Harvard University Press, 1990.

Bryant, B. I., and J. E. Crowfoot. *Making Desegregation Work: A Professional's Guide to Effecting Change.* Beverly Hills, Calif.: Sage Publications, 1981.

Buber, M. *Between Man and Man.* New York: Macmillan, 1965.

Bullock, C. *School Desegregation, Interracial Contact and Prejudice.* Washington, D.C.: National Institute of Education, 1976.

Byrne, D. "Parental Antecedents of Authoritarianism." *Journal of Personality and Social Psychology* 1 (1965): 369–73.

Byrnes, D. and G. Kiger, eds. *Common Bonds: Anti-Bias Teaching in a Diverse Society.* Wheaton, Mass.: Association for Childhood Education International, 1992.

Carkhuff, R. R. *The Art of Helping: An Introduction to Life Skills.* Amherst, Mass.: Human Resource Development Press, 1977.

Carkhuff, R. R., and G. Banks. "Training as a Preferred Method of Facilitating Relations between Races and Generations." *Journal of Counseling Psychology* 17 (1970): 413–18.

Carlson, R. V., and E. R. Ducharme, eds. *School Improvement: Theory and Practice.* Lanham, Md.: University Press of America, 1987.

Carnegie Council on Adolescent Development. *Turning Points: Preparing American Youth for the 21st Century. Report of the Task Force on Education of Young Adolescents.* Washington, D.C.: Carnegie Council, 1989.

Carney, M. *Inservice Education for Desegregation, A Review of the Literature.* Santa Monica, Calif.: Rand Corporation, 1979.

Carr, D. *Educating the Virtues.* New York: Routledge and Kegan Paul, 1991.

Carrington, B., and B. Troyna, eds. *Children and Controversial Issues: Strategies for the Early and Middle Years of Schooling.* New York: The Falmer Press, 1988.

Carter, R. *Dimensions of Moral Education.* Toronto: University of Toronto Press, 1984.

Casey, W. M., and R. V. Burton. "Training Children to be Consistently Honest through Verbal Self-Instructions." *Child Development* 53 (1982): 911–19.

Chandler, M. J. "Social Cognition: A Selective Review of Current Research." In

Knowledge and Development, edited by W. Overton and J. Gallagher. New York: Plenum, 1976.

Chesler, M., B. Bryant, and J. Crowfoot. *Making Desegregation Work: A Professional Guide to Effecting Change*. Beverly Hills, Calif.: Sage, 1981.

Clark, A., D. Hocevar, and M. Dembo. "The Role of Cognitive Development in Children's Explanations and Preferences of Skin Color." *Developmental Psychology* 16 (1980): 332–39.

Clark, K. *Prejudice and Your Child*. 2d ed. Boston, Mass.: Beacon Press, 1963.

Cohen, D. *Piaget: Critique and Reassessment*. New York: St. Martin's Press, 1983.

Cohen, H., and G. Weil. *Tasks of Emotional Development: A Projective Test for Children and Adolescents*. Lexington, Mass.: D. C. Heath, 1971.

Colby, A., and L. Kohlberg. *The Measurement of Moral Judgment*. New York: Cambridge University Press, 1986.

Cole, M., ed. *Education for Equality: Some Guidelines for Good Practice*. London: Routledge, 1987.

Coleman, J. S., and T. Hoffer. *Public and Private High Schools: The Impact of Communities*. New York: Basic Books, 1987.

____. *High School Achievement: Public, Catholic and Private Schools Compared*. New York: Basic Books, 1982.

Coleman, J. S., E. Campbell, C. Hobson, J. McPartland, F. Weinfeld, and R. York. *Equality of Educational Opportunity*. Washington, D.C.: Government Printing Office, 1966.

Coles, R. *The Moral Life of Children*. Boston: Atlantic Monthly Press, 1986.

Collins, M., and C. Tamarkin. *Marva Collins' Way*. New York: St. Martin's Press, 1982.

Comer, J. P. *A Conversation between James Comer and Ronald Edmunds: Fundamentals of Effective School Improvement*. Dubuque, Iowa: Kendall Publishing, 1989.

____. *Maggie's American Dream*. New York: New American Library, 1988.

____."Educating Poor Minority Children." *Scientific American* 259 (1992): 42–48.

____. *School Power: Implications of an Intervention Project*. New York: Free Press, 1980.

Community Board. *Conflict Resolution: A Secondary School Curriculum*. San Francisco: Community Board, 1987.

Conard, B. "Co-operative Learning and Prejudice Reduction." *Social Education* 52 (1988): 283–86.

Condry, J., and M. Simon. "An Experimental Study of Adult versus Peer Orientation." Unpublished manuscript, Cornell University, Department of Child Development, 1968.

Condry, J., M. Simon, and U. Bronfenbrenner. "Characteristics of Peer- and Adult-Oriented Children." Unpublished manuscript, Cornell University, Department of Child Development, 1968.

Cook, S. W. "Cooperative Interaction in Multiethnic Groups." In *Groups in Contact: The Psychology of Desegregation*, edited by N. Miller and M. Brewer. New York: Academic Press, 1984.

____. "Interpersonal and Attitudinal Outcome in Cooperating Racial Groups." *Journal of Research and Development in Education* 12 (1978): 97–113.

Coopersmith, S. *The Antecedents of Self-Esteem*. San Francisco: Freeman, 1967.

Corcoran, T., L. Walker, and J. L. White. *Working in Urban Schools*. Washington, D.C.: Institute of Educational Leadership, 1988.

Crain, R., R. Mahard, and R. Narot. *Making Desegregation Work: How Schools Create Social Climates*. Cambridge, Mass.: Ballinger Publishing, 1982.

Crushschon, I. J. *Peer Tutoring: A Strategy for Building on Cultural Strengths.* Chicago, Ill.: Center for New Schools, 1977.

Cummins, J. "Empowering Minority Students." In *Facing Racism in Education,* edited by N. Hidalgo, C. McDowell, and E. V. Siddle. Cambridge, Mass.: Harvard Educational Review Reprint 21 (1990): 62–65.

Curcio, J. L., and P. F. First. *Violence in the Schools: How to Proactively Prevent and Defuse It.* Newbury Park, Calif.: Corwin Press, 1993.

Cushman, K. "Managing the Change Process." *Horace* 9 (1993): 3.

Daloz, L. A. *Effective Teaching and Mentoring.* San Francisco: Jossey-Bass, 1986.

Damon, W. *The Moral Child: Nurturing Children's Natural Moral Growth.* New York: Free Press, 1988.

____. *The Social World of the Child.* San Francisco: Jossey-Bass, 1977.

Damon, W., and M. Killen. "Peer Interaction and the Process of Change in Children's Moral Reasoning." *Merrill-Palmer Quarterly* 28 (1982): 347–68.

Darmon-Sparks, L. *Anti-Bias Curriculum: Tools for Empowering Young Children.* Washington, D.C.: National Association for the Education of Young Children, 1989.

Davey, A. G. *Learning to Be Prejudiced: Growing Up in Multiethnic Britain.* London: Edward Arnold, 1983.

Davidson, F. H. "Respect for Persons and Ethnic Prejudice in Childhood: A Cognitive-Developmental Approach." In *Pluralism in a Democratic Society,* edited by M. M. Tumin and W. Plotch. New York: Praeger, 1977.

____. "Ability to Respect Persons Compared to Ethnic Prejudice in Childhood." *Journal of Personality and Social Psychology* 34 (1976): 1256–67.

____. "Respect for Human Dignity and Ethnic Judgments in Childhood." Ed.D. dissertation, Harvard University, 1974.

Department of Education. *One on One, A Guide for Establishing Mentor Programs.* Washington, D.C.: Government Printing Office, 1990.

Dryfoos, J. G. *Adolescents at Risk: Prevalence and Prevention.* New York: Oxford University Press, 1990.

Durkheim, E. *Moral Education: A Study in the Theory and Application in the Sociology of Education.* New York: Free Press, 1961.

____. *Sociology and Philosophy.* Glencoe, Ill.: Free Press, 1953.

Dykstra, C. "What Are People Like? An Alternative to Kohlberg's View." In *Moral Development Foundations: Christian Alternatives to Piaget / Kohlberg,* edited by D. M. Joy, pp. 13–62. Nashville, Tenn.: Abingdon Press, 1983.

Eaton, S. "Forty Years after *Brown,* Cities and Suburbs Face a Rising Tide of Racial Isolation." *The Harvard Educational Letter* 10 (1994): 1–5.

Eberly, D., ed. *National Youth Service: A Democratic Institution for the 21st Century.* Washington, D.C.: National Service Secretariat, 1991.

Eckert, P. *Jocks and Burnouts: Social Categories and Identity in the High School.* New York: Teachers College Press, 1989.

Edmunds, R. "Effective Schools for the Urban Poor." *Educational Leadership* 37 (1979): 15–18, 20–24.

Education Commission of the States, Task Force on Education for Economic Growth. *Action for Excellence.* Denver, Colo.: Education Commission of the States, 1983.

Eisenberg, N. *The Caring Child.* Cambridge: Harvard University Press, 1992.

____. *Altruistic Emotion, Cognition and Behavior.* Hillsdale, N.J.: Lawrence Erlbaum, 1986.

Eisenberg, N., and P. Miller. "The Relation of Empathy to Prosocial and Related Behaviors." *Psychological Bulletin* 101 (1987): 91–119.

Emler, N., and J. Rushton. "Cognitive-Developmental Factors in Children's

Generosity." *British Journal of Social and Clinical Psychology* 13 (1974): 227–81.

Enright, R. D., W. F. Enright, L. A. Manheim, and B. E. Harris. "Distributive Justice Development and Social Class." *Developmental Psychology* 16 (1980): 555–63.

Epstein, R., and S. S. Komorita. "Parental Discipline, Stimulus Characteristics of Outgroups, and Social Distance in Children." *Journal of Personality and Social Psychology* 2 (1965): 416–20.

Erikson, E. *Childhood and Society*. New York: W. W. Norton, 1963.

____. "The Concept of Identity and Race Relations: Notes and Queries." *Daedalus* 95 (1966): 145–71.

Feshbach, N. D. "Studies of Empathic Behavior in Children." In *Progress in Experimental Personality Research*, Vol. 8, edited by B. Maher. New York: Academic Press, 1978.

Fischer, K. W., ed. *Levels and Transitions in Children's Development*. San Francisco: Jossey-Bass, 1983.

Fischer, K. W., D. Bullock, A. Rotenberg, and P. Raya. "The Dynamics of Competence: How Context Contributes Directly to Skill." In *Development in Context: Acting and Thinking in Specific Environments*, edited by R. H. Wozniak and K. W. Fischer. Hillsdale, N.J.: Lawrence Erlbaum, 1993.

Fischer, K. W., and R. L. Canfield. "The Ambiguity of Stage Structure in Behavior: Person and Environment in the Development of Psychological Structure." In *Stage and Structure: Reopening the Debate*, edited by I. Levin. Norwood, N.J.: Ablex, 1986.

Fischer, K. W., and S. L. Pipp. "Processes of Cognitive Development: Optimal Level and Skill Acquisition." In *Mechanisms of Cognitive Development*, edited by R. J. Sternberg. San Francisco: Freeman, 1984.

Fiske, E. B. *Smart Schools, Smart Kids: Why Do Some Schools Work?* New York: Simon and Schuster, 1991.

____. "Lessons." *New York Times*, November 30, 1988, p. B14.

Flavell, J. H. "The Development of Inferences about Others." In *Understanding Other Persons*, edited by T. Mischel. New York: Basil Blackwell, 1974.

____. "On Cognitive Development. *Child Development* 53 (1982): 1–10.

Fliegel, S, and J. MacGuire. *Miracle in East Harlem: The Fight for Choice in Public Education*. New York: Random House, 1993.

Fox, D. J., and V. B. Jordan. "Racial Preference and Identification of Black, American Chinese, and White Children." *Genetic Psychology Monographs* 88 (1973): 229–86.

Franklin, D. "Charm School for Bullies." *Hypocrites* 3 (1989): 75–77.

Freire, P. *Education for Critical Consciousness*. New York: Continuum, 1983.

Frenkel-Brunswik, E. "Children's Attitudes." *Journal of Orthopsychiatry* 21 (1951): 543–58.

Frenkel-Brunswik, E., and J. Havel. "Prejudice in the Interviews of Children. I: Attitudes toward Minority Groups." *Journal of Genetic Psychology* 82 (1953): 91–136.

Freud, A. *The Ego and the Mechanisms of Defense*. New York: International Universities Press, 1966.

Freud, S. *The Basic Writings of Sigmund Freud*. New York: Modern Library, 1938.

Froming, W. J., L. Allen, and R. Jensen. "Altruism, Role-taking, and Self-Awareness: The Acquisition of Norms Governing Altruistic Behavior. *Child Development* 56 (1985): 1223–28.

Furth, H. G. *The World of Grown-Ups: Children's Conceptions of Society*. New York: Elsevier, 1980.

Gagnon, P. "Why Study History?" *The Atlantic* 262 (1988): 43–80.

Galbraith, R., and T. Jones. *Moral Development and Moral Education*. London: George Allen and Unwin, 1981.

____. *Moral Reasoning: A Teaching Handbook for Adapting Kohlberg to the Classroom*. Minneapolis: Greenhaven Press, 1976.

Gallup Poll, June–July 1989, reported in *National Service Newsletter* 55 (October 1989). National Service Secretariat, Washington, D.C.

Gardner, G. "Personality Development and Childhood Behavioral Disabilities." In *Psychiatry and Medicine*, edited by N. Brill. Los Angeles: University of California Press, 1962.

Gardner, H. *To Open Minds: Chinese Clues to the Dilemma of Contemporary Education*. New York: Basic Books, 1989.

Garrod, A. "Promoting Moral Development through a High School English Curriculum." *The Alberta Journal of Educational Research*, 35 (1989): 61–79.

Getzels, J. W. "The School and the Acquisition of Values." In *From Youth to Constructive Adult Life: The Role of the Public School*, edited by R. W. Tyler, pp. 43–66. Berkeley, Calif.: McCutchan Publishing Co., 1978.

Garrod, A., ed. *Approaches to Moral Development: New Research and Emerging Themes*. New York: Teachers College Press, 1993.

Gibbs, J. C. "Social Processes in Delinquency: The Need to Facilitate Empathy as well as Sociomoral Reasoning." In *Moral Development through Social Interaction*, edited by W. Kurtines and J. Gewirtz. New York: Wiley, 1987.

____. "Kohlberg's Stages of Moral Judgment: A Constructive Critique." *Harvard Educational Review* 47 (1977): 1.

Gibbs, J. C., and K. F. Widamon. *Social Intelligence: Measuring the Development of Socio-Moral Reflection*. Englewood Cliffs, N.J.: Prentice-Hall, 1982.

Gibson, J. *The Intergroup Relations Curriculum*. Medford, Mass.: Tufts University, Lincoln Filene Center, 1969.

Gilligan, C. *In a Different Voice: Psychological Theory and Women's Development*. Cambridge, Mass.: Harvard University Press, 1982.

Gilligan, C., N. P. Lyons, and T. J. Hammer. *Making Connections: The Relational Worlds of Adolescent Girls at Emma Willard School*. Troy, N.Y.: Emma Willard School, 1989.

Gilligan, C., J. V. Ward, J. M. Taylor, and B. Bardage. *Mapping the Moral Domain: A Contribution of Women's Thinking to Psychological Theory and Education*. Cambridge, Mass.: Harvard University Press, 1988.

Gillispie, P. H. *Learning through Simulation Games*. New York: Paulist Press, 1973.

Giroux, H., and D. Purpel., eds. *The Hidden Curriculum and Moral Education: Deception or Discovery*. Berkeley, Calif.: McCutchan, 1983.

Glasser, W. *Control Theory in the Classroom*. New York: Harper & Row, 1990.

____. *Schools without Failure*. New York: Harper & Row, 1969.

Glock, C., R. Wuthnow, J. Piliavin, M. Spencer. *Adolescent Prejudice*. New York: Harper & Row, 1975.

Goldsmith, S. A. *City Year: On the Streets and in the Neighborhoods with Twelve Young Community Service Volunteers*. New York: New Press, 1993.

Goldstein, A. *The Prepare Curriculum: Teaching Prosocial Competencies*. Champaign, Ill.: Research Press, 1988.

Goldstein, C., E. Koopmen, and H. Goldstein. "Racial Attitudes in Young Children as a Function of Interracial Contact in the Public Schools." *American Journal of Orthopsychiatry* 49 (1979): 89–99.

Goleman, D. "Study of Play Yields Clues to Success." *New York Times*, October 2, 1990.

Goodlad, J. I. *A Place Called School: Prospects for the Future*. New York: McGraw-Hill, 1983.

Goodlad, J. I., R. Soder, and K. A. Sirotnik, eds. *The Moral Dimensions of Teaching.* San Francisco: Jossey-Bass, 1990.

Goodman, M. E. *Race Awareness in Young Children.* 2d ed. Cambridge, Mass.: Addison-Wesley, 1964.

Goodwin, M. Quoted in *The Boston Globe,* December 20, 1989.

Gough, H., D. Harris, W. Martin, and M. Edwards. "Children's Ethnic Attitudes. I: Relationship to Certain Personality Factors." *Child Development* 21 (1950): 83–91.

Gould, R. *Child Studies through Fantasy: Cognitive Affective Patterns in Development.* New York: Quadrangle Books, 1972.

Gow, K. *Yes, Virginia, There is Right and Wrong.* Toronto: John Wiley and Sons, 1980.

Grant, C. A., and C. E. Sleeter. "Equality and Excellence: A Critique." In *Excellence in Education,* edited by P. Altbach, G. Kelly, and L. Weis. Buffalo, N.Y.: Prometheus, 1985.

Grant, G. "The Character of Education and the Education of Character." *Daedalus* 110 (1981): 145–46.

Green, L. "Motivational Antecedents to Maturity of Moral Judgment." Ph.D. dissertation, University of Chicago, 1974.

Green, P. "Tolerance Teaching and the Self Concept in the Multiethnic Classroom." *Multi-Ethnic Review* 1 (1982): 8–11.

Grusec, J. E., and L. Kuczynski. "Teaching Children to Punish Themselves, and Effects on Subsequent Compliance." *Child Development* 48 (1972): 1296–1300.

Haan, N. "Can Research on Motality be Scientific? *American Psychologist,* 37 (1982): 1096–1104.

———. *Coping and Defending.* New York: Academic Press, 1977.

Hannaway, J., and M. Carnoy, eds. *Decentralization and School Improvement: Can We Fulfill the Promise?* San Francisco: Jossey-Bass, 1993.

Hall, W. S., and P. E. Jose. "Cultural Effects on the Development of Equality and Inequality." In *The Child's Construction of Social Inequality,* edited by R. L. Leahy. New York: Academic Press, 1983.

Harding, J., H. Proshansky, B. Kutner, and I. Chein. "Prejudice and Ethnic Attitudes." In *Handbook of Social Psychology,* 2d ed., Vol. 5, edited by G. Lindsey and E. Aronson. Reading, Mass.: Addison-Wesley, 1969.

Harrington, A., and M. Curtis. "Basic Writing: Moving the Voices on the Margin to the Center." *Harvard Educational Review* 60 (1990): 4.

Harris, D., H. Gough, and W. Martin. "Children's Ethnic Attitudes: II. Relationship to Parental Beliefs Concerning Child Training." *Child Development* 21 (1950): 169–81.

Harris, P. L. *Children and Emotion: The Development of Psychological Understanding.* New York: Basil Blackwell, 1989.

Harris, V. J. *Teaching Multicultural Literature in Grades K–8.* Norwood, Mass.: Christopher Gordon Publishers, 1992.

Harter, S. "Effectance Motivation Reconsidered: Toward a Developmental Model." *Human Development* 21 (1976): 34–64.

Hartman, R. S. *The Structure of Value.* Carbondale: Southern Illinois University Press, 1969.

Hawley, W., R. Crain, C. Rossell, M. Smylie, R. Fernandez, J. Schofield, R. Tompkins, W. Trent, and M. Zlotnik. *Strategies for Effective School Desegregation: Lessons from Research.* Lexington, Mass.: Lexington Books, 1983.

Hawley, W., ed. *Effective School Desegregation, Equity, Quality and Feasibility.* Beverly Hills, Calif.: Sage Publications, 1981.

Hess, R. D. "Social Class and Ethnic Influences on Socialization." In *Carmichael's*

Manual of Child Psychology, edited by P. Mussen, pp. 457–57. New York: John Wiley and Sons, 1970.

Hewstone, M., and R. Brown. "Contact is not Enough: An Intergroup Perspective on the Contact Hypothesis." In *Contact and Conflict in Intergroup Encounters*, edited by M. Hewstone and R. Brown. New York: Blackwell, 1986.

Higgins, A., C. Power, and L. Kohlberg. "The Relationship of Moral Atmosphere to Judgments of Responsibility. In *Morality, Moral Behavior, and Moral Development*, edited by W. Kurtines and J. Gewirtz. New York: Wiley-Interscience, 1984.

Higgins, A. "Research and Measurement Issues in Moral Education Interventions." In *Moral Education: A First Generation of Research and Development*, edited by R. L. Mosher, p. 91. New York: Praeger, 1980.

Hilliard, A. *Strengths: African-American Children and Families*. New York: City College School of Education, 1982.

Hoffman, M. L. "Affective and Cognitive Processes in Moral Socialization." In *Cognition and Social Behavior: Developmental Perspectives*, edited by E. T. Higgins, D. N. Rubble, and W. W. Hartup. New York: Cambridge University Press, 1981.

____. "Empathy, Role-taking, Guilt, and Development of Altruistic Motives." in *Moral Development and Behavior*, edited by T. Lickona, pp. 124–43. New York: Holt, Rinehart and Winston, 1976.

____. "Developmental Synthesis of Affect and Cognition and Its Implications for Altruistic Motivation." *Developmental Psychology* 11 (1975): 607–22.

Hogan, R., J. Johnson, and N. Emler. "A Socioanalytic Theory of Moral Development." In *New Directions for Child Development*, Vol. II, edited by W. Damon. San Francisco, Calif.: Jossey-Bass, 1978.

Hoppe-Graff, S. "The Study of Transitions in Development, Potentialities of the Longitudinal Approach." In *Transition Mechanisms in Child Development*, edited by A. DeRibaupierre, pp. 1–30. Cambridge: Cambridge University Press, 1989.

Howe, H. II. *Thinking about Our Kids: An Agenda for American Education*. New York: Free Press, 1993.

____. "Giving Equity a Chance in the Excellence Game." In *The Great School Debate: Which Way for American Education?* edited by B. Gross and R. Gross. New York: Simon and Schuster, 1985.

Hraba, J., and G. Grant. "Black is Beautiful: A Reexamination of Racial Preference and Identification." *Journal of Personality and Social Psychology* 16 (1970): 398–402.

Hunt, T. C., and M. M. Maxson, eds. *Religion and Morality in American Schooling*. Washington, D.C.: University Press of America, 1981.

Ionotti, R. "The Effects of Role Taking Experiences on Altruism, Empathy, and Aggression." Paper presented to the Society for Research in Child Development, Denver, April 1975.

Isen, H. M. "Success, Failure, Attention and Reaction to Others: The Warm Glow of Success." *Journal of Personality and Social Psychology* 15 (1970): 294–301.

Izard, C. E. *Human Emotions*. New York: Plenum Press, 1977.

Jackson, P. W., R. E. Boostrom, and D. T. Hansen. *The Moral Life of Schools*. San Francisco: Jossey-Bass, 1993.

Johnson, D. W., and R. L. Johnson. *Circles of Learning: Cooperation in the Classroom*. Edina, Minn.: Interaction Books, 1986.

____. "Critical Thinking through Structural Controversy." *Educational Leadership* 45 (1988): 58–64.

____. "Effects of Cooperative and Individualistic Learning Experiences on Interaction." *Journal of Educational Psychology* 73 (1981): 444–49.

Joy, D. M., ed. *Moral Development Foundations: Christian Alternatives to Piaget/Kohlberg*. Nashville, Tenn.: Abingdon Press, 1983.

Junior Great Books Shared Inquiry Handbook. Chicago: Great Books Foundation, 1984.

Kagan, H. E. *Changing the Attitudes of Christians toward Jews: A Psychological Approach through Religion*. New York: Columbia University Press, 1952.

Kagan, J. *The Nature of the Child*. New York: Basic Books, 1984.

Kagan, J., and S. Lamb. *The Emergence of Morality in Young Children*. Chicago: University of Chicago Press, 1987.

Kagan, J., and H. Moss. *Birth to Maturity*. New York: Wiley, 1962.

Katz, N. H., and J. W. Lawyer. *Conflict Resolution: Building Bridges*. Newbury Park, Calif.: Corwin Press, 1993.

Katz, P. A. *Towards the Elimination of Racism*, p. 84. New York: Pergamon, 1976.

____. "Stimulus Predifferentiation and Modification of Children's Racial Attitudes." *Child Development* 44 (1973): 232–37.

Katz, P. A., and S. R. Zalk. "Modification of Children's Racial Attitudes." *Developmental Psychology* 14 (1978): 447–61.

Kilpatrick, W. *Why Johnny Can't Tell Right from Wrong: Moral Illiteracy and the Case for Character Education*. New York: Simon and Schuster, 1992.

Kirscht, J., and R. Dillehay. *Dimensions of Authoritarianism: A Review of Research and Theory*. Lexington: University of Kentucky Press, 1967.

Knowles, R., and G. McLean, eds. *Psychological Foundations of Moral Education and Character Development, An Integrated Theory of Moral Development*. Lanham, Md.: University Press of America, 1986.

Kochman, T. *Black and White Styles in Conflict*. Chicago: University of Chicago Press, 1981.

Kohl, H. *I Won't Learn from You*. Bellevue, Wash.: Thistle Press, 1992.

Kohlberg, L. *Essays on Moral Development* Vol. 2: *Moral Stages and the Idea of Justice*. San Francisco: Harper & Row, 1985.

____. "An Evaluation of the Effects of High School Democratic Governance of Students' Moral Judgment and Action." Revised proposal to the Grant Foundation, Harvard Graduate School of Education, 1985.

____. *Essays on Moral Development* Vol. 1: *Moral Stages and the Idea of Justice*. San Francisco: Harper & Row, 1981.

____. *The Meaning and Measurement of Moral Development*, Vol. XIII. Heinz Werner Lecture Series. Worcester, Mass.: Clark University Press, 1981.

____. "Moral Education Reappraised." *The Humanist*, 6 (1978): 14–15.

____. "The Moral Atmosphere of Schools." In *The Unstudied Curriculum*, edited by N. Overly. Monograph of the Association for Supervision and Curriculum Development, Washington, D.C., 1970.

____. "A Cognitive-Developmental Analysis of Children's Sex-role Attitudes." In *The Development of Sex Differences*, edited by E. Maccoby. Stanford, Calif.: Stanford University Press, 1966.

Kohlberg, L., and D. Candee. "The Relationship of Moral Judgment to Moral Action." In *Morality, Moral Behavior and Moral Development*, edited by W. M. Kurtines and J. L. Gewirtz. New York: Wiley, 1984.

Kohlberg, L., and C. Gilligan. "The Adolescent as a Philosopher: The Discovery of the Self in a Postconventional World." *Daedalus* 100 (1971): 1051–86.

Kohlberg, L., C. Levine, and A. Hewer. *Moral Stages: A Current Formulation and a Response to Critics*. New York: Karger, 1983.

Kohlberg, L., and R. Meyer. "Development as the Aim of Education." *Harvard Educational Review* 42 (1972): 449–96.

Kohn, A. "P Is for Prosocial Teaching." *The Boston Globe Magazine*, November 6, 1988, pp. 25, 61–71.

Kovel, J. *White Racism: A Psychohistory.* New York: Random House, 1970.

Krebs, D. L. "Empathy and Altruism." *Journal of Personality and Social Psychology* 32 (1975): 1134–46.

Krebs, D. L., and B. Stirrup. "Role-Taking Ability and Altruistic Behavior in Elementary School Children." *Journal of Moral Education* 11 (1982): 94–100.

Kreidler, W. J. *Creative Conflict Resolution: More than 200 Activities for Keeping Peace in the Classroom.* Glenview, Ill.: Scott-Foresman, 1984.

Kretovics, J., and E. J. Nussel. *Transforming Urban Education.* Boston: Allyn and Bacon, 1994.

Kuhmerker, L., M. Mentkowski, and V. Erikson, eds. *Evaluating Moral Development and Evaluating Educational Programs that Have a Value Dimension.* Schenectady, N.Y.: Character Research Press, 1980.

Kutner, B. "Patterns of Mental Functioning Associated with Prejudice in Children." *Psychological Monographs* 72 (1958): 460.

Larrieu, J., and P. Mussen. "Some Personality and Motivational Correlates of Children's Behavior." *Journal of Genetic Psychology* 147 (1986): 529–542.

Lasker, B. *Race Attitudes in Children.* New York: Henry Holt, 1929.

Leahy, R. L. "The Development of the Concept of Social Class." In *The Child's Construction of Social Inequality*, edited by R. L. Leahy. New York: Academic Press, 1983.

———. "The Development of the Conception of Economic Inequality. II. Explanations, Justifications, and Conceptions of Social Mobility and Social Change." *Developmental Psychology* 19 (1983): 111–25.

———. "The Development of the Conception of Economic Inequality. I. Descriptions and Comparisons of Rich and Poor People." *Child Development* 52 (1981): 523–32.

———. "Parental Practices and the Development of Moral Judgment and Self-image Disparity during Adolescence." *Developmental Psychology* 17 (1981): 580–94.

Leahy, R. L., and M. Eiter. "Moral Judgment and the Development of Real and Ideal Self-Image during Adolescence and Young Adulthood." *Developmental Psychology* 16 (1980): 362–70.

Leahy, R. L., and T. M. Hunt. "An Approach to the Development of Conceptions of Intelligence." In *The Child's Construction of Social Inequality*, ed. R. L. Leahy, p. 149. New York: Academic Press, 1983.

Leming, J. S. "An Evaluation of Kohlberg-Based Educational Programs in the Schools." In *Lawrence Kohlberg, Consensus and Controversy*, edited by S. Modgil and C. Modgil. Philadelphia: Falmer Press, 1986.

Lessing, E., and C. Clarke. "An Attempt to Reduce Ethnic Prejudice and Assess Its Correlates in a Junior High School Sample." *Education Research Quarterly* 4 (1976): 3–16.

Levin, H. M. *Building School Capacity for Effective Teacher Empowerment: Applications to Elementary Schools with At-Risk Students.* New Brunswick, N.J.: Rutgers University, Center for Policy Research in Education, 1991.

———. *Accelerated Schools for At-Risk Students.* New Brunswick, N.J.: Center for Policy Research in Education, 1988.

Lickona, T. *Educating for Character: How Our Schools Can Teach Respect and Responsibility.* New York: Bantam, 1991.

Lickona, T., ed. *Moral Development and Behavior: Theory, Research and Social Issues.* New York: Holt, Rinehart and Winston, 1976.

Lifton, P. "Individual Differences in Moral Development." *Journal of Personality* 53 (1985): 306–34.

____. "Should Heinz Read This Book? (Review of Essays on Moral Development: Vol. I by L. Kohlberg)." *Journal of Personality Assessment* 46 (1982): 323–24.

Lightfoot, S. L. *The Good High School: Portraits of Character and Culture.* New York: Basic Books, 1983.

Lindzey, G., and D. Byrne. "Measurement of Social Choice and Interpersonal Attractiveness." In *The Handbook of Social Psychology* Vol. 2: *Research Methods,* 2d ed., edited by G. Lindzey and E. Aronson, pp. 452–525. Reading, Mass.: Addison-Wesley, 1968.

Lippman, W. *Public Opinion.* New York: Harcourt Brace, 1922.

Lively, W., and D. Bromley. *Person Perception in Childhood and Adolescence.* London: Wiley, 1973.

Lockwood, A. "The Effects of Values Clarification and Moral Development Curricula on School-Age Subjects: A Critical Review of Recent Research." *Review of Educational Research* 48 (1979): 325–64.

Lockwood, A., and D. Harris. *Reasoning with Democratic Values: Ethical Problems in United States History,* Vols. I and II. New York: Teachers College Press, 1985.

Lukas, J. A. *Common Ground: A Turbulent Decade in the Lives of Three American Families.* New York: Alfred A. Knopf, 1985.

Lyeseight-Jones, P. "A Management of Change Perspective: Turning the Whole School Around." In *Education for Equality, Some Guidelines for Good Practices,* edited by M. Cole, pp. 38–52. London: Routledge, 1989.

Lynch, J. *Prejudice Reduction and the Schools.* New York: Nichols, 1987.

MacDonald, S., and R. Gallimore. *Battle in the Classroom: Innovations in Classroom Techniques.* Scranton, Pa.: Intext, 1971.

Maeroff, G. *The School-Smart Parent.* New York: Henry Holt, 1989.

Martz, L. *Making Schools Better: How Parents and Teachers across the Country Are Taking Action — And How You Can, Too.* New York: Random House, 1992.

Massachusetts Teachers' Association. "Needed: Bold Plans to Help Schools." *Massachusetts Education Today* 7 (1991): 3–4.

Matthews, R. "Hawlemont Regional Elementary School." *The Boston Sunday Globe,* July 7, 1991, pp. 57–58.

McConkey, R. *Working with Parents: A Practical Guide for Teachers and Therapists.* London: Croom Helm, 1985.

McCormick, C., and R. Karbinus. "Relationship of Ethnic Groups' Self-Esteem and Anxiety to School Success." *Education and Psychological Measurement* 36 (1976): 1098.

McGoldrick, S. M., J. K. Pearce, and J. Giordano, eds. *Ethnicity and Family Therapy,* pp. 340–61. New York: Guilford Press, 1982.

Meier, D. "In Education Small Is Sensible." *New York Times,* September 8, 1989, I25.

Michael, B., ed. *Volunteers in Public Schools.* Washington, D.C.: National Academy Press, 1990.

Michaelis, J. U. *Social Studies for Children: A Guide to Basic Instruction.* Englewood Cliffs, N.J.: Prentice-Hall, 1980.

Miller, H., and M. Brewer, eds. *Groups in Contact: The Psychology of Desegregation.* New York: Academic Press, 1984.

Milner, D. *Children and Race.* Beverly Hills, Calif.: Sage, 1983.

Mischel, W., and H. Mischel. "The Development of Children's Knowledge of Self Control Strategies." *Child Development* 54 (1983): 603–9.

Modgil, S., and C. Modgil. *Lawrence Kohlberg, Consensus and Controversy.* Philadelphia: Falmer Press, 1986.

Moir, D. J. "Egocentrism and the Emergence of Conventional Morality in Adolescent Girls." *Child Development* 45 (1974): 299–309.

Morland, J. K, and E. Suthers. "Racial Attitudes of Children: Perspectives on the Structural-Normative Theory of Prejudice." *Phylon* 41 (1980): 267–75.

Moses, R. P., M. Kamii, S. M. Swap, and J. Howard. "The Algebra Project: Organizing in the Spirit of Ella." *Harvard Educational Review* 5 (1989): 423–43.

Mosher, D. L., and A. Scodel. "Relationships between Ethnocentrism in Children and the Ethnocentrism and Authoritarian Rearing Practices of Their Mothers." *Child Development* 31 (1960): 369–76.

Mosher, R., ed. *Moral Education, A First Generation of Research and Development*. New York: Praeger, 1980.

Murray, F. B. "Teaching through Social Conflict." *Contemporary Educational Psychology* 7 (1982): 257–71.

Mussen, P., ed. *Handbook of Child Psychology*, 4th ed. New York: John Wiley, 1983.

Mussen, P., and N. Eisenberg-Berg. *Roots of Caring, Sharing and Helping*. San Francisco: W. H. Freeman, 1977.

National Commission on Excellence in Education. *A Nation at Risk: The Imperative for Educational Reform*. Washington, D.C.: Government Printing Office, 1983.

Noddings, N. *The Challenge to Care in Schools: An Alternative Approach to Education*. New York: Teachers College Press, 1992.

——. *Caring: A Feminine Approach to Ethnics and Moral Education*. Los Angeles: University of California Press, 1984.

——. "An Ethic of Caring and Its Implications for Instructional Arrangements." *American Journal of Education* 96 (1988): 215–30.

Oakes, J. *Keeping Track: How American Schools Structure Inequality*. New Haven: Yale University Press, 1985.

Oser, F. K. "Moral Education and Values Education: The Discourse Perspective." In *Handbook of Research on Teaching*, 3rd ed., edited by M. C. Wittrock, pp. 917–41. New York: Macmillan, 1986.

Paley, V. G. *You Can't Say You Can't Play*. Cambridge, Mass.: Harvard University Press, 1992.

Parr, S. R. *The Moral of the Story: Literature, Values, and American Education*. New York: Teachers College Press, 1982.

Patchen, M. *Black-White Contact in Schools: Its Social and Academic Effects*. West Lafayette, Ind.: Purdue University Press, 1982.

Peel, E. *The Psychological Basis of Education*. London: Oliver and Boyd, 1967.

Perlmutter, M., ed. *Cognitive Perspectives on Children's Social Development*. Hillsdale, N.J.: Erlbaum, 1986.

R. S. Peters, *Moral Development and Moral Education*. London: Allen and Unwin, 1981.

——. "Moral Development, a Plea for Pluralism." In *Cognitive Development and Epistemology*, edited by T. Mischel. New York: Academic Press, 1971.

Pettigrew, T. S. "Busing: A Review of the Evidence." *The Public Interest* 30 (1973): 88–118.

——. "Social Evaluation Theory: Convergences and Applications." In *Nebraska Symposium on Motivation*, Vol. 15, edited by D. Levine, pp. 241–318. Lincoln: University of Nebraska Press, 1967.

——. "Personality and Socio-Cultural Factors in Intergroup Attitudes: A Cross-National Comparison." *Journal of Conflict Resolution* 2 (1958): 29–42.

Phillips, D. A., and E. Zigler. "Children's Self-Image Disparity: Effects of Age, Socioeconomic Status, Ethnicity, and Gender." *Journal of Personality and Social Psychology* 39 (1980): 689–700.

Phinney, J. S., and M. J. Rotheman. *Children's Ethnic Socialization: Pluralism and Development.* Newbury Park, Calif.: Sage Publications, 1987.

Piaget, J. *To Understand Is to Invent: The Future of Education.* New York: Grossman, 1973.

___. *The Child's Conception of Physical Causality,* trans. M. Gabain. Patterson, N.J.: Littlefield, Adams, 1960.

___. *The Moral Judgment of the Child.* Glencoe, Ill.: Free Press, 1932, 1948.

___. *Judgment and Reasoning in the Child.* New York: Teachers College Press, 1928.

___. *The Language and Thought of the Child,.* New York: Harcourt Brace, 1926.

Piaget, J., and B. Inhelder. *Mental Imagery in the Child: A Study of Imaginal Representation,* trans. P. A. Chilton, pp. 270–82. London: Routledge and Kegan Paul, 1971.

Pink, W. T., and A. Hyde, eds. *Effective Staff Development for School Change.* Norwood, N.J.: Ablex, 1992.

Porter, J. *Black Child, White Child: The Development of Racial Attitudes.* Cambridge, Mass.: Harvard University Press, 1971.

Powell, A. G., E. Farrar, and D. K. Cohen. *The Shopping Mall High School: Winners and Losers in the Educational Marketplace.* Boston: Houghton Mifflin, 1985.

Powell, M., and J. Solity, eds. *Teachers in Control: Cracking the Code.* New York: Routledge, 1990.

Power, C. "Democracy in the Larger High School: The Case of Brookline." In *Moral Education, Interactional Perspectives,* edited by L. Berkowitz and F. Oser. Hillsdale, N.J.: Lawrence Erlbaum, 1983.

Power, C., A. Higgins, and L. Kohlberg. *Lawrence Kohlberg's Approach to Moral Education.* New York: Columbia University Press, 1988.

Power, C., and J. Reimer. "Moral Atmosphere: An Educational Bridge between Moral Judgment and Action." In *New Directions for Child Development* 2 (1978): 105–16.

Powers, S. I. "Moral Judgment Development within the Family." *Journal of Moral Education* 17 (1988): 209–10.

Proshansky, H. "The Development of Intergroup Attitudes." In *Review of Child Development Research,* Vol. 2, edited by I. W. Hoffman and M. L. Hoffman. New York: Russell Sage Foundation, 1966.

Purpel, D. *The Moral and Spiritual Crisis in Education: A Curriculum for Justice and Compassion in Education.* Granby, Mass.: Bergin and Garvey, 1989.

Purpel, D., and K. Ryan, eds. *Moral Education . . . It Comes with the Territory.* Berkeley, Calif.: McCutchan Publishing, 1976.

Radke, M., H. Trager, and H. Davis. "Social Perceptions in Attitudes of Children." *Genetic Psychology Monographs* 40 (1949): 440.

Radke-Yarrow, M., H. Trager, and J. Miller. "The Role of Parents in the Development of Young Children's Ethnic Attitudes." *Child Development* 23 (1952): 13–53.

Rawls, J. *A Theory of Justice.* Cambridge, Mass.: Harvard University Press, 1971.

Reimer, J., D. P. Paolitto, and R. H. Hersh. *Promoting Moral Growth: From Piaget to Kohlberg.* New York: Longman, 1983.

Rest, J. *Moral Development: Advances in Research and Theory.* New York: Praeger, 1986.

Riordan, R. C. "High School Writing Centers: Students Find Their Voices." *The Harvard Education Letter* 6 (1990): 6–7.

Rist, R. C. *The Invisible Children: School Integration in American Society.* Cambridge, Mass.: Harvard University Press, 1978.

___. "Student Social Class and Teacher Expectations: The Self-Fulfilling Prophecy in Ghetto Education." *Harvard Educational Review* 40 (1970): 411–51.

Rist, R. C., ed. *Desegregated Schools, Appraisals of an American Experiment*. New York: Academic Press, 1979.

Robinson, J. "Mr. Robinson Regrets." *The Boston Globe*, October 30, 1991, p. 59.

Roe, M. *Multiculturalism, Racism, and the Classroom*. Ontario: Canadian Education Association, 1983.

Rogers, C. R. *On Becoming a Person: A Therapist's View of Psychotherapy*. Boston: Houghton Mifflin, 1961.

Rokeach, M. *The Nature of Human Values*. New York: Free Press, 1973.

____. "Long-Range Experimental Modification of Values, Attitudes and Behavior." *American Psychologist* 26 (1971): 453–59.

Roosevelt, M. Quoted in *The Boston Globe*, May 17, 1993.

Rosenberg, M., and R. Simmons. *Black and White Self-Esteem, The Urban School Child*. Washington, D.C.: American Sociological Association, 1971.

Rosenfeld, D. "Classroom Structure and Prejudice in Desegregated Schools." *Journal of Educational Psychology* 73 (1981): 17–26.

Rubenstein, R. ed. *Great Courtroom Battles*. Chicago: Playboy Press, 1973.

Rubin, K. H., and F. W. Schneider. "The Relationship between Moral Judgment, Egocentrism and Altruistic Behavior." *Child Development* 44 (1973): 661–65.

Rutter, M., B. Maughan, J. Mortimore, and A. Smith. *Fifteen Thousand Hours: Secondary Schools and Their Effects on Children*. Cambridge, Mass.: Harvard University Press, 1979.

Ryan, K. "In Defense of Character Education." In *Moral Development and Character Education: A Dialogue*, edited by L. Nucci, pp. 358–79. Berkeley, Calif.: McCutchan, 1989.

____. "The Moral Education of Teachers." In *Character Development in Schools and Beyond*, edited by K. Ryan and G. F. McLean, pp. 358–629. New York: Praeger, 1987.

St. John, N. *School Desegregation, Outcomes for Children*. New York: Wiley Interscience, 1975.

Sandler, J., and A. Freud. *The Analysis of Defense: The Ego and the Mechanisms of Defense Revisited*. New York: International Universities Press, 1985.

Sandler, J., H. Kennedy, and R. Tyson. *The Technique of Child Psychoanalysis: Discussions with Anna Freud*. Cambridge, Mass.: Harvard University Press, 1980.

Sarason, S. B. *The Predictable Failure of Educational Reform*. San Francisco, Calif.: Jossey-Bass, 1990.

Schaeffer, C. E., and T. F. DiGeronimo. *Help Your Child Get the Most Out of School*. New York: Penguin Books, 1990.

Schaps, E., D. Solomon, and A. Watson. "A Program That Combines Character Development and Academic Achievement." *Educational Leadership* 43 (1986): 32–35.

Scheffler, I. "Moral Education beyond Moral Reasoning." In *The Legacy of Lawrence Kohlberg*, edited by D. Schrader, pp. 99–102. San Francisco, Calif.: Jossey-Bass, 1990.

Schmuck, R. A., and P. A. Schmuck. *Group Processes in the Classroom*. Dubuque, Iowa: W. C. Brown, 1979.

____. *A Humanistic Psychology of Education: Making the School Everybody's House*. Palo Alto, Calif.: National Press Books, 1974.

Schofield, J. W. *Black and White in School: Trust, Tension, or Tolerance*. New York: Praeger, 1982.

Schofield, J. W., and H. A. Sager. "The Social Context of Learning in an Interracial School." In *Desegregated Schools: Appraisals of an American Experiment*, edited by R. C. Rist, pp. 155–97. New York: Academic Press, 1979.

Schorr, L., and D. Schorr. *Within Our Reach: Breaking the Cycle of Disadvantage.* New York: Doubleday, 1988.

Selman, R. J. *The Growth of Interpersonal Understanding: Developmental and Clinical Analyses.* New York: Academic Press, 1980.

Selman, R. L. "The Relation of Role Taking to the Development of Moral Judgment in Children." *Child Development* 42 (1971): 79–91.

Selman, R. J., and L. H. Schultz. *Making a Friend in Youth: Developmental Theory and Pair Therapy.* Chicago: University of Chicago Press, 1990.

Semaj, L. "The Development of Racial Evaluation and Preference: A Cognitive Approach." *Journal of Black Psychology* 6 (1980): 59–79.

Sennett, R. *The Uses of Disorder: Personal Identity and City Life.* New York: Knopf, 1970.

Shaffer, D. R., and G. H. Brody. "Parental and Peer Influences on Moral Development." In *Parent-Child Interaction: Theory, Research and Prospects,* edited by R. W. Henderson. New York: Academic Press, 1981.

Sherif, M. *In Common Predicament: Social Psychology of Intergroup Conflict and Cooperation.* Boston: Houghton Mifflin, 1966.

Shoreham-Wading River Middle School. *Advisory Handbook.* Shoreham, New York, 1989.

Shor, I. *Empowering Education: Critical Teaching for Social Change.* Chicago, Ill.: University of Chicago Press, 1992.

Sichel, B. A. *Moral Education: Character, Community and Ideals.* Philadelphia: Temple University Press, 1988.

Sizer, T. R. *Horace's School: Redesigning the American High School.* Boston: Houghton Mifflin, 1992.

———. *Horace's Compromise: The Dilemma of the American High School.* Boston: Houghton Mifflin, 1984.

Slavin, R. E. *Cooperative Learning: Theory, Research and Practice.* Englewood Cliffs, N.J.: Prentice-Hall, 1990.

———. "Student Team Learning: A Manual for Teachers." In *Cooperation in Education,* edited by S. Sharan, P. Hare, C. Webb, and R. Hertz-Lazarowitz. Provo, Utah: Brigham Young University Press, 1981.

Slavin, R. E., and N. Madden. "School Practices that Improve Race Relations." *American Education Research Journal* 16 (1979): 169–80.

Slavin, R. E., S. Sharon, S. Kagan, R. Hertz-Lazarowitz, C. Webb, and R. Schmuck, eds. *Learning to Cooperate, Cooperating to Learn.* New York: Plenum Press, 1985.

Sleeter, C. E. *Empowerment through Multicultural Education.* Albany: State University of New York Press, 1991.

Sleeter, C. E., and C. A. Grant. *Making Choices for Multicultural Education: Five Approaches to Race, Class, and Gender.* New York: Macmillan, 1994.

Sleeter, C. E., and W. Robertson. "In-Service Staff Development for Desegregated Schooling." *Phi Delta Kappan* 72 (1990): 33–40.

Smetana, J. G. "Children's Impressions of Moral and Conventional Transgressions." *Developmental Psychology* 21 (1985): 715–24.

Smylie, M., and W. Hawley. *Increasing the Effectiveness of In-Service Training for Desegregation: A Synthesis of Current Research.* Washington, D.C.: National Education Association, 1982.

Solomon, D., M. Watson, K. Delucchi, E. Schaps, and V. Battistich. "Enhancing Children's Prosocial Behavior in the Classroom." *American Educational Research Journal* 25 (1988): 527–54.

Splitter, L. "Educational Reform through Philosophy for Children." *Thinking, the Journal of Philosophy for Children* 7 (1988): 32–39.

Sprinthall, N. A. "Learning Psychology by Doing Psychology: A High School Curriculum in the Psychology of Counseling." In *Adolescents' Development and Education*, edited by R. Mosher. Berkeley, Calif.: McCutchan, 1979.

Staub, E. "Steps toward a Comprehensive Theory of Moral Conduct: Goal Orientation, Social Behavior, Kindness, and Cruelty." In *Morality, Moral Behavior, and Moral Development*, edited by W. M. Kurtines and J. L. Gewirtz. New York: Wiley, 1984.

____. "Use of Role Playing and Induction in Training for Prosocial Behavior." *Child Development* 42 (1971): 805–81.

Steinberg, A., ed. "Reading Problems: Is Quick Recovery Possible?" In *The Best of the Harvard Education Letter*, pp. 10–12. Cambridge, Mass.: Harvard Graduate School of Education, 1993.

Steinberg, A., ed. *Adolescents and Schools: Improving the Fit*. Cambridge, Mass.: The Harvard Education Letter Reprint Series, 1993.

Stephan, W. G. "Intergroup Relations." In *Handbook of Social Psychology*, edited by G. Lindzey and E. Aronson, p. 600. New York: Random House, 1985.

Stephan, W. G., and J. R. Feagin, eds. *School Desegregation, Past, Present and Future*. New York: Plenum, 1980.

Stephan, W. G., and D. Rosenfeld. "Black Self-Rejection: Another Look." *Journal of Educational Psychology* 71 (1979): 708–16.

____. "Effects of Desegregation on Racial Attitudes." *Journal of Personality and Social Psychology* 36 (1978): 795–804.

Stevenson, H. W., and J. W. Stigler. *The Learning Gap: Why Our Schools Are Failing and What We Can Learn from Japanese and Chinese Education*. New York: Simon and Schuster, 1992.

Stoskopf, A. L., and M. Strom. *Choosing to Participate: A Critical Examination of Citizenship in American History*. Brookline, Mass.: Facing History and Ourselves National Foundation, 1990.

Sullivan, E. V. *Kohlberg's Structuralism: A Critical Appraisal*. Toronto: Ontario Institute for Studies in Education, 1977.

Sullivan, H. S. *The Interpersonal Theory of Psychiatry,*. New York: Norton, 1953.

Tajfel, H. "Intergroup Behavior I: Individualistic Perspectives." In *Introducing Social Psychology*, edited by H. Tajfel and C. Fraser. Hammondsworth: Penguin Books, 1978.

____. "The Roots of Prejudice: Cognitive Aspects." In *Psychology and Race*, edited by P. Watson. Chicago: Aldine, 1973.

____. "Cognitive Aspects of Prejudice." *Journal of Social Issues* 25 (1969): 79–97.

Tajfel, H., ed. *Differentiation between Social Groups*. New York: Academic Press, 1978.

Tajfel, H., and M. Billig. "Familiarity and Categorization in Intergroup Behavior." *Journal of Experimental Social Psychology* 10 (1974): 159–70.

Tajfel H. and J. Turner. "An Integrative Theory of Intergroup Conflict." In *The Social Psychology of Intergroup Relations*, edited by W. G. Austin and S. Worchel. Monterey, Calif.: Brooks Cole, 1979.

Teaching Tolerance. Montgomery, Ala.: Southern Poverty Law Center, 1993–94.

Tessman, H. *Children of Parting Parents*. New York: Jason Aronson, 1978.

Tiedt, P. L., and I. M. Tiedt. *Multicultural Teaching: A Handbook of Activities, Information and Resources*, 3rd ed. Boston: Allyn and Bacon, 1990.

Timm, J. S., and H. S. Timm. *Athena's Mirror: Moral Reasoning in Poetry, Short Story and Drama*. Schenectady, N.Y.: Character Research Press, 1983.

Towne, J. Quoted in *The Westtonian* (Westtown Friends' School, Westtown, Pa.) Winter 1989: ix.

Trager, H., and M. Radke-Yarrow. *They Learn What They Live.* New York: Harper, 1952.

Troyna, B., and B. Carrington, eds. *Education, Racism and Reform.* New York: Routledge, 1990.

Turiel, E. *The Development of Social Knowledge: Morality and Convention.* New York: Cambridge University Press, 1983.

____. "Conflict and Transition in Adolescent Moral Development." *Child Development* 45 (1974): 14–29.

____. "An Experimental Test of the Sequentiality of Developmental Stages in the Child's Moral Judgments." *Journal of Personality and Social Psychology* 3 (1966): 611–18.

Underwood, B., and B. Moore. "Perspective Taking and Altruism." *Psychological Bulletin* 91 (1982): 143–73.

U.S. Commission on Civil Rights. *Reanalysis of Coleman's Equality of Educational Opportunity.* Washington, D.C.: Government Printing Office,1970.

Useem, E. "White Suburban Secondary Students in Schools with Token Desegregation: Correlates of Racial Attitudes." Ed.D. dissertation, Harvard University, 1971.

Valdivieso, R. Quoted in *The Boston Globe,* June 12, 1990, p. 16.

Walberg, H. J., ed. *Educational Environments and Effects: Evaluation, Policy and Productivity.* Berkeley, Calif.: McCutchan Publishing, 1979.

Walker, L. J., and B. S. Richards. "Stimulating Transitions in Moral Reasoning as a Function of Stage of Cognitive Development." *Developmental Psychology* 15 (1979): 95–103.

Wasserman, E. R. "Implementing Kohlberg's 'Just Community Concept' in an Alternative High School." *Social Education* 4 (1976): 203–7.

Watson, M., D. Solomon, V. Battistich, E. Schaps, and J. Solomon. "The Child Development Project: Combining Traditional and Developmental Approaches to Values Education." In *Moral Development and Character Education: A Dialogue,* edited by L. Nucci, pp. 51–92. Berkeley, Calif.: McCutchan, 1989.

Weigel, R., P. Weiser, and S. Cook. "The Impact of Cooperative Learning on Ethnic Relations and Attitudes." *Journal of Social Issues* 31 (1975): 219–43.

Weinberg, M. *The Search for Quality Integrated Education: Policy and Research on Minority Students in School and College.* Westport, Conn.: Greenwood Press, 1983.

Weiskopf, W. A. "The Dialectics of Equality." *Annals of the American Academy of Political and Social Science* 409 (1973): 163–73.

Welch, F., and A. Light. *New Evidence on School Desegregation.* Washington, D.C.: U.S. Commission on Civil Rights, 1987.

Werner, E. E., and R. S. Smith. *Vulnerable but Invincible.* New York: McGraw Hill, 1982.

"Where Prejudice Takes Root." *Human Behavior* 6 (1977): 37–38.

Whiting, B., and J. Whiting. *Children of Six Cultures: A Psychocultural Analysis.* Cambridge, Mass.: Harvard University Press, 1975.

Williams, J. E., and J. K. Morland. *Race, Color and the Young Child.* Chapel Hill: University of North Carolina Press, 1976.

Windmiller, M., N. Lambert, and E. Turiel, eds. *Moral Development and Socialization.* Boston: Allyn and Bacon, 1980.

Winnicott, D. W. *Human Nature.* New York: Schocken Books, 1988.

Winnicott, D. W. *Deprivation and Delinquency,* edited by C. Winnicott, R. Shepherd, and M. Davis. New York: Tavistock Publications, 1984.

Wozniak, R. H., and K. W. Fischer. *Development in Context: Acting and Thinking in Specific Environments.* Hillsdale, N.J.: L. Erlbaum, 1983.

Wynne, E. A., ed. *Character Policy*. Washington, D.C.: University Press of America, 1982.

Yarrow, M. R., P. Scott, and C. Z. Waxler. "Learning Concern for Others." *Developmental Psychology* 8 (1973): 240–60.

Yarrow, M. R., and C. Z. Waxler. "Dimensions and Correlates of Prosocial Behavior in Young Children." *Child Development* 47 (1976): 118–25.

Yeats, W. B. *The Poems of W. B. Yeats*, edited by J. R. Finneran. New York: Macmillan, 1989.

Youniss, J. *Parents and Peers in Social Development: A Sullivan-Piaget Perspective.* Chicago: University of Chicago Press, 1980.

Zahn-Waxler, C., M. Radke-Yarrow, and R. King. "Child Rearing and Children's Prosocial Initiatives toward Victims of Distress." *Child Development* 50 (1979): 319–30.

Zinsser, W. *Writing to Learn: How to Write — and Think — Clearly about Any Subject at All*. New York: Harper & Row, 1988.

Index

ABOUT THE AUTHORS

Florence H. Davidson is a child psychologist in private practice in the Boston area. She is affiliated with the Graduate School of Education at Harvard University.

Miriam M. Davidson is a journalist and freelance writer.

ISBN 0-89789-395-6

HARDCOVER BAR CODE